Listening to the Heart of Genesis

Listening to the Heart of Genesis

A Contemplative Path

by
Rabbi Leila Gal Berner

CASCADE Books • Eugene, Oregon

LISTENING TO THE HEART OF GENESIS
A Contemplative Path

Copyright © 2021 Leila Gal Berner. All rights reserved. Except for brief quotations in critical publications or reviews, no part of this book may be reproduced in any manner without prior written permission from the publisher. Write: Permissions, Wipf and Stock Publishers, 199 W. 8th Ave., Suite 3, Eugene, OR 97401.

Cascade Books
An Imprint of Wipf and Stock Publishers
199 W. 8th Ave., Suite 3
Eugene, OR 97401

www.wipfandstock.com

PAPERBACK ISBN: 978-1-4982-0592-4
HARDCOVER ISBN: 978-1-4982-0594-8
EBOOK ISBN: 978-1-4982-0593-1

Cataloguing-in-Publication data:

Names: Berner, Leila Gal, author.

Title: Listening to the heart of Genesis : a contemplative path / by Leila Gal Berner.

Description: Eugene, OR: Cascade Books, 2021 | Includes bibliographical references and index.

Identifiers: ISBN 978-1-4982-0592-4 (paperback) | ISBN 978-1-4982-0594-8 (hardcover) | ISBN 978-1-4982-0593-1 (ebook)

Subjects: LCSH: Spiritual life—Judaism | Bible—Genesis | Bible—Devotional use | Bible—Reading

Classification: BM723 B47 2021 (print) | BM723 (ebook)

02/02/21

For my beloved wife Franna—
sine qua non.

For my amazing daughter, Kayla Moriya—
I love you "infinity yardsticks"

For my exquisite granddaughters, Olivia, Aliya, and Lucy—
In delight, may we listen to your wisdom,
in gentle love, may we impart our own to you.

and

For my beloved teacher and rebbe, Reb Zalman Schachter-Shalomi
—of blessed memory:

Rabbi Abraham Joshua Heschel wrote "What we need more than anything is not more textbooks, but textpeople. It is the personality of the teacher which is the text that the pupils read; the text that they will never forget."

Thank you, Reb Zalman, for giving so abundantly of yourself
—you are the text I will always cherish and never forget.

Contents

A Word to the Reader | ix
Path Clearers | xi
Gratitude | xv
What Is the "Hebrew Bible"? | xix
How to Use this Book | xxiii

Introduction | 1
Chapter 1: *Bereshit*: Adam Hides from God | 21
Chapter 2: *Bereshit*: Finding Our Hineni—Here I Am
 —to the Ayeka Question | 31
Chapter 3: *Noach*: Murder and Drunkenness | 40
Chapter 4: *Lech Lecha I*: Exploring a New World | 61
Chapter 5: *Lech Lecha II*: Infertility and Sorrow | 73
Chapter 6: *Lech Lecha III*: Hagar Flees | 85
Chapter 7: *Vayera I*: Jealousy and Discord | 89
Chapter 8: *Vayera II*: Sin, Consequences, and Grief | 101
Chapter 9: *Vayera III*: Sacrifice, Fear, and Trembling | 111
Chapter 10: *Chayei Sarah*: Death, Burial, and New Love | 129
Chapter 11: *Toldot*: Sibling Rivalry | 139
Chapter 12: *Vayeitzei I*: Awakening | 150
Chapter 13: *Vayeitzei II*: Two Sisters | 161
Chapter 14: *Vayishlach I*: God Wrestling and Reunion | 171
Chapter 15: *Vayishlach II*: Rape and Revenge | 180
Chapter 16: *Vayeshev I*: Parental Favoritism | 188

Chapter 17: *Vayeshev II*: Joseph and the Stranger | 194

Chapter 18: *Vayeshev III*: Murderous Thoughts | 200

Chapter 19: *Mikkets and Vayiggash:* The Stuff of Dreams
    —and Reunion | 208

Chapter 20: *Vayiggash-Vayechi:* The Curse of Blessings | 221

Guidelines for Group Facilitation of Kriat Hakodesh | 231

Bibliography | 237

Index | 243

Non-Genesis Biblical, Midrash, and Talmud References | 247

A Word to the Reader

I write from my heart to yours. Though this book is a very "Jewish" book, I hope that others will choose to read it. If you are reading these words, you are a spiritual seeker. I write to you if you are a Jew, a Christian, a Muslim, an adherent of another faith-tradition, or if you are an atheist or an agnostic, one who finds greatest meaning in Nature, a Gaia world philosophy, or if you are simply (!) yearning for something and you may not even know what that "something" is.

This book is not a religious tract, treatise, or an attempt to convert anyone to any faith-tradition, credo, sect, or cult. It is an invitation to learn about the stories of the Hebrew Bible to find wisdom and personal meaning in them.

This book emerges from my own great spiritual adventure with a Catholic practice called *lectio divina* and the Hebrew Bible (called the *TaNaKH*). It emerges from my experiences with meditation and my love of silence as a way of making sense out of the Bible's words and stories.

I am an unabashedly passionate, committed, observant Jew who honors, embraces, and celebrates a spiritual kinship with peoples of all faiths and also with those who seek "spirit" beyond conventionalized religious traditions. I am a rabbi and a university professor of religion, philosophy, history, feminism, and feminist ritual. I have studied and taught with Jews, Christians, Muslims, Buddhists, Sufis, and anthropologists of religion and also non-believers. I have learned from each of my colleagues and have been enriched by every encounter.

Almost a century ago, a German Jewish philosopher, Franz Rosenzweig, wrote about a "new learning" that had been born among modern German Jews—a learning that came from their assimilation into a larger national German culture: "*a learning that no longer starts from the Torah and leads into life, but the other way around: from life . . . back to the Torah.*[1] We may be different in myriad ways. We may be Muslim, Christian, Jew, skeptic, or non-believer, but we are each united in our humanity and the stories of the Bible bond us through that essential humanity. This book is based on this premise: that our very lives inform the way we enter the biblical text, and that the biblical text "speaks" to us through the context of our lives. We cannot think as the ancients did; we read biblical stories through the prism of our present-day context, and we respond to the text via our current values, mores, and our deepest and most mundane daily concerns. I invite you to join me on the journey. Welcome!

---

1. Franz Rosenzweig (1886–1929), excerpted from an address given at the opening of the *Freies Judisches Lehrhaus* in Frankfurt, Germany, August, 1920, adapted from Glatzer, *Franz Rosenzweig: His Life and Work*, 231.

Path Clearers

In every person's life, there are those who rise up to clear a path for that person to follow. Such individuals understand that ancient traditions call out for "newness" that will speak to the hearts, minds, and souls of contemporary people. These path clearers reflect back on the distant past and discern that long-dormant meditative practices might be revived to bring spiritual meaning to our generation. In my work in contemplative spiritual practice, I am deeply indebted to these agents of renewal, who have cleared my path, so illuminating it that I might see new entry points into the Hebrew Bible. I give heartfelt thanks for their wisdom and prescience.

In the last decades of the twentieth century, a number of teachings began to appear about Jewish meditation, mysticism, and the Hebrew Bible. One stellar teacher, Rabbi Aryeh Kaplan, was a pioneer in these fertile fields. How tragic was his premature death at the age of forty-eight. Nonetheless, though I never had the privilege of meeting him, I consider Rabbi Kaplan—author of *Inner Space: Introduction to Kabbalah, Meditation and Prophecy* and *Meditation and the Bible* and *Meditation and Kabbalah*—as one of my significant teachers.

For the contributions of others to our understanding of Jewish meditative practices, too numerous to list here, I refer the reader to the bibliography at the end of this book. Beyond that list, some teachers stand out:

I was honored to study meditation with three master teachers: Sylvia Boorstein and Rabbis Jeff Roth and Sheila Peltz Weinberg. Sylvia is a founding teacher at Spirit Rock, an Insight Meditation Center in northern California, and author of *That's Funny, You Don't Look Buddhist: On Being a Faithful Jew and a Passionate Buddhist*. Rabbi Roth is the co-founder of Elat Chayyim, Center for Jewish Spirituality and author of *Jewish Meditation Practices for Everyday Life: Awakening Your Heart, Connecting with God* and *Me, Myself, and God: A Theology of Mindfulness*. Rabbi Sheila Peltz

Weinberg is a founder of the Institute for Jewish Spirituality and a nationally recognized pioneer in contemplative practice.

I was also fortunate to study in the Lev Shomea Institute for the Training of Spiritual Directors[1] in the Jewish Tradition, founded by Rabbi Howard (Abruhm) Addison, Dr. Barbara Breitman, and Rabbi Zari Weiss. It was in this program that I was first introduced to the Christian practice of lectio divina, which set me on the path toward writing this book.

Rabbi Jonathan Slater, a founder of the Institute for Jewish Spirituality, has also been a pioneer in Jewish contemplative practice. His book *Mindful Jewish Living: Compassionate Practice* was crucial to me in my connecting Judaism and mindful practice, and his most recent book, *A Partner in Holiness: Deepening Mindfulness, Practicing Compassion, and Enriching Our Lives through the Wisdom of R. Levi Yitzchak of Berdichev's Kedushat Levi*, vol. 1, has been a guiding light for me in my own contemplative entry into the Book of Genesis. I regret only that I have never studied with him in person.

Early on in my spiritual journey, Rabbi Rami Shapiro's work deeply influenced me. Though his earlier works were not written directly about meditation or a contemplative approach, I felt the seeds of such work blossoming in Rabbi Shapiro's poetry and liturgical creativity. More recent books such as *Fully Awake and Truly Alive: Spiritual Practices to Nurture Your Soul* and *Perennial Wisdom for the Spiritually Independent* (co-authored with Fr. Richard Rohr) have guided my thinking toward the contemplative approach I offer here.[2]

Spiritual seekers in various faith traditions make a variety of distinctions between meditation and contemplation. Indeed, it would be far beyond the scope of my offerings here to enter into such a complex discussion. I will only declare that in the territory of my heart and mind, there is little distance between the two. For me, meditation leads to a deeply contemplative spiritual state—and back again. Sometimes, as with Christian *lectio divina* (please see my Introduction), I might flow from meditation via a prayerful journey to contemplation and then find myself returning to meditation again, and then re-turning to an even deeper place of contemplation. If meditation is the place where text interacts "with our thoughts, hopes, memories and desires," and contemplation is when we "rest in the presence of the One,"[3] we may rest assured that any questions about our lives

---

1. There are a number of other Jewish spiritual direction training programs: The "*Hashp'ah*" program in the ALEPH: Alliance for Jewish Renewal Ordination Program, the Yedidya Center, Morei Derekh and others.

2. See bibliography for more works by Rabbi Rami Shapiro.

3. Fr. Luke Dysinger, O.S.B., "Accepting the Embrace of God: The Ancient Art of Lectio Divina," http://www.valyermo.com/ld-art.html. Fr. Dysinger writes that: The

that emerge will be answered within God's shelter—what a safe place to be when we might flow back into meditation—a different path than traditional Christian *lectio divina*, but certainly a more authentically Jewish trajectory: to flow *between* meditation and contemplation!

In sum, my own training in meditation with the aforementioned teachers and my studies of the writings of many pioneers in the field of meditation and contemplative practice (both Christian and Jewish) have guided me on a path that I have felt has been cleared before me by spiritual seekers who have preceded me on this sacred journey. I thank them with all my heart, for without them, I would still be clearing away the spiritual thicket.

---

author considers this article to be in the Public Domain. This article may therefore be downloaded, reproduced, and distributed without special permission from the author. It was first published in *Valyermo Benedictine*, vol. 1, no. 1 (Spring, 1990). It has subsequently been reprinted as (1) "Appendix 2" in *The Art and Vocation of Caring for People in Pain* by Karl A. Schultz (Paulist Press, 1993), 98-110; and in (2) *An Invitation to Centering Prayer with and Introduction to Lectio Divina*, by Basil Pennington and Luke Dysinger (Liguori/Triumph, 2001)

Gratitude

Kosi revaya—my cup runs over with gratitude to the many people who have given of their time, hearts, and insights to the creation of this book. They have offered ideas, suggestions, honest critique, some skepticism, and lots of gentle encouragement to me. When I felt like Moses who couldn't hold his arms up any longer, they lifted me up—and so my mind kept thinking and my fingers kept typing. With all humility, and with all the inevitable flaws and weaknesses of this work, its strengths are due in no small measure to the support of the people named here.

With all my heart, I thank:

Rabbi Howard (Avruhm) Addison who read early parts of this work and turned me in a significant new direction that has helped shape this book.

Rabbi Addison, Dr. Barbara Breitman, and Rabbi Zari Weiss, all co-founders of *Lev Shomea* [A Listening Heart], Institute for the Training of Spiritual Directors in the Jewish Tradition, helped sow the seeds for my current work in Contemplative Torah. Rabbi Addison first introduced me to *lectio divina*, Dr. Breitman, with her brilliant feminist passion, helped me to see the link between spiritual direction and *midrash* and Rabbi Weiss, with her quiet wisdom, helped me to learn how to "be still" and feel God's Presence. These were my first steps toward a contemplative approach to Torah.

Rabbi Sue Levi-Elwell, dear friend and fellow traveler on a Jewish feminist path, who has shown me through her own work that teaching the "Torah of our lives" can bring us to a new friendship, indeed intimacy, with the biblical text. And likewise, to my friend, teacher, and modern prophet in our broken world, Rabbi Arthur Waskow, who modeled a way to both love and wrestle with the Bible.

Rabbi Ruth Gan Kagan, who helped me in one important conversation to learn about wider horizons and more open questions.

Rabbi Jason Mann and his wonderful wife Belle gave me a home to write in for several weeks at the inception of writing. Thank you! Rabbi Ilyse Kramer who studied with me and offered friendship and helped me to be open to new questions and ways of teasing out text and "arguing" with the Divine. Rabbi Gilah Langner, who not only offered her sweet friendship when I most needed it, but also her wonderful editorial skills, which helped keep me on track and illumine my way.

Rabbis Judy Kummer, Marcia Plumb, and Benjamin Shalva who, in the gestational stages of this book, shared their midrashic insights and enthusiasm with me. More recently, Avi West has helped me craft several chapters of this work into a keener work than it would have been without his wisdom. I am greatly indebted to him. I have much gratitude for my beloved friend and colleague Rabbi Marcia Prager, for her wisdom in the final stages of writing. I am also indebted to Reverend Gerald Fuss, my new neighbor, who shared his experience in the ministry with me.

Poetry about the Hebrew Bible has significantly informed my thoughts and feelings. Dr. Laurie Patton, President of Middlebury College, who has been my dear friend, colleague, and cheerleader for years, shared "Angel's Task" with me before its publication, and her poems touched my soul. Rabbi Ruth Sohn, whose magnificent poem, "I Shall Sing to the Lord a New Song" has inspired me for years to take "leaps of faith" (including this book) that have been transformative for me.

Maimonides once wrote that "Students increase a teacher's wisdom and broaden [the teacher's] mind. The sages said, 'Much wisdom I have learned from my teachers, more from my colleagues, [and] from my students most of all.'"[1] One of my greatest joys is to be able to thank several individuals with whom I have studied as a classmate, then served as a teacher, and now call my rabbinic colleagues. With humility, I thank my former classmates in the *Lev Shomea* Jewish Spiritual Directors' Training program, Rabbi Eva Sax-Bolder, Rabbi Hannah Nathans, and Rabbi Simcha Zevit, all of whom later became my students and colleagues in the ALEPH Ordination Program. As students, each one contributed to increasing my own knowledge and wisdom—with insights into Torah, with excellent essays on *midrash*, biblical history and civilization, and more, all of which were thrown into the spicy "soup" that is my brain, heart, and soul and have helped to shape the person, writer, and teacher that I am.

I am deeply indebted for what I now share with my beloved former student and now, wonderful friend, colleague, and writing buddy, Rabbi Mark Elber. We share a universe that includes poetry, *midrash*, and the agonies

---

1. Maimonides, *Mishnah Torah*, "Laws Concerning the Study of Torah," ch. 5:13.

and ecstasies of writing books. Sharing the journey with Rabbi Elber has been a deep joy and lots of fun too! I thank Jinks (Jennifer) Hoffman for her spiritual guidance and gentle encouragement as I worked on this book. I would also like to thank Dr. Irene Landsman for her wise guidance as I grappled with the challenge of writing.

I am grateful to have had the honor of having had the opportunity to teach several cohorts of students in Contemplative Torah in the ALEPH Ordination Program and also two cohorts of the students in the ALEPH *Ruach Ha-Aretz* Program. I am grateful for the chance to hone the *kriat ha-kodesh* method with them, and to gain insights from their responses to my offerings.

I am also honored and grateful to have taught *kriat ha-kodesh* at the congregation I served for sixteen years as rabbi—*Kol Ami:* The Northern Virginia Reconstructionist Community in Arlington, Virginia. To all my students in these communities, I offer my sincerest thanks.

I thank my wonderful editor, Reverend Dr. Robin Parry for his work and his kindness.

I offer my most heartfelt gratitude to my rebbe, greatest teacher and friend with whom I shared many conversations and good chocolate, Reb Zalman Schachter-Shalomi of blessed memory. He taught me more than "book knowledge." He taught me the ways of the gentle, the deeply thoughtful, the non-judgmental, and the profoundly kind. As much for his *menschlichkeit* as for his wisdom, I am beyond grateful.

I thank my sister Ilana Berner and her life-partner Tzviya Yedidya for offering me their home, a lovely haven on the Mediterranean Sea, a place in which to write undisturbed for several weeks. This is where this book got launched, amidst palm trees, sea breezes, and a peaceful garden. I will always be indebted to them for their generosity in offering me that refuge for one sweet summer.

I am deeply grateful to my wife, Franna Ruddell, who sustains me in countless ways. She is my *besherte,* my purveyor of tea, backrubs, sweet and savory snacks, encouragement and more. . . . Franna is an astute editor, though any flaws in writing or editing are solely my own.

—I have found the one whom my soul loves.[2]

---

2. Song of Songs 3:4

What Is the "Hebrew Bible"?

Often referred to as the "Old Testament," the Hebrew Bible is the Holy Scriptures that guide the Jewish tradition. The entire corpus consists of twenty-four books divided into three sections:

TORAH (The Teaching):
- Genesis
- Exodus
- Leviticus
- Numbers
- Deuteronomy

NEVI'IM (Prophets):
- Joshua
- Judges
- First Samuel
- Second Samuel
- First Kings
- Second Kings
- Isaiah
- Jeremiah
- Ezekiel

- Hosea
- Joel
- Amos
- Obadiah
- Jonah
- Micah
- Nahum
- Habakkuk
- Zephaniah
- Haggai
- Zechariah
- Malachi

KETHUVIM (Writings):

- Psalms
- Proverbs
- Job
- The Song of Songs
- Ruth
- Lamentations
- Ecclesiastes
- Esther
- Daniel
- Ezra
- Nehemiah
- First Chronicles
- Second Chronicles

The Hebrew Bible contains the stories of the creation of the world, the first human beings, Adam and Eve in the Garden of Eden, the fate of their children, Cain and Abel, Noah and the Great Flood that destroyed the world, and the re-creation of the world by God. Then, the text tells us of the origins of a people, beginning with Avram (later renamed Abraham) and his wife Sarai (later renamed Sarah), who are the first ancestors of the people who come to be known as the "Israelites," who later come to be known as the Jews.

The stories of this people encompass complex family dynamics over their first three generations, under their patriarchs and matriarchs, Abraham and Sarah, Isaac and Rebecca, Jacob and his two wives, Leah and Rachel. Then the sacred Scripture recounts the dramatic story of Israelite slavery in Egypt, liberation from bondage, miracles and wonders in the wilderness, the appearance of the God of Israel to Moses in the desert that will come to be known as Sinai and the magnificent and awesome revelation at Mount Sinai where the Law is given by Moses to the people in the form of the Ten Commandments.

From here, the saga continues through the desert to the conquest of the land of Canaan and the slow, inexorable maturation of a people into a religion with its belief, tenets, practices, and customs—and with its very human tales of politics, passion, love and war, conquest and community, poetry and prophesy. The Hebrew Bible is the story of a people, the story of a faith, the story of hundreds of human beings struggling to carve out lives for themselves in a harsh, inhospitable climate and land, facing challenges all along the way—in other words, *this* biblical story is a story about LIFE, and it teaches us exquisite lessons all along the way.

How to Use This Book

Each chapter of this book follows a similar format. First, I retell the biblical story, so that you will be familiar with the plot of each story. I try to provide continuity from one Torah portion (called a *parsha* in Hebrew) of this book to the next. In the Table of Contents, you will find that each chapter is named by the *parsha* and a title that hints of the theme I have chosen to address in the chapter.

Next, I offer teachings about the biblical text. I bring these teachings from a variety of Jewish sources—ancient rabbinic commentaries (from the genre of *midrash*),[1] contemporary rabbinic and lay *midrash*, poetry, music, art, and my own observations about life.[2] These reflections offer different perspectives about some aspect of life, interactions between humans, and interactions between humans and God. Some of these thoughts will reappear as contemplative questions in the "Exploring the Text Within" section of the chapter. Next I offer a section called "From Text to Life," which are

---

1. *Midrash* is a millennia-old Jewish practice of interpreting biblical text to derive manifold meaning in the text. Some *midrashim* (plural of *midrash;* generically called *midrash halacha*) are focused on understanding God's commandments, and discerning ways to live in adherence to divine commandment. Other *midrashim* (generically called *midrash aggadah*) are of a folkloristic, or folk tale nature, aimed at deriving moral or ethical lessons from the biblical text.

2. There is some debate as to whether contemporary rabbinic and lay commentaries on biblical text, poetry, music, art, and dance constitute forms that may be defined as *midrash*. I take the position that they are *midrash*, as legitimate as ancient rabbinic commentaries. Any modality that opens up the text and illuminates its meaning beyond pure intellect, penetrating into the realm of emotion, heart and soul, is, in my view, a form of *midrash,* and serves the purpose originally intended by the ancient rabbis: to understand the divine word more deeply and clearly.

true life stories—moments in the lives of people just like you and me who have found resonance in the Bible stories that are explored in each chapter.

A bit more about the simple questions I offer to you in each chapter: Here I invite you to sit in contemplative silence and consider your own life's experience. Ask yourself: what do the biblical text and the midrashic teachings offered here mean *to me* in *my* life?

An example: after Adam and Eve had eaten from the forbidden tree of knowledge—"the eyes of both of them were opened and they perceived that they were naked" (Gen 3:7). Suddenly, with their newfound knowledge, the first humans experienced shame and vulnerability for the first time. Have *you* ever felt vulnerable when you have gained increased knowledge? Sometimes knowledge empowers us, and sometimes it intimidates us.

In the "Exploring the Text Within" section for this chapter, you are asked the question: "Can I recall when new knowledge has expanded my awareness *and* my sense of vulnerability?" I invite you to enter into a silent internal conversation. This conversation may simply be a time when no one else is present—just you; or, you may feel a Presence (I choose to call God) and you might choose to explore the inner rooms of your heart in a conversation with God. Ask yourself: Can I recall when too much knowledge has frightened me? Has there been a time when newly discovered information has made me aware of how complex things are? Has that awareness of complexity caused me to feel more open to risk? Conversely, your awareness of the complicated insights your new knowledge brings might give you insights (IN-"sights") that illumine your understanding of the next steps on your life's journey. You never know!

As you explore these questions, delve deeper: enter into an even deeper contemplative silence and engage in the practice of *kriat ha-kodesh* as outlined in this book: deep listening to the text as it is read several times, paying attention to its teachings, attending to the questions posed, and meditating on your memories. There is no designated destination to which you "must" arrive. Let your mind, heart, and soul wander freely—they will guide you in the most authentic direction(s).

After you have explored the questions, try "praying" on what is happening within you. By "prayer," I mean a reflective, spiritually oriented inner way of exploring that asks what *deep* meaning this all has for you and your own life. It is a religious act, but not doctrinal or dogmatic in the conventional sense, and it *is* most certainly addressed to your spirit. The Latin word "religion" means to re-tie, or re-connect, *re-ligio* (as in ligature). In its original meaning, it signified the re-connection of humans to the divine. Here I suggest a more expansive definition of the word "religion" to embrace not only the "divine" but any power, force, spirit that brings us awe and wonder—some call this God, others call it Nature. The jargon doesn't matter—but the feeling does.

Don't think too much and try not to analyze. Just let the feelings and sensations wash over you. Whatever happens is good—whether the emotions bring tears of sadness or joy, understanding or further questions, it is all good. They are all part of the journey. Remember always that "prayer" takes many forms—silence, breathing intentionally and slowly in a mindfully rhythmic way, song, chant, journaling, walking quietly—whatever is gentle, quiet, and nurturing.

This practice may be part of an individual daily spiritual practice or as part of a group led by a facilitator.[3] The key is that it become a regular part of your life, so that once you are accustomed to the practice, you spend less time in learning the method and give more time and attention to what is happening within.

Keeping a Journal

You might want to keep your own journal as you read each chapter of this book.

Perhaps dating your entries will give you insights later as to what was happening in your life at the time of your entry and how that entry related to the biblical story or your life experience. You might gain some insight into where you were/are on your own spiritual journey and how that phase of your journey might be illumined by your journey with Torah!

In the journal, you might jot down any questions or thoughts that emerge for you from the *biblical story, the teachings or the questions for silent contemplation*—does the biblical story remind you of a story in your own life? What feelings in you does the story evoke?

- Do the teachings spark some new insights or responses within you? New questions or associations with times in your life?
- Do the questions for contemplation lead you to unanticipated "rooms" in your heart? Your mind? Your soul?
- Do questions lead to new questions? New memories? New insights?

Let your journal become a record for you of the "history" of this journey. It needn't be organized or systematic. Let yourself meander wherever your heart and mind might lead you—you might discover fascinating things along the way!

---

3. See pages 231–36 for Guidelines for Group Facilitation of *Kriat Hakodesh*.

Introduction

Have you ever heard or read a story that has turned your heart even just a few degrees toward a new direction? Has a book or poem so touched you that it has given you insight at a perplexing moment in your own life? Have you ever been alone long enough to reflect deeply on a truly important situation in your life, and *because* you were alone, you were able to reach clarity as to what to do next?

Have you ever been still and silent enough to let the stillness guide you? Have you ever journeyed emotionally, spiritually, or even geographically until you have found your way to a new and more serene state of being?

Where have your stopped on your way? When have your moments of insight come? In the din of daily life? Or in quieter, more reflective times?

I want to share a story with you—it is actually a collection of stories, and thousands of words that have guided me on my own spiritual, emotional, and very personal life journey. As I have sat alone, still and silent, reading the stories of people who I have been told lived millennia ago, I have even wondered if they ever even lived. I have questioned if these were "real" people or just archetypes, and finally, I have come to understand that their humanity, whether real or created by a Divine or human author, reaches deep into my heart, touching my soul—because their lives and my life have so much in common. I resonate with their struggles, I weep as I read about their sadness and their tragedies, I become angry at the injustices they endured, I laugh at their joys and I chuckle at their foibles.

What was this rich collection of oh-so-human stories? It was the 419,687 words of the Hebrew Bible.

"Hold on!" you might be thinking. "I don't want to read a religious tract! I'm not looking to be converted! I'll stop reading now. This is *not* for me!"

Please read on.

Do you believe in God? Are you questioning? Are you a non-believer? Do you believe in a some sort of Great Spirit, but choose not to call this Spirit "God?" Are you a member of an organized religion? Do you reject organized religion? Do you like *dis*organized religion? Are you utterly disinterested in religion? *None of this really matters.*

I am a person of faith. I believe in God; not the God of "pediatric religion"—the old man with a long white beard sitting high on a lofty throne in a wispy-white clouded heaven, surrounded by cherubic creatures playing harps, producing sticky-sweet Muzak. I believe in Something Else—an Energy that comforts me, energizes me, makes me think hard, inspires me, disturbs me, moves me along in a bewildering, complex universe. Something Else speaks to me through experience, through other human beings, through kind and fearful looks in the eyes of strangers, through nature and music and sublime and terrifying moments and also words on the page and words in poems and words in books.

I believe in Something Else that communicates with me through the Hebrew Bible and sometimes has conversations with me through stories I read and hear from the mouths of ancient peoples whose skin shines in many hues, whose words (alas) I must hear and read only in translation. I believe in traveling in both wild and sensible directions and I am thrilled by as many moments and journeys as life can offer.

My passionate embrace of the Hebrew Bible has brought me to a place of a deep desire to share what I have learned, *with dogma set aside*, and with an enthusiastic invitation to you, the reader, to join me in a voyage of heart, soul, and perhaps discovery of new meaning for your life's journey.

How My Road Began

About four decades ago, I faced a profound personal challenge. Because of a secret, my life was chokingly constrained. I knew that there was so much more that I wanted to do and be in my life, so much more I wanted to give. I wanted to live more richly, more passionately, more openly. In my own heart, I defined all of this as a search to connect with the Great Spirit I choose to call God.

At some point in my journey, I came across words that changed my life:

"I, Miriam, stand at the sea

and turn

to face the desert . . .

I want to sing the song rising inside me.

My mouth open

INTRODUCTION

I stop . . .
Can I take a step
Without knowing a
Destination?
Will I falter?
Will I fall
Will the ground sink away from under me?

Rabbi and poet, Ruth Sohn, eloquently writing in the voice of the biblical Miriam, Moses's older sister, was describing the moment when the Israelites stood at the sea, too terrified to take the leap into the waters that would take them across the great divide between them and the Egyptians, petrified, frozen in place, unable to jump from slavery to freedom.

To take the first step—
To sing a new song
Is to close one's eyes
And dive
Into unknown waters
For a moment knowing nothing risking all—
But then to discover—
The waters are friendly
The ground is firm
And the song— . . .
the song
the song rises again . . .
And I hear
for the first
the song
that has been in my heart
silent
unknown
even to me.[1]

---

1. "I Shall Sing to the Lord a New Song," by Rabbi Ruth Sohn, first published in *Kol Haneshamah: Shabbat VeHagim*, 768–69.

Rabbi Sohn was singing through Miriam, the biblical prophetess, and Miriam was singing to *me!* And when I read those words, the Hebrew Bible, which had been whispering in my ear for some time, finally touched my heart in a way that turned my life's direction. On that morning, my secret no long held me in its grip. I began to cross my own personal sea. A biblical story experienced through the words of a contemporary rabbi-poet, imagining a courageous biblical woman, and listening to the stirrings of my own heart brought me to the beginnings of a new journey on which I still travel today.

At another moment in my life, I experienced a profound loneliness. Surrounded by people, I found myself unable to authentically connect with anyone. So, I decided to take action—to isolate myself even more, in order to come back into the world, I hoped, to more connection. Taking a leave from my studies and my job, I drove out into the desert for ten days. Now *that's* a pretty crazy thing to do! If you're lonely, go away from people and be lonelier! On this trek out into nowhere, I took very little with me: a few favorite books of poetry, my camera, and, for some reason I can't quite explain, the Hebrew Bible.

I lodged in a small rented cabin, with one "luxury" item—air conditioning. Eating on my own, I saw no other humans. I spent my mornings watching the skies and the hawks and a few desert animals who roamed in the distance. When the day grew too hot, I settled down inside to read and nap.

In the evenings, I sat on the cabin's porch and gazed at the stars, so bright out in the desert without artificial light. The skies shone with a kind of luminescence I had rarely been blessed to see before. Today I am reminded of what a beloved friend tells me about her devout Methodist mother. This remarkable woman, for whom the eloquence of the King James translation of the Bible was like mother's milk, would gather her three daughters whenever they saw a particularly wondrous sunset and encouraged them to recite: "The heavens declare the glory of God and the firmament showeth His handiwork!" (Psalm 19:1).

An amazing thing happened. After a day or two, my mind began to grow still, yet, paradoxically, I enjoyed vivid and wonderful dreams. In the mornings, I awoke with a sense of joy and tranquility, remembering only fragments of the dreams, but sensing a gentle gratitude for having had them.

On about the third day of my sojourn in the desert, I began to leaf through the Bible in a completely unsystematic way—and my eyes began to rest on certain phrases,

"*Ayeka?*"—"*Where are You?*" (3:9), God asks Adam in the Garden.

"Well, Certainly God knows where Adam is!" I thought to myself—and then I thought—*where am I?* And I walked in the desert and kept asking myself that question: "Leila, where are you? Where are you?" Answers didn't come—but the question didn't frighten me. It was almost as if the question was my guide as I walked. I had no idea where I was going. Rabbi Sohn's words echoed within me: "To take a step without knowing a destination . . . ." This time, I walked without fear.

Another phrase: *"Surely, God is in this place, and I, did not know it!"* (28:16). Jacob, fleeing after having stolen his brother Esau's birthright and their father Isaac's blessing, lies down to sleep, puts his head on the earth, has a dream about a stairway, a ladder reaching right up to heaven, with angels, ascending and descending on the stairway. And when Jacob awakens, he understands what he has not perceived before: there is holiness in this place! This phrase jumped off the page at me as I looked out on the arid plain before me, as bramblebush tumbled along in the wind, as the hawks circled in the sunsets, pink and red and crimson descending on the horizon—*Indeed, God is in this place, and I, i did not know it!* I discovered that God had been an intellectual concept for me, an idea, but not a reality of the heart. Did the words on the page help God enter my soul along with my sojourn in the desert? I believe with absolute faith that they did.

And yet another phrase: "Come up to Me on the mountain, and be there" (Exodus 24:12). Here God is instructing Moses to come up to Mt. Sinai to receive the tablets of the Law to bring down to the Israelites. What an odd invitation, I thought. It's kind of like saying to someone, "Come and have a drink, and have some coffee." It's redundant! What does it mean, "Come up to Me and *be there?*" If somebody comes, they're already there! Then, in the quiet of the afternoon, as I sat on my cabin porch, I thought more deeply. Haven't I gone to lots of places and not really *"been* there"? Surely there is a difference between attending and being fully *present!* I thought about all of the times I had attended parties, dinners, and other events and I hadn't been fully present. My body was there, but my heart, my mind were elsewhere. No wonder I was so lonely, even when surrounded by small crowds. Reading that one, odd biblical phrase, I began to crack through my loneliness. I began to understand that when one is fully present, one makes connections. Authentic presence dispels loneliness. What a concept!

My ten days in the desert passed more quickly than I had thought possible, and when I returned to the city, much had changed within me.

My baggage had changed too. My formerly crisp, unused Hebrew Bible was now well-worn.

Assuredly, my experience in the arid wilderness and the epiphany I experienced because of Rabbi Sohn's poem were dramatic moments. But my encounters with the Bible continued—in much more prosaic places.

One day at the supermarket checkout counter, I greeted the checker, an older African-American woman with whom I was friendly. She had worked at this store for years, and I was a regular customer.

"How are you, Gladys?" I inquired.

"Well, not so good. Marvin has been very sick, the bills aren't getting paid, and we need a new hot water heater."

And then, in an instant, Gladys' face brightened. "But don't you worry about us! 'Weeping may last through the night, but joy cometh with the morning!'" Gladys exclaimed, quoting Psalm 30:5 to me. This devout woman turned to the Bible to raise herself up from despair, to elevate her mood and to restore her innate optimism. Indeed, joy cometh in the morning.

A few days after my encounter with Gladys, I was with my old friend Michael[2] when we heard the news of a terrorist bombing at a beachfront nightclub in Tel-Aviv. Four young people had been killed, including one of Michael's distant cousins.

"I didn't really know him very well," Michael said. "I only met him once, when he was a little boy."

We listened to the news report. Then, Michael, who was a completely secular Jew, a self-proclaimed atheist, began to sing in Hebrew, "*V'chit'tu charvotam l'itim* . . . And they shall beat their swords into ploughshares and they shall study war no more." Michael and I sang that song over and over again, with tears streaming down our faces. A believer and an atheist comforted by the words of an Israeli folksong that were actually the words of the biblical prophets Isaiah (2:4) and Micah (4:3). Then Michael and I sang the African-American spiritual version of the song, "Gonna lay down my sword and shield, down by the riverside and study war no more!" Once again, biblical words sustained us. Once again, we found meaning in the Hebrew Bible.

On yet another ordinary day, I sat in an airport waiting to board a plane. Sitting next to me in the waiting area was a young, uniformed Marine. After a while, we struck up a typical airport conversation.

"Where are you headed?" I asked. He responded that he was on his way home to Colorado to visit his wife and young son before heading back to Iraq. We chatted for a while about his family, his hometown, and

---

2. Unless otherwise indicated, I have changed names, for the sake of individuals' privacy.

his war experiences. He proudly showed me photos of his baby boy. We smiled, we laughed.

I don't know what moved me to turn the conversation in a serious direction, but I asked him if he was scared in combat. Quietly and intently, he simply looked at me and said, "Ma'am, though I walk through the valley of the shadow of death, I shall fear no evil, for the Lord is with me," echoing the words of Psalm 23.

"Amen," I responded, and then I touched him gently on the shoulder and we were silent. After a few minutes, our flight was called. We boarded, smiled at each other, and I never saw the young man again. I hope and pray that he is safe and well and back at home with his wife and son. I know that the Bible comforted him and gave him courage. Its words accompanied him on his life's journey.

On my way in life, I continue each day to explore the words and the people of the Hebrew Bible. I have come to see that the pathos of biblical people's lives, their dramatic and their mundane experiences, often mirror our lives today. Despite the very different landscape of biblical times from our own lives today, human nature is the same then and now. The Bible's words, moments, and journeys are worthy guides and tools to helps us draw meaning from our own lives' challenges and experiences—not necessarily because we are all people of faith, not necessarily because we all believe in Divine Word, but because there is *something about the words themselves or about the journeys of those who came before us in biblical times that resonates for us. Their stories are our stories.* We learn from their stories, we reflect on their stories, we find meaning in their stories. *The words speak our lives.*

The words speak our lives. It's clear that I have the Bible's words hold great personal power for me. *But how do I know that this might be true for others?*

Some moments I have experienced with others:

A few years ago, when I was teaching Torah to a group of women on the Oregon Coast, one of the participants, Amy, said to me "I don't understand why everyone is so jazzed by Torah. All those antiquated stories about people who may or may not have lived thousands of years ago. It doesn't do a thing for me." I encouraged Amy to wait until the end of the weekend.

That morning, we listened to the biblical story of Rebecca's very painful pregnancy with twins, the boys' births, and then (with Rebecca's assistance), the deception of her husband by the younger son, and the younger son's theft of his brother's birthright and paternal blessing. We listened to the text three times and in between we sat in contemplative silence considering Rebecca's favoritism toward the younger boy, the increasing tension between the brothers, the elder brother's pain at not receiving his father's "innermost"[3] blessing, and the younger brother's fleeing to escape his brother's wrath.

A bit later in the afternoon, I found Amy weeping as she stared out at the ocean. "That's my story," she said, between her tears. "Not exactly, but it's so similar." I am a widow. I have two sons, not twins, but twenty months apart in age. The younger is really smart, and the older is strong and athletic, but not very intellectual. They're now grown and my younger son has manipulated my older son out of his part of their father's inheritance. The boys are estranged from each other and there is nothing I can do to get them back together. It hurts so much! You were right. These Bible stories really *do* speak to my life."

Several years ago I taught a class on *midrash* in the Hebrew Bible at Emory University in Atlanta, Georgia. *Midrash* is the genre of commentary of biblical text. It takes two forms: legal (called *midrash halacha*), which deals with divine commandments that have become the basis for Jewish ritual rules and daily behavior, and homiletic or folkloristic (called *midrash aggadah*), which is a collection of stories and parables to teach ethical and moral lessons.

As the final assignment for the class, I challenged the students to write their own *midrash*, based on one of the biblical narratives we had studied during the semester. One young man, Nick, wrote an extremely moving *midrash* identifying himself in the paper as Ishmael, the biblical Abraham's older son.

In the biblical account, Sarah, the older woman, offers Hagar to Abraham, so that he might have sexual relations with her and sire a child (preferably a son) with Hagar. Sarah's expectations, however, are that *she*, not Hagar, will be recognized as the baby's mother, since the Egyptian maid is simply that, and Sarah is the mistress of the tribe. Sarah's yearning to be a mother are so strong that she is even willing to resort to surrogacy to do so. But things do not turn out as Sarah hoped:

> He [Abram] cohabited with Hagar and she conceived, and when she saw that she had conceived, her mistressed was lowered in her esteem. And Sarai said to Abram, "The wrong done me is your fault! I myself put my maid in your bosom; now that she sees that she is pregnant, I am lowered in her esteem. The Lord decide between you and me!" (Gen 16:4–5)

Tensions mount between the two women, ultimately resulting in Sarah's demanding that Hagar and her son Ishmael be cast out into the desert.

---

3. This is the word used in the Torah to describe the blessing.

Abraham very reluctantly complies, sending his older son and Hagar out into the wilderness with only one flask of water.

Back to my student Nick. I felt that my student's midrashic version of the story of Hagar and Ishmael was so poignant that I invited him to tell me more. Stunningly, Nick said to me with a shaking voice, "I am Ishmael and my mother is Hagar." A story of divorce, his father's second marriage and departure for the other side of the country, a baby step-brother, a profound sense of abandonment and Nick's estrangement from his father, all spilled from my young student's heart. Indeed, this biblical story of a broken and embittered family mirrored Nick's own life.

To make a long story short, when Nick's dad read the *midrash* and came to understand its deeper meaning, when he listened "with the ears of [his] heart," a reconciliation between father and son eventually took place. Nick's understanding of the biblical story, reading it again and again, and his own reflections on it became the agents for love and reconnection to emerge.

In a class that I taught using a contemplative approach to Bible. Matt, a psychotherapist in Chicago, encountered the text of Moses at the Burning Bush (Exodus 3:1–6).

> In response to . . . the question you asked: "What are the old habits (that is, the old 'shoes' you have to take off as you stand on holy ground) you need to remove so you can walk on life's holy path?" I was struck by the metaphor of the burning bush as anger. Moses' anger led to him striking down the Egyptian taskmaster and his banishment into the wilderness. My personal anger has also cost me relationships, job opportunities, etc. However, God reveals an anger (fire) that does not consume (the bush), and thus allows for changing old habits of responding destructively to anger and Moses becoming a leader of his people. This led to my personal work throughout the week on identifying triggers/hurts that lead to my anger, ways of healing the hurts, and changing my bad habits of responding to anger so I also may walk on a more holy path through life."

Matt had begun a new path in life—and this all occurred because of one compelling biblical story.

Deborah, a rabbi, spent a week in a class I taught, which incorporated repeated readings of the biblical text, teachings based on ancient rabbinic commentaries (*midrashim*) on the text, and periods of deep contemplative silence preceded by very pointed and intimate questions regarding the connections between text, commentary, and the students' personal life experiences. At the end of the week, referring to Exodus 3:1–6, Rabbi Deborah told me,

> *God only spoke to Moses after he stopped long enough to look at the burning bush to see that it wasn't consumed.*[4] He practiced what we would call today "mindfulness." The process that you offered to us in class—text, midrashic teachings, and the guiding questions helped me reflect and focus attention on what is most important in my life. I recommitted to slowing down, listening more carefully, and concentrating on appreciating the good that surrounds me.

Helen, a community professional at a university in the Midwestern United States, wrote of her experience with a contemplative approach to the Hebrew Bible:

> [This] was for me both a gentle, safe, and easy channel in which to access biblical text, and a deep, cleansing, psycho-spiritual breath connecting one with the stories of our ancients and the bedrock of Jewish wisdom tradition. This process allowed me "feel" the stories in new and surprising way and connect, for example, with the unnamed and previously one-dimensional character of Potiphar's wife in the Joseph parable. We are used to seeing her only as the foil to Joseph's strength of character, a "walk-on," bit part without even a name beyond "wife," placed there only to create a plot-twist that furthers Joseph's journey in Egypt and his character development. But through the contemplative use of the biblical text, midrashic teachings, and guiding questions, silence, and soft singing, I found myself weeping for the love, pain, and sadness I was surprised to discover in the story of Potiphar's wife. She had always been merely a wicked temptress—one-dimensional, sinful, pathetic, deceitful. But in the quiet space following the words, she became a whole, complex, and deeply wounded woman. During the moments of quiet contemplation and spiritual sanctuary, created lovingly by my teacher, I was able to notice the beauty, strength, and sadness of this woman. I was able to identify with her wounds and appreciate the differences between her circumstances and mine. I felt deeply grateful for the freedom and support that so many women have today, while also grieving the servitude and

---

4. Rabbi Lawrence Kushner points out that it takes some time for a bush to be completely consumed by fire, so "the 'burning bush' was not a miracle. It was a test. God wanted to find out whether or not Moses could pay attention to something for more than a few minutes. When Moses did, God spoke: See, *God was in this Place and I, i did Not Know: Find Self, Spirituality and Ultimate Meaning*, 25.

humiliation that so many women still suffer—living without love or kindness or appreciation for their gifts. I was able to cry for her as I released some of the sadness over the decay and bitterness of my own marriage, appreciating that I have been able to move out and on and through that pain of my own divorce. Identifying with Potiphar's wife in this way also reminded me that I often judge others too harshly or too quickly and with too little information. I am so grateful to have had the opportunity to experience this process . . . .

What Helen had just experienced was similar to a centuries-old process—with a Jewish twist. Let me explain. For many centuries, people have been finding meaning in biblical text. Clergy of many faiths have used the words of the Hebrew Bible to teach moral and ethical lessons, explain life's mysteries, and draw parallels to their own people's life experiences. Ordinary folk through time and circumstance have read the Bible's stories to try to understand God's will and teachings and seek models (both positive and negative) of response to life's dilemmas. And some who were more mystical in their nature, sought to approach the inner heart of Torah so that their own hearts could be touched by the Bible's words. As they encountered the text and traditional methods of studying it, they sought to go beyond an intellectual scriptural analysis; they wanted to delve deeper into the mysterious nature of the Torah, and the great Mystery of God.

In the late eighteenth century, Rabbi Menachem Nachum Twersky of Chernobyl (Ukraine), author of an early Hassidic[5] work called the *Me'or Eynayim* (Light of the Eyes), wrote that if one approached Torah from a purely cognitive perspective *without deeper contemplation,* one could not fully derive the deepest meaning from the sacred words. He further taught that if one sought to live a morally exemplary life, one must dig deep, and find Torah's "inner light," its "Nothingness," the no-thing-ness that went beyond all material, concrete ideas and words.

Torah radiates a dimension of the heart and soul, Rabbi Twersky wrote, that can only be grasped through spiritual meditation:

> The Torah is composed of letters, vowel points, musical notations (*te'amim*), and crownlets. But this is only the revealed Torah; all of it can be accessed by the human mind, each according to one's own level. But the light within Torah, that of which the

---

5. Hassidism is a mystical-ecstatic movement that emerged in eighteenth-century Eastern Europe under the leadership of Rabbi Yisroel (Israel) ben Eliezer (born circa 1700; died 1760) and gained thousands of adherents in the subsequent decades. Today, there are many hundreds of Hassidic sects throughout the world, the most well-known being the Lubavitcher Hassidim.

sages said, "the light within it will bring them to goodness"[6] is the quality of Nothing, that which cannot be grasped. It is beyond any reason (*ta'am*). It is the source from which Torah flows, the Creator. In this way Y-H-W-H and Torah are one.... When your inner self cleaves to Torah's inner light, you become the throne for God's presence as it flows through Torah.... So if you want Torah to be effective in making you good, seek out the flowing light within it, that from which Torah itself is formed.[7]

Whether you are a believer or an atheist, an agnostic or "just" a spiritual person, or a seeker or questioner or simply someone who is curious about what biblical stories might offer you, I invite you to move beyond intellectual analysis, beyond cognition and a purely rational approach to the Bible, and take this journey with me into a contemplative approach to the Book of Genesis.

We begin in the medieval Christian world. In those times, Christian mystics sought to draw closer to God using a spiritual practice called *lectio divina*, which literally means "divine reading," or "reading of the Divine." Through mindful *listening* to a biblical text (rather than visual reading) and then sitting in an extended time of prayerful silence, the mystics tried to integrate God's most profound life lessons into their souls. Then these spiritual seekers would listen to the text again and again they would enter into prayerful silence, and then *again* they would listen, and *again* they would become silent.

Franciscan friar Fr. Richard Rohr, founder of the Center for Action and Contemplation in New Mexico, offers the following instructions for someone who wants to engage in *lectio divina*:

> Read [a biblical] passage slowly and aloud four times. With the first reading, listen with your heart's ear for a phrase or word that stands out for you. During the second reading, reflect on what touches you, perhaps speaking that response aloud or writing in a journal. Third, respond with a prayer or expression of what you have experienced and what it calls you to. Fourth, rest in silence after the reading.[8]

---

6. Lamentations Rabbah, Petihta 2.

7. *Me'or Eynayim* by commentary on Numbers 19:1–2, quoted in Green et al., *Speaking Torah*, 38–39.

8. Fr. Richard Rohr, adapted from the webcast *What is the Emerging Church?* (CD, DVD, MP3 download). These are included in Fr. Richard's book *Yes, And . . .*

Fr. Rohr continues: "During *lectio divina*, a person listens to or reads the text of the Bible with the 'ear of the heart,' as if he or she is in conversation with God and God is suggesting the topics for discussion."

A Benedictine[9] friar, Fr. Luke Dysinger, explains the progression of steps in the *lectio divina* process:

Lectio

> When we read the Scriptures we should . . . allow ourselves to become women and men who are able to listen for the "still, small voice of God"[10]; the "faint murmuring sound" which is God's word for us, God's voice touching our hearts. This gentle listening is an "atunement" to the presence of God in that special part of God's creation which is the Scriptures. . . . In order to hear someone speaking softly we must learn to be silent. We must learn to love silence. . . . The practice of lectio divina . . . requires that we first quiet down in order to hear God's word to us. This is the first step of lectio divina, appropriately called *lectio*—reading. . . . Once we have found a word or a passage in the Scriptures that speaks to us in a personal way, we must take it in and "ruminate" on it.[11]

Meditatio

Fr. Lysinger evokes the image of a cow chewing it cud, gently and methodically *digesting*: the words enter our hearts, our minds, our bodies, our souls. This is what classical *lectio divina* calls the second step in the process: *meditatio*.

Oratio

As we delve even further into our listening, we enter into what the German-Jewish philosopher Martin Buber called the "I-Thou" relationship with God, an intimate conversation between our heart and the Heart of the World: it is as if no one else on the planet is privy to this Heart-to-heart conversation; the

---

9. The Benedictine monastic order was founded in 529 C.E. by St. Benedict of Nursia in Subiaco, Italy during the rule of the Roman Emperor of Justinian I, "the Great."
10. 1 Kings 19:12.
11. Dysinger, "Accepting the Embrace of God."

words now quietly speak our lives and each of us reaches out, and each of us catches the words, and sends them out to God, who quietly, non-verbally engages in the most profound and intimate dialogue just with each of us alone. Christians call this dialogue *prayer*, in Latin *oratio*. Indeed, this sacred conversation *is* prayer. In Hebrew, the infinitive for the verb "to pray," *l'hitpalel*, is a reflexive verb. Like a soft, grammatical boomerang, the words begin with each of us and soar from us to the firmament and back to earth again to each of us privately. When a Jew prays, she prays *very* personally in a sacred conversation with God—even in a room full of other worshippers. She can be alone and together with her community at the same time. This is indeed *oratio* in the same sense as understood by contemplative Christians.

Contemplatio

The final step in the Christian contemplative practice known as *lectio divina* is known as *contemplatio*—deep silence in which we integrate the words of the biblical text, their meaning for our own lives, and we begin to understand that through Scripture's words, God is speaking directly to each of us very personally. Again, in the loving, intimate silence of these moments, we must listen with the "ears of the heart" as if we were held in God's most intimate embrace, as if the Author of all Creation is whispering sublime messages of profound and everlasting love only for each of us, especially for each of us. The text has words, but now in our silent contemplation, words float away and what remains is pure sacred connection. Fr. Lysinger writes:

> No one who has ever been in love needs to be reminded that there are moments in loving relationships when words are unnecessary. It is the same in our relationship with God. Wordless, quiet rest in the presence of the One who loves us has a name in the Christian tradition—*contemplatio*, contemplation. Once again we practice silence, letting go of our own words; this time simply enjoying the experience of being in the presence of God.[12]

And how does all this relate to Jews and Judaism and this book's purpose?

A story:

---

12. Dysinger, "Accepting the Embrace of God."

INTRODUCTION

In 2006, I was training to become a Jewish spiritual director. My esteemed teachers were Rabbi Howard (Avruhm) Addison, Barbara Breitman,[13] and Rabbi Zari Weiss.[14]

As my classmates and I sat down for one session, Rabbi Avruhm began to sing a *niggun*, a slow, lilting, wordless Hassidic melody. We all joined in. Together we sang—and the space became transformed by our voices undulating in sacred energy. Rabbis Avruhm and Zari and Barbara led us gently, first bringing the volume to a louder pitch and then quieting us down. Together we sang, without words, for about twenty minutes and then, without preface, Rabbi Avruhm began to read a text from the Book of Genesis: *"Jacob was left alone. And a man wrestled with him until the break of dawn. . . ."*[15] Avruhm read slowly, quietly—articulating each word.

I felt my heart awaken, but my mind was restless. "What is he doing?" I wondered.

After the reading—silence. Nothing. "What's going on?" I thought.

My heart was beating a little faster. I was a little scared of this deep silence. Still, nothing. It seemed like an eternity.

Then, Avruhm's voice once more: "Jacob was left alone. And a man wrestled with him until the break of dawn. . . ." The same text—*again?* Now, I was getting annoyed. "What's this all about?"

After the reading—again, silence. Nothing.

My heart was more fully awake, but this time, my mind was just a *bit* less restless.

As we all sat quietly, I began to recline into the quiet. The lyrics of a sweet song by one of my favorite Jewish singers and most honored spiritual guides, Rabbi David Zeller, of blessed memory, came to me: "Listen, listen, listen to my heart's song . . . ." I began to settle down and soon I caught what my beloved father, of blessed memory, used to call "a sliver of a glimmer of a hint" of what Fr. Lysinger described as "wordless, quiet rest in the presence of the One Who loves us."

I found myself wandering in Torah's words: "And Jacob was left alone . . . ."

Soon, I was *ruminating*—about times of *aloneness*, in my own life. I asked myself: Had positive change or movement come? Was *aloneness* the same as loneliness? In those silent moments, I began to understand that I

---

13. Rabbi Addison and Dr. Breitman are co-editors of *Jewish Spiritual Direction: An Innovative Guide from Traditional and Contemporary Sources* (Jewish Lights, 2006).

14. Rabbi Weiss is currently the spiritual leader of Kol HaNeshamah congregation (Reform) in Seattle, Washington.

15. Genesis 32:25–32.

had embarked on a path of self-exploration—and I palpably felt God's Presence right there with me.

Soon, Avruhm was reading the text for a third time. This time, I listened with the ears of my heart—and when silence came, I welcomed it. I could feel myself beginning what would become a *very* long conversation with God—a dialogue that continues to this very moment.

Afterwards, Avruhm and Zari and Barbara were leading us once again in the *niggun*, the wordless melody. Five minutes, ten, fifteen, reaching crescendos—rising and ebbing, like the tides within our hearts, blood coursing through us—our souls embodied, our hearts wide open—open to the wondrous possibilities of the I-Thou dialogue of our futures.

When it was all over, I was stunned by my deep need for quiet. A loquacious and gregarious person, now I simply wanted to remain in silence. Where was a hermitage, I wondered?

Back home—back to earth: crash! I should have known that I couldn't capture the sublime feeling I had as Avruhm read and reread the biblical verses interspersed by silence and a *niggun*. A few days after my return to my *regular life*, I enthusiastically invited two friends to try to replicate my *lectio divina* experience with me. Alas, the experiment didn't work! No sublime insights, not a hint of spirituality. I had bombed! I should have realized that any deep spiritual practice just doesn't come that easy! It takes discipline and yes, *practice*! I very quickly realized that I needed a *lot* of practice—and I resolved to learn with the "pros"—Catholic contemplatives who practiced *lectio divina* on a regular basis.

Back at home in the Washington D.C. metro area, I found a small Christian group that practiced *lectio divina* on a weekly basis. I asked to join the group and was welcomed graciously. I was the only Jew and non-Christian in the group of six individuals. For the next six months, I sat with my new friends and each week, one person took responsibility to be the *reader*. We followed the classic *lectio divina* format:

- short silence (about two minutes)
- first reading of text—either from the Hebrew Bible or Christian Scriptures (*lectio*) [reading]
- silence (about ten minutes) (*meditatio*) [gentle rumination or reflection]
- second reading of text
- silence (about ten minutes) *(oratio)* [prayer]
- third reading of text
- silence (about ten minutes) (*contemplatio*) [contemplation]

Fr. Lysinger teaches that the purpose of the third reading is "experiencing Christ 'calling us forth' into *doing* or *being*. Members ask themselves what Christ in the text is calling them to *do* or to *become* today or this week. After the silence, each [participant] shares [his/her thoughts] and the exercise concludes with each person praying for the person on the right."[16]

Every week, as I left our sessions, I became ever more determined to find a way to adapt this profound Christian spiritual practice into a shape that would *work* for my own people.

What I absolutely *knew* was that a classic Christian design would not work well with Jews. Jews are a talkative people. Our Torah study, mostly cognitive, is like a wonderful intellectual ping pong game: one person expresses an idea—using her paddle to whack the idea across the table to another, who slams another idea back! Lots of words, lots of argumentation (which we assert is a *machloket l'shem shamayim*—a controversy for the sake of heaven!). Learning and advancing knowledge in Jewish tradition has always been based on *sacred arguing*.[17] Maybe that's why culturally, we are considered such a contentious people!

I concluded that extended periods of silence, *with no cognitive or learning element,* just wouldn't work with Jews. I set myself a challenge: how to advance a spiritual discipline for Jews, a people for whom words have immense power,[18] with silent contemplation at its core. I sought to find that delicate balance between speech and silence, between matters of the mind and matters of the heart and soul. I was (and still am) absolutely convinced that *life's most important concerns must flow through the mind and ultimately be dealt with within one's soul.* If they reside only in one's mind, we remain stuck: if soul and heart remain unengaged, we cannot grow.

I began to ask friends, students, and colleagues whether *traditional* Torah study and discussion touched their hearts and souls, as well as their minds, whether Torah's words really spoke to them about the challenges, delights, and dilemmas of their own lives.

Sam, a scientist with a strong spiritual bent, told me, "Very rarely. I am excited by the intellectual *tussle* of Torah study, but only once in a very long

---

16. Dysinger, "Accepting the Embrace of God." This is a slightly different format to that described by Fr. Richard Rohr. Different *lectio divina* groups vary formats and modalities, according to the group's needs. Some groups include prayerful chant as well.

17. For more about sacred arguing in the Jewish tradition, see Rabbi Anson Laytner's book *Arguing with God: A Jewish Tradition*.

18. Words have such immense power in Jewish tradition because the very act of Creation was accomplished through Divine speech: in Genesis 1:3, we read: "God *said*, 'let there be light,' and there was light." This idea is echoed in Christian Scripture in The Gospel according to John 1:1: "In the beginning was the Word, and the Word was with God, and the Word was God."

time do I feel a tug at my heart. It usually doesn't relate much to my daily life. I would love to feel more of that."

Judy, a yoga instructor and observant Jew, expressed her frustration that each time she attended synagogue and listened to a *"dvar Torah"*—a sermon or homily, whether delivered by the rabbi or by a layperson—she was *left cold* because they were always so *heady*, with long-winded explications of the origins of biblical words, or derivatives from other ancient Mesopotamian languages, anthropological observations about life in biblical times, and esoteric points of Israelite law that "have nothing to do with me! Once, just once, I wish they would speak about life in *my* times, about things that matter to me!"

I asked Judy how the words of Torah might come alive for her, and she asked me to give her some time to think about it. Several weeks later, Judy returned to me and said: "[Biblical] Sarah was infertile; I gave birth to Jamie via in-vitro fertilization after Michael and I tried for years to have a baby. *Sarah's story speaks my life!* I would *love* to focus for a while on her story—but without so many back-and-forth arguments about how many angels dance on a pin of one word! I'm a yoga teacher! I like to feel my body and also to feel silence!"

Judy would have loved the experience that Merle, a speech therapist working in the public school system, shared with me:

> I was blessed to experience a synthesis of *lectio divina* with Torah text. I was being guided through a text by using *lectio divina*, a prayerful, personal method of engaging with the text. Our teacher shared this process as a way to connect the text of Torah with the Torah of our hearts. I had never learned Torah from the inside out, being asked questions like "How does this passage relate to what is going on in your life?" or "How does God show up for you when you hear this phrase?" I remember feeling a resonating sensation in my body, inviting me into deep discernment through silence. This process was in contrast to the model I had learned growing up of verbally wrestling with text. By inviting God to be present with me as I read or listened to sacred passages, followed by periods of contemplation, I was able to infuse a new depth of meaning into my understanding of the text. When engaged in the practice of *lectio divina*, I open my heart to God's love and wisdom and am able to witness how the selected texts can have transformative powers in my life.

In just a few words, Judy had articulated the essence of my own desire to find a way to bring the best of *lectio divina* into a creative interplay with Jewish teachings and Merle had described a good bit of what I wanted to create in a systematic process merging Hebrew Scripture, ancient and contemporary Jewish teachings about the biblical text, and guiding personal questions preceding contemplative silence as a spiritual practice,

For years now, I have been experimenting with different ways to accomplish just this spiritual merger, and I have been *field testing* with rabbinic, cantorial and rabbinic pastor students, and Jewish laypeople from different communities.[19] Each experiment has yielded new insights as to how to birth a Jewish form of *lectio divina* into the world.

I believe it is finally time for the Jewish baby to be born, and—just like a Jewish baby boy or girl—to be given a Hebrew name. That name is *Kriat Hakodesh*—in English: *Reading the Holy*. This practice is crafted around what we Jews share with our Christian and Muslim brothers and sisters: a strong encouragement to listen to the *heart* of the text, with all that is in us, with every fiber of our beings.

One of the central prayers of Judaism is called the *Shema—Listen, O Israel* (you Godwrestling people),[20] Y-H-V-H, your God, Y-H-V-H, is One![21] The key teaching of this prayer is that we must listen not only with our ears, but with *all* of who and what we are.

In Jewish liturgy, immediately following the *Shema*, we are taught that we must strive to love God: "*b'chol levavcha, b'chol nafshecha, u-v'chol me'odecha*"—with all our heart(s), with all our soul and with all our [physical] might, that is, our earthly and earthy energy.[22]

---

19. I thank the students of the ALEPH: Alliance for Jewish Renewal Ordination Program, who have studied the method I have developed and have *piloted* it throughout North America and Canada, with much positive response. I especially thank my beloved student (and now colleague) Rabbi Eva Sax-Bolder and my "Kedems" Torah Study group with which I shared Torah learning for thirteen years. I am also indebted to members of the Adat Shalom Reconstructionist Congregation of Bethesda, Maryland for engaging with *contemplative Torah* with me.

20. The notion of "Israel" as a "Godwrestling people" was first introduced in contemporary times by Rabbi Arthur Waskow in his books *Godwrestling* (1987) and *Godwrestling, Round 2* (1998). Rabbi Waskow explains this interpretation from Genesis 32:29 in which Jacob wrestles with an angel and his name is changed to "Israel": "Your name shall no longer be Jacob, but Israel, for you have striven (i.e., wrestled) with beings divine and human and have prevailed."

21. Deuteronomy 6:4. I consciously use the Y-H-V-H name for God here, because it is unpronounceable. Biblical philologists believe that the sounds that might be made from these consonants might be a deep "breath" sound—the wind or spirit—the *ruach* in Hebrew (which literally means both *wind* and *spirit*) of the Divine.

22. Deuteronomy 6:5–9. The word *levavcha* literally means "hearts" in the plural. Certainly human beings do not possess more than one cardiac organ! The deeper meaning is that in Israelite (and later Jewish) belief, the "heart" was the locus of not only emotion (as we think of the heart today), but also of the intellect—our minds.

Thus, from our earliest spiritual formation, Israelites (and later who we collectively became—Jews) have been guided toward *deep listening* and *deep living based on Torah's words*. I have titled this book, *Listening to the Heart of Genesis*, to reflect what we have been taught from our earliest beginnings: the words of our sacred texts are to be woven *first* into everything we feel (emotionally and physically) and then into everything we understand and teach to our young ones, and finally into everything we do and how we live our lives. First and foremost is to *listen*.

> [T]ake these words that I [God] command you now to heart. Teach them intently to your children. Speak them when you sit inside your house or walk upon the road, when you lie down and when you rise up . And bind them as a sign upon your hand, and keep them visible before your eyes. Inscribe them on the doorposts of your house and on your gates.[23]

A holistic and whole contemplative approach tells us that we may take Torah's words into our bodies, into our muscles, so that we may have "muscle memory" of our lives' experiences, even from young childhood, drawn into the rhythm and cadence of our breathing, into "all the openings and vessels of the body."[24]

A contemplative approach tells us that we may welcome Torah's words into the deepest corners of our lives—into the shadow places and the brightest spots, into our family joys and most bitter sorrows, into our most harmonious experiences and our greatest and most painful conflict. It tells us that we may use the stories of Torah's people—Abraham and Sarah, Hagar, Isaac, Jacob, Dinah, and all the others, *midrashically*—that is, metaphorically, as allegories and parables about our own lives' experiences. Such an approach enables us to embrace Torah's stories and tales *as reflections of our own lives and struggles, our own triumphs, our defeats, our own dreams and disappointments*. Torah's words do indeed speak our lives. I invite you to journey with me into the words, into the rugged territory of your own heart, into the cracks and crevices of your own hearts and souls. However complex, however painful, however exhilarating, may it be a blessed journey!

---

23. Deuteronomy 6:4–9

24. In Jewish daily prayer, we express gratitude for God's creation and sustenance of our bodies: "*Blessed are you,* Y-H-V-H, our God, Sovereign of the universe, who has created the human being with wisdom, making for us all the openings and vessels of the body. It is revealed and known before your Throne of Glory that if one of these passageways should be open when it should be closed, or blocked up when it should be free, one could not stay alive or stand before you. Blessed are you, Y-H-V-H, the wondrous healer of all flesh." (Translation by Joel Rosenberg [adapted] in *Kol Haneshamah Shabbat Vehagim*, Wyncote, PA: Reconstructionist, 1996, 162.)

Chapter 1

Bereshit

Adam Hides from God

> *"Where are you?"*
>
> —Genesis 3:1–12

They heard the sound of the Holy One moving about in the garden at the breezy time of day; and the man and his wife hid from the Holy One among the trees of the garden. God called out to the man and said to him, "Where are you?"

—Genesis 3:8–9

When the world was not yet born, God had a vision of a magnificent universe filled with the sun and moon and all the stars of the heavens, with clouds and rain, with glistening oceans and winding rivers, lofty mountains, forests, savannahs, green meadows, and amber deserts, an earth teeming with wildlife of all kinds. And so God went about the work of creation. Biblical tradition tells us that all this took six days—perhaps this was a metaphor for six hundred million years, or at least a *long, long, long* time.

Finally, toward the end of Creation, a lonely God envisioned a being who could be His/Her[1] companion in this splendid universe. Men and

---

1. A note on language: God has no gender. Indeed, in Kabbalah, the Jewish mystical tradition, the Holy One has always been imagined as male *and* female—one named the *Kadosh Baruch Hu*—the Holy One, Blessed be He and the Shechinah, the *[female]* Indwelling Presence. How good it would be if we could re-imagine the Holy One in gender-neutral or even multi-gendered terms! For this reason, I have chosen to alternate my use of the male and female pronouns in English. Sometimes I refer to God as "He," "His," "Him" and sometimes as "She," "Hers," or "Her." There is no specific thematic linkage to the way I use these terms. I am simply trying to make the point

women came into the world. The first human being was an called an *adam*, an "earth creature," whose name derives from the Hebrew word *adamah*, which means earth. (Some ancient rabbis believed that this first person was an *androgynos*, a hermaphrodite, only split later into male and female bodies.) Once this separation occurred, two humans, universally known as Adam and Eve, dwelled in a Garden called Eden, naked, unaware, and unashamed of their nudity.

Follow me into the Garden. What might we see there? Luscious trees ripe with fruit, verdant foliage hiding birds and creeping creatures. And these first two people who have never seen any others like themselves, who have never experienced suffering or loss, who know nothing about the complexity of the world as now we know it. They are true and pure innocents. As they walk in the Garden, they come upon many trees. God forbids them to eat from the fruit of the tree of the knowledge of good and evil.

Good and evil? What are they? Such concepts that seem so elementary to us are unknown to them. What is "knowledge"? Adam and Eve don't understand what that means, just that God warns them that of *this* tree they may not eat. They may enjoy the fruit of all the other trees in the Garden, but not the fruit of *this* tree, for if they eat of it, they will die.

Temptation overcomes Adam and Eve. Their tempter comes in the form of *"the shrewdest of all the wild beasts that the Lord God had made"* (3:1), the serpent, who offers a most attractive lure. Speaking to Eve, the serpent says, *"You are not going to die, but God knows that as soon as you eat of it your eyes will be opened and you will be like divine beings who know good and bad"* (3:5).

Eve, more adventurous than Adam, eats of the tree, and then offers its fruit to her mate, who also eats. Immediately, *"the eyes of both of them were opened and they perceived that they were naked."* Now, instead of feeling *"like divine beings"* who have the great power of knowledge, as the serpent promised, Adam and Eve feel ashamed at their nakedness, and they "sewed together fig leaves and made themselves loincloths" (3:7).

Now *self-consciousness* and *shame* have come into the human world—and "bad" has come along as well. Before Adam and Eve walked freely in the Garden, happy in their naked state, unaware that there was anything wrong with their nudity. *Now* they are uncomfortable, and begin to feel that their genitalia (and exposing them) is shameful. How tragic that the most life-giving parts of themselves, where as sexual beings they would derive the most pleasure, are now sources of shame for them! Now, with

---

that these pronouns are mere gender-symbols and that just as there are infinite human minds to imagine God, so there is an infinity of legitimate names for the Holy One. Choose your own as your spirit moves you! You will *never* run out of images!

self-consciousness, the radiant beauty of the human body is diminished. Forever more, we humans will be ashamed of our bodies. And *inhibition* has come into the world. The pure, innocent spontaneity that was born with Adam and Eve is now gone forever.

Temptation is the first of many trials that Adam and Eve will endure in their lives. It is the first of life's tribulations that they will experience. They are beginning to learn life's lessons, that life on this earth will not always be easy.

Hearing the sound of God moving in the Garden, Adam and Eve hide among the trees and God calls out to Adam, "*Ayeka?* (אַיֶּכָּה)— *Where are you?*" Adam responds, "*I heard the sound of You in the garden, and I was afraid because I was naked, so I hid.*" If God is everywhere, then the Holy One certainly knows where Adam is in the Garden. Then why does God ask Adam, " *Ayeka?—where are you?*" This question is not about location. Let's explore.

When I first encountered this text, I wanted to understand the deeper meaning of God's question, *Ayeka?* I turned to ancient rabbinic wisdom for help, to the sages of Judaism of the first centuries of the Common Era, who also sought to understand this biblical story. These early rabbis struggled for understanding by engaging in an elaborate conversation. In this conversation, which took place over centuries, the rabbis would spin tales relating to the text to bring forth (through metaphor and analogy) the spiritual meaning of the biblical story. This type of tale-telling or folkloric style is known as *midrash aggadah*.

Midrash aggadah comprises a vast corpus of interpretive commentary on the biblical text with the goal of explaining and elucidating it. One such collection is known as *Midrash Rabbah*—the "Great" (*Rabbah*) Interpretation.

A remarkable example of such interpretive commentary is found in *Bereshit Rabbah* (Genesis Rabbah), where we find two rabbis playing with the Hebrew spelling of the word *ayeka* (אַיֶּכָּה)—"*where are you?*"—and the word, *eicha* (אֵיכָה).[2] Both are spelled with the same consonants, but with different vowels. *Ayeka* means "where?" as in "where are you?" *Eicha* is used in the sense of "how did you get into this mess?" OR "how have you fallen so far?" *Eicha* is also the first word and the Hebrew title of the biblical book of Lamentations, which mourns the destruction of the First Temple in Jerusalem by the Babylonians in 586 B.C.E. *Eicha* is a profoundly plaintif and sad word. In this midrashic reading, *ayeka* and *eicha* are two sides of a single question. God's calling out *ayeka* to Adam in the Garden is

---

2. Genesis Rabbah 19:9.

a mournful question, "Where are you, my child?" "How have you strayed? How have you become so lost? Can you find your way back home, to your center, to your own groundedness, to your own *adamah* (earth) (for you are *Adam*, man—or human)?"

In life, we sometimes find ourselves on a much different path than the one we envisioned or dreamed about when we were younger. If we are introspective, we might look back and wonder "Where has the time gone? How did I stray from my original dreams and visions?" We may regret all that we haven't done or accomplished in all the years that we have been blessed to live. We may dwell upon our mistakes, and the ways in which we have strayed during the journey from the pure innocence of childhood into adulthood, into that state of being in which we have inevitably done wrong, hurt others, and have been hurt ourselves. We might be dissatisfied with our lives and even ask ourselves, "*Eicha*—how did I get myself into this mess?" At moments like these, we dig deep within our hearts, minds, and souls and ask ourselves, "*Ayeka?*"—where am I—*now*—at this moment in my life, at *this very moment?*" And then we ask ourselves, "What's next? How do I live my life from this moment forward?"

From a different perspective, we may simply muse more neutrally on time gone by and how differently life has turned out for us. We may be sad about all that has been left undone or disappointed about unrealized dreams or plans left unfinished. For some of us, rather than dwelling on our mistakes and the ways we have gone astray, things are less complicated—we are able to simply accept that our life's trajectory has turned out differently than we had originally intended; we live more by that common dictum, "It is what it is." Nonetheless, as reflective people, we still might stop to ask ourselves, "*Eicha?*—how did we get here?" and "*Ayeka?*—where are we now?" We might stop to contemplate the directions in which our lives have progressed, where we are in the present moment, and what comes next.

The poet, Jinks (Jennifer) Hoffmann, expresses our human ponderings beautifully:

> Where are you today?
>
> As this summer draws to a close
>
> and summers and summers
>
> and winters and winters
>
> have both prodded you and lifted you up
>
> to this moment,
>
> where are you, today?
>
> As you look back

generation upon generation,
ancestors and ancestors
a jagged line behind you,
their stories for good and bad
alive yet in you,
where are you at this moment?
If you listen inward
to the place, the still, small place
that is inscribed
with only your name
where are you
and why are you
in this blessed circle
at this moment in time?
Indubitably you too have had
your measure of jaggedness
and gratitude
in your summers and in your winters.
How is the full measure
of this moment, this summer,
past summers, past winters
ancestors and generations,
how is the full measure
of who you are in this moment,
a gift to the life of this circle
and the larger circle
of Spiritual Life in the world?[3]

We are challenged as human beings with the existential question, *ayeka*? How do we answer with strength and affirmation *hineni*—here I am?

Adam answers God's questions "where are you?" and "how did you get into this mess?" by hiding. Most of us, however, are capable of reflective answers to these profound questions. At a number of points in our lives, we are faced with situations that demand of us to look courageously

---

3. Used with the poet's permission.

in the mirror and decide where we stand, what is most important to us, and how we will proceed with our lives. It is at those moments that we realize where we are and plan how we will extricate ourselves from unhealthy situations, deciding how to begin to move toward a more life-affirming stance for our futures.

Text to Life

> *Sascha, a former dental hygienist, came to ask her ayeka question after decades of marriage. As she did, she embarked on a journey toward wholeness. Here is her story.*
>
> I got married young to a man for whom I felt deep affection, but no passion. Gene was a kind and responsible man who loved me and I felt cherished. I had dreams of exploring many lands and peoples, and researching *something*, but I was too timid to venture off on my own. Gene was my safety net.
>
> I was a good wife, and Gene was an excellent husband. Like many wives of the 1970s, I helped support Gene through school. As he pursued his studies, I worked, kept house, and soon our first child, a beautiful daughter, Rachel, was born.
>
> After Gene's graduation, we lived a moderately affluent life. We had two more wonderful children, Monica and David, and I stopped working outside our home. I poured all of my creativity into being a great mom. I became very involved in my children's activities, socialized with other mothers, and was generally bored with my life. Nonetheless, I would say that life was "good"—safe, self-contained, limited, sometimes interesting, but usually rather prosaic. What was missing for me was the juicy part! Increasingly over time, I would ask myself, "Sascha, where are you? Where is that young woman who dreamed of foreign lands and exploring different cultures? Where is that young girl who read voraciously and was curious about the world?" My world seemed to have contracted so very much. I was hungry for more. My inner hunger began to manifest on the outside as I gained weight each year.
>
> When I was fifty-three, my longings for a different life turned outward. I explored meditation, *spiritual* self-help books, yoga and spiritual retreats. Finally, I found a Unitarian Universalist Church. Gene did not join me at services. He once had said to me, "I really don't understand what you mean by

spiritual. For me, I guess *spiritual* means watching the kids grow up and loving you, and going on an occasional hike." On the most basic level, I think he is right—all of this *is* spirituality. But my need for spirituality seemed to pull me beyond the borders of my home.

I became active at the Unitarian church, and especially loved a Bible study class in which I first encountered the story of Adam and Eve in the Garden of Eden and God's question to Adam *"where are you?"* (3:9). "It's really an existential question," my minister said. "It's a question we should each ask ourselves every day, and the answer should prod us into some movement if we keep hearing *nowhere* or *somewhere I don't want to be*."

I was astounded by the minister's comment. I began to tremble. I tried to banish the question from my mind, but I just couldn't shake it—"Where are you, Sascha?" My ears were pounding, as if my heart had taken up residence in my brain. Years later, after meeting several Christians and Jews who were engaged in contemplative practice and after I had learned the phrase "listening with the ears of the heart," from Fr. Richard Rohr's teaching, I came to understand that what was happening to me was an important spiritual breakthrough. For the first time I was listening with the ears of my own heart.

All of this happened in the Fall. By January, when the weather was very cold, I kept thinking, "Now is the winter of our discontent."[4] I was clearly discontent. The biblical question *"where are you?"* kept echoing within me, prodding me to seek an answer. Finally, I sought counsel with my minister. "I don't know why the question keeps hounding me," I said—and the tears came. "I have a good life, a fine husband and friends. It's all good. Why am I so unhappy?" The minister quietly responded, "Perhaps you are searching for something deeper. Maybe you need to explore this with your husband."

"I saw that I was naked—and I was afraid" (3:10). This phrase now almost constantly resonated in my mind. One afternoon, our Bible study group was studying the story of God's call to Abram when God said to him *"Go forth from your native land and from your father's house, to the land that I will show you . . ."* (12:1).

The group was observing my minister and a visiting rabbi in conversation about this sentence, and my minister was pointing out that to venture forth from everything that one knows

---

4. William Shakespeare, *Richard III*, Act I, Scene I.

takes a huge leap of faith and that it had to be a very scary thing to do. Everyone agreed. The rabbi commented that in one of the *midrashim* about this verse, the first Hebrew words, *lech lecha* (לך לך), might be translated as "take *yourself* and go forth" or "go forth *to yourself*," meaning that God was instructing Abram to go to his own soul's territory—to find *himself*, to go on an inner journey and become his most authentic self.

I was thunderstruck. The "winter of my discontent" had became a year-round condition for me and after that day's Bible study, I *knew* that I had to *go forth*, speak to Gene, and see if there was any way we could venture forward together.

Gene and I talked that very night. I tried to explain what I was feeling and had been feeling for a long time. Needless to say, Gene was perplexed, and surprised, as he had been feeling no discontent. He asked that we begin marriage counseling together. Though I doubted that such therapy could help us, I agreed to give it a try.

After almost a year of counseling, I knew that I needed to make my way forward alone and I asked Gene for a divorce. In the same dignified and responsible manner that he had always acted in our marriage, Gene agreed to the divorce and within days I moved out to begin my new life on my own. Though I felt sadness at our parting, I felt more excitement (and much trepidation) as I headed out of the safe "garden" I had inhabited for three and half decades. I was indeed naked and exposed to a world in which I no longer enjoyed the protections of Gene's steady guidance. I now needed to navigate all the mundane demands of life on my own.

I found a job and a new home for myself and began carving out a new relationship with my grown children. I explained as honestly as I could what I had been feeling over time. Each one of my children received this news differently, and each one accepted my news with love and pledged their complete support. Today, I enjoy loving relationships with each of them. I continue to face the challenge of living life as a single woman, but I am increasingly finding a natural path for myself. I have new friends and have kept some friends from my married days. I travel alone or with friends to some of those exotic places I dreamed of when I was younger. I live a more spiritually and intellectually rich life, and my sense of awe and connection to God is very strong. I feel free to let my heart and my mind (and my feet!) travel to lands

> (inner and outer) of my own choosing—and I feel that my life is abundantly vibrant and full.
>
> The feminist poet Marge Piercy once wrote, "a strong woman is a woman strongly afraid."[5] While sometimes I still feel naked in the world, more often than not I feel my own strength and I feel less afraid. My first "going forth," like the patriarch Abram—leaving the security of a *good* marriage—has led to new "goings forth" that have deeply enriched my life. More often than not these days, I can answer the question, *ayeka*—where are you?—with clarity and confidence. For this, I am grateful and proud to be "a strong woman who is strongly afraid."

Exploring the Text Within

Find a quiet and comfortable place to sit in contemplative silence with the above teachings and with the following questions about you and your life's experience. You may choose to focus on one question or sit with several. Ask yourself: what do the biblical text and these teachings mean to me in my life?

> *Then the eyes of both of them were opened and they perceived that they were naked; and they sewed together fig leaves and made themselves loincloths.*
>
> (Genesis 3:7)

> Has there been a time in my life when I have experienced profound shame?

> *I was afraid because I was naked, so I hid.*
>
> (Genesis 3:10)

> Has there been a time in my life when I have avoided or hidden from an essential truth about myself?
>
> Am I hiding now?

---

5. Marge Piercy, from her poem, "For Strong Women."

God called out to the man and said to him, "Ayeka—where are you?"
(Genesis 3:9)

> *Ayeka?* Where am I in my life now?
>
> Are there changes I need or want to make in order to be in a different place?

Chapter 2

Bereishit

Finding Our *Hineni*—Here I Am
—to the *Ayeka* Question

They heard the sound of Holy One moving about in the garden at the breezy time of day; and the man and his wife hid from the Holy One among the trees of the garden. God called out to the man and said to him, "Where are you?"

—Genesis 3:8–9

The profound question, *"Ayeka,"* "where are you?" deserves further exploration. How will we respond? Adam was not yet ready to respond to this question because he was frightened and hid from God's presence. But many others in the Book of Genesis and elsewhere in the Hebrew Bible answer with the word, *"hineni*—here I am."

Let us consider our own answers.

"Ayeka? is the first question posed in the Hebrew Bible and sometimes appears with another transformational word, the answer *"hineni*—here I am," as a pair, and they are a formula for life. Like an antiphonal song, a call and response, we hear a voice calling to us—the voice of God, the voice of a lover, a friend, even an adversary that challenges us to respond to *"Ayeka?"*

—"Where are you my child?" God calls out.

—"Where are you my beloved one?" our lover, our spouse, our partner beseeches us.

—"Where are you, dear one?" our friend, our ally cries out to us.

—"Where are you?" our enemy screams.

Sometimes, when I hear that question—whether from the Holy One, from my beloved, from a friend or foe, like Adam, I want to hide—because I don't really know myself well enough at that moment to respond with clarity. And then, there are times when my mind is clear, when I have done the work of deep contemplation, when I have been given insight (in-sight) and I can answer with lucidity and certainty, "*Hineni, here I am.*"

What brings me clarity? What allows me to stand strong and claim my center? I am most able to respond in the fullness of my own *hineini* when I am able to get out of my own way and banish all the old negative messages in my head, messages learned over a lifetime, messages that tell me that I am unworthy. When I falter I try to return to these truths. Then I am able to respond in the fullness of my own *hineni* when I am most able to truly have confidence in (believe?) what Jewish tradition teaches me in three simple, but ultimately quite profound, affirmations that return me to the "home of my soul."[1]

The first affirmation is that *I was created in the Divine image* ("*Let us make the earth creature/human being in Our Image . . . male and female God created them*"; 1:26–27). What a radical concept! I am a mirror of God! I reflect the Divine within me! Of course, this does not mean that God has two eyes, two ears, a nose, and a mouth (indeed, then God would look like us humans!). Rather, being created in the "image" of God is beyond the visual. It means that something of the mystery, something of the godly and *goodly* Essence is within us, and that not only does this elevate us above the rest of created sentient beings, but it also places upon us a responsibility to live in harmony with that Essence. Given this challenge of responsibility, how can I *not* respond with a determined "*Hineni*—here I am"?

The second affirmation is that *I am endowed with a pure soul,* unsullied by sin or misdeed. In the Jewish traditional morning liturgy, one line is striking to me: אלהי נשמה שנתתה בי טהורה היא "My God, the soul you have planted within me is pure." What a powerful vote of confidence in the beauty and goodness of humankind! Unlike teachings that all human beings are tainted by "original sin," Judaism asserts that our souls are pure. It is only as our life unfolds, only as we act in the world, that our souls become tarnished by the wrongs that we commit; there is no supposition that from birth we are already blemished by the sin and "fall" of the first man and woman in the Garden of Eden when they ate from the tree of knowledge of good and evil. Given this Jewish assertion of the purity of the human soul, how can I *not* respond with a commitment to keep my soul as pure as possible in the way I act in the world, by declaring with faith, *hineni, here I am?*

---

1. Rabbi Shlomo Carlebach—song lyric.

The third affirmation is that *God loves me with an "unending love"* (in Hebrew, *ahavat olam*) (אהבת עולם).² In traditional Judaism, this boundless love is manifested through God's bestowing upon the Jewish people the gift of Torah and commandments, guidance by which to live our lives—and these are deeply cherished parts of a Jewish heritage. Beyond these, however, are the manifestations of God's love that we experience daily in our interactions with other human beings. In a poem entitled "Unending Love," which has become part of the liturgy in many contemporary prayer books, Rabbi Rami Shapiro writes,

> Embraced, touched, soothed, and counseled . . .
>
> ours are the arms, the fingers, the voices;
>
> ours are the hands, the eyes, the smiles;
>
> We are loved by an unending love.³

With these three affirmations, I can stand before the Holy One knowing that I intend with all my heart to live in harmony with my best essence, which is a reflection of God's Essence, and that my best essence reflects a pure soul. I also believe that in my most ardent efforts to live a life that reflects the goodly and the godly, I am held in God's loving embrace—endlessly. What more could I ask? Strengthened and fortified by these affirmations, I respond, *"Hineni—here I am"* to even the most giant challenges and thus I answer the question posed to me by God or other humans—*"Ayeka—where are you?"*⁴

I find myself in my most authentic place, where I can truly say *hineni*—here I am—when I am happiest and most fulfilled. To some, depending on the affirmations I have outlined may seem a naïve and simplistic way of thinking. I acknowledge that it flies in the face of logic and reason to believe in pure souls, humans as created in the Divine image, or God's endless love. The skeptical among us might scoff. Nonetheless, I insist that such belief is a worthy philosophy to live by. For me they are step stones on a road to happiness—a path that is grounded in a relationship with God based on the eighteenth-century Hassidic master Reb Nachman of Bratslav's simple dictum: "It is a great *mitzvah* to live in joy!" But joy doesn't always come so

---

2. Though Jewish liturgy states that this "unending love" is to the "House of Israel," many Jews (including me!) feel strongly that such love is not limited to the Jewish people—and that God's love extends to *all* people, Jew and non-Jew alike.

3. See Rabbi Shapiro's poem as liturgy in *Kol Haneshamah: Shabbat Vehagim*, 61.

4. For an inspiring treatment of Ayeka and Hineini, see Leonard Felder's book, *Here I Am*, chapter 1.

easily to us, and for many, finding happiness in one's life requires effort, a pursuit of our desire to enjoy life.

Professor Tal Ben-Shahar of Harvard University, who teaches the university's most popular course based on a series of lectures with the theme "Happier: Learn the Secrets to Daily Joy and Lasting Fulfillment," writes: "Attaining lasting happiness requires that we enjoy the journey on our way toward a destination we deem valuable. Happiness, therefore, is not about making it to the peak of the mountain, nor is it about climbing aimlessly around the mountain: happiness is the experience of climbing toward the peak."[5]

Reb Nachman taught about "climbing toward the peak" when he counseled his followers to always live in joy. This wasn't so easy for Nachman himself, who lived in poverty and was prone to deep depression (he was called a "tormented master" by one of his best biographers),[6] but his pursuit of joy enabled him to sing and pray to God with great fervor and to survive his melancholy and teach with great wisdom. Indeed, his insistence on living joyfully allowed him to stand and say *hineni* to God and to his disciples.

I believe with absolute faith that the pursuit of joy through the three understandings I have articulated can well save our lives. A 2007 study that followed more than six thousand men and women between the ages of twenty-five and seventy-four, for example, yielded the results that "emotional vitality—a sense of enthusiasm, of hopefulness, of engagement in life"—in other words, happiness—"appears to reduce the risk of coronary heart disease."[7] And if you are still a skeptic, then I suggest falling back on the concept of a "suspension of disbelief" and try to live your life that way! Life is certainly more pleasant and after a while it becomes a felicitous habit! One is more present to life when one is happy and fulfilled, when one can say *hineni* to life.

Awe, wonder, gratitude, and praise.

Ayeka? Where are you, Adam?

A very ancient text, *Midrash Tanhuma*, offers us a different perspective on God's question to Adam. The midrash situates Adam in the Garden of Eden, telling us that Adam is singing the words of praise and exaltation

---

5. Several reports on Professor Ben-Shahar's course may be found at http://daringtolivefully.com/happier-tal-ben-shahar and http://www.npr.org/templates/story/story.php?storyId=5295168. See also Ben-Shahar, *Happier* and *Choose the Life You Want*.

6. Green, *Tormented Master*.

7. See a report on this study conducted by Laura Kubzansky, Associate Professor at the Harvard School of Public Health, chronicled at http://www.hsph.harvard.edu/news/magazine/happiness-stress-heart-disease/.

to God, who has created the world. It is as if Adam is able to gaze out beyond the Garden and see the entire universe, his heart bursting with awe and wonder. He is filled with what the great modern rabbi, Rabbi Abraham Joshua Heschel, called "radical amazement." All Adam can do is utter words extolling God's glory:

> The Lord is King
>
> He is robed in grandeur
>
> The Lord is robed,
>
> He is girded with strength.
>
> The world stands firm;
>
> It cannot be shaken.
>
> Your throne stands firm from of old;
>
> From eternity you have existed.
>
> The Ocean sounds, O Lord,
>
> The ocean sounds its thunder,
>
> The ocean sounds is pounding
>
> Above the thunder of the mighty waters,
>
> More majestic than of the breakers of the sea
>
> Is the Lord, majestic on high.
>
> Your decrees are indeed enduring;
>
> Holiness befits Your house
>
> O Lord, for all times.[8]

These eloquent words from Psalm 93 speak in the language of royalty and majesty: God is "King," sitting in exalted realms. This image is often echoed in Jewish liturgy, especially on the High Holy Days. Indeed, one of the central prayers of these "Days of Awe" is known as "*Ha-Melech*, the King"—"The King, sitting on a high and lofty throne...."

Whatever we may feel about the exclusive masculinity of the imagery (Why can't God be Queen?), each of us can feel a heart-resonance with

---

8. These are the words of Psalm 93 that *Midrash Tanhuma* places in Adam's mouth. How could Adam, the first human, know the words of the Psalms? Clearly *Tanhuma* is wildly anachronistic here! Such anachronism is characteristic of a common midrashic device; for the ancient rabbinic sages, chronological time as we understand it was less important than God's eternity. That is, for them there was "neither early nor late in the Torah" or in the entire Hebrew Bible for that matter. They would utilize quotes from anywhere in Scripture to illustrate their points, because in their understanding, all was part of Divine Truth that transcended both time and place.

Majesty, "purple mountains' majesty," as "America the Beautiful" sings to us, "spacious skies, amber waves of grain." All of these images are meant to evoke in us feelings of awe and wonder.

Like the midrashic Adam have you ever seen such overwhelming natural beauty that you have been left breathless? Have you found yourself so filled with awe that you cannot describe in words the feelings within you? At one such moment in my own life all I could feel was wonder at the mysterious ways of the universe, astonishment at the magnificence of God's artistry. At that moment, the sensation within me was that I was in the Presence of Majesty—a Majesty enfolding me in an overwhelming and nurturing embrace, a Majesty taking my breath away and restoring it to me in an inspiring rush. At that moment, I felt "breathed" by God and I truly understood for the first time the words of the Hebrew liturgy:

נשמת כל חי תברך את שמך, יהוה אלהינו
nishmat kol chai t'varech et shimcha, Adonai Eloheinu
The soul of every living thing shall bless Your Name, Holy One, our God. . .

This moment came for me many years ago, when I visited New Mexico's Carlsbad Caverns, enormous stalactite and stalagmite caves: beautiful; truly awesome. And as the sun began to set, I sat at the entrance of an opening in the caves where hundreds of thousands of bats reside. Just at dusk, the bats emerge to soar through the desert in search of food. All the assembled visitors who had come to witness this remarkable sight became very still as soon a faint but steadily increasing fluttering of wings could be heard. Within moments, thousands of bats swooped out of the cave's mouth and ascended into the crimson sky.

The fluttering sound increased in volume, then ebbed as the bats raced upward. With tears in my eyes, my mouth formed a blessing: ברוך עושה נפלאות/*Baruch oseh nifla'ot* ("Blessed is the One who creates wonders"). *This* was MAJESTY—that is what *Ha-Melech*—the King/the Queen (it really didn't matter which) meant to me.

For anyone who has been blessed to have experienced such a moment of Majesty in their lives, a moment of absolutely pure joy or wonder, a sense of gratitude *and place* are inevitable emotions—gratitude for having witnessed such a sight and a sense that *we were in the exact* right place at the exact right moment. Somehow I cannot help but feel that Midrash Tanhuma got it just right: Adam could answer with awe, "*Hineni, here I am*" to God's call of "*Ayeka?—where are you?*" because he knew that being in that awesome Garden of Delights was exactly where he needed to be, witnessing the Monarch, "robed in grandeur," who has just created a world of indescribable beauty. Unlike the more commonly told story of sin and shame in a literal interpretation of the story in Genesis, the midrash offers sublime reading, one filled with awe, wonder, gratitude, and praise.

Rabbi Arthur Green suggests for us an *Ayeka* response focused on an increased commitment to responsibility in our lives, responsibility of heart, mind, and deed. In his exciting and provocative book, *Radical Judaism: Rethinking God and Tradition*, Rabbi Green writes about God's *ayeka* question and asks us three compelling questions:

First, "Are you stretching your mind to move forward . . . as we think in ever more sophisticated and refined ways about the nature of existence and its unity?"[9]

Second, "Are [you] stretching [your] hearts to become more open, more aware[?]" Rabbi Green teaches that the divine question, *ayeka*, "demands of us a greater openness to our own vulnerability and dependence on forces beyond ourselves than our frail ego is willing to accept. . . . Liberation into the life of the spirit means doing the hard work of breaking through . . . [and] coming face to face with the ultimate frailty of our lives . . . ."

Third, "Are you engaged in the work given to you by the call of God?"[10] Rabbi Green asks if we can we move into the realm of *deed* and *act* to transform the world? By reminding us that the ills of our broken world (such as hunger, extreme poverty, and hatred leading to violence) all prevent the world's healing, Rabbi Green urges us to enter into the realm of "deed," understanding full well that we must battle all of society's "barriers" that are obstacles to healing.[11] Rabbi Green's *ayeka* is the most universal and existential question of all: are we humans ready and able to engage mind, heart, and hands and feet in the active pursuit of what Judaism calls *tikkun olam*, the healing of a profoundly wounded global society? *Ayeka* is a call to action on all fronts for us to marshall all our God-given human capacity and potential to work for the good of our planet. Ultimately, he concludes that if we are cast in the Divine image, then we alone are capable of bringing godliness into the world through our intellectual and emotional capacities and through our actions. If we fail to use these capacities and live up to our potential, then why indeed were we placed on this precious planet?

One of my greatest teachers, Reb Zalman Schachter Shalomi (of blessed memory), taught that each day we should rise from bed and ask God, "how should I be deployed today?" Given Arthur Green's notion of *Ayeka*, I like to think that in his context, *Ayeka* is indeed deployment into the world—to do

---

9. Green, *Radical Judaism*, 28.
10. Green, *Radical Judaism*, 30.
11. Green, *Radical Judaism*, 30.

the best work of healing the world that we can. In the *Mishna,* Judaism's first code of customary law, compiled in the third century C.E., in a tractate called *Avot* ("Ancestors"), we read, "The day is short, the work is great, the workers are lazy, the wages are great and the Householder is insistent.... It is not up to you to finish the work, yet you are not free to avoid it."[12]

So here we are, faced with our task as humans—to use all that we have—mind, heart-spirit, and body to work for the repair of our world. *This is the reason for our existence, the reason for our creation, the reason for our lives*—will we meet God's challenge?

Text to Life

> When I was fourteen years old, my family lived in San Francisco at the height of the civil rights movement. As a socially conscious teenager, I joined with CORE (the Congress of Racial Equality) and other groups in demonstrations at the city's Auto Row to protest the fact that in all the car showrooms there was not one African-American salesperson. For many days in the springtime of 1964, we stood in large groups on Van Ness Avenue in front of the Cadillac showroom singing songs of freedom and shouting words demanding justice. On April 11, the peaceful demonstrations escalated into a full-scale sit-in, in which I participated, and many of us were about to be arrested. That was an *ayeka-hineni* moment for me. Where was I? Was I going to stand with my fellow demonstrators and take a risk for the freedom and well-being of others? Was I willing to go to jail? I decided to sit down and engage in passive resistance along with the others. I was taken with friends in a paddy wagon to the San Francisco City Jail. Because I was a juvenile, I was released into my father's custody fairly quickly. Fearing my father's anger, but clear that what I was doing was right, I was feeling defiant when my father appeared at the jail to bail me out.
>
> I will never forget my father's words. With tears in his eyes, my gentle father simply said to me, "Leila, I am proud of you. For doesn't it say in the Bible, 'Justice, Justice, you shall pursue?'[13] I may not be a religious man, but sometimes, the Bible is right. You stood your ground. Come on, let's get out of here—I'll buy

---

12. *Mishna, Pirke Avot,* 2:15–16. We humans are the "workers" and the "Householder" is God. Here I use the translation of Kravitz and Olitzky, *Pirke Avot,* 29–30.

13. Deuteronomy 16:20.

you a milkshake." The next day I was back out on the picket line in front of the Cadillac showroom—with my father's blessing.

Those biblical words, "justice, justice you shall pursue" and God's question to Adam have been my companions ever since. I often ask myself, "where am I?" as I try to discern whether what I am about to do is the right pursuit of justice. Through my father and ever since, the Bible had given me wisdom.

LGB

Exploring the Text Within

Find a quiet and comfortable place to sit in contemplative silence with the above teachings and with the following questions about you and your life's experience. You may choose to focus on one question or sit with several. Ask yourself: what do the biblical text and these teachings mean to me in my life?

I am created in the image of the Divine, endowed with a pure soul and I am loved by an unending love.

Do I believe this, or do I struggle to believe?

When I believe, how does my faith manifest in my life?

When I struggle to believe, how might I seek a path toward faith?

When I have experienced awe and wonder, how do I express my gratitude—in word and in deed?

Where *am* I at this moment in my life?

As a human being created by God for the sacred purpose of healing our world, I am called to responsibility in mind, heart, and deed.

Where am I—In my own mind and heart and in my ability to take action in the world for its healing?

Chapter 3
Noach

Murder and Drunkenness

Now the man knew his wife Eve, and she conceived and bore Cain, saying, "I have gained a male child with the help of the Lord." She then bore his brother Abel. Abel became a keeper of sheep, and Cain became a tiller of the soil. In the course of time, Cain brought an offering to the Lord from the fruit of the soil; and Abel, for his part, brought the choicest of the firstlings of his flock. The Lord paid heed to Abel and his offering, but to Cain and his offering He paid no heed. Cain was much distressed and his face fell. And the Lord said to Cain, "Why are you distressed, and why is your face fallen? Surely, if you do right, there is uplift. But if you do not do right Sin crouches at the door; Its urge is toward you, yet you can be its master." Cain said to his brother Abel . . . and when they were in the field, Cain set upon his brother and killed him. The Lord said to Cain, "Where is your brother Abel?" And he said, "Am I my brother's keeper"

—Genesis 4:1–9

"Cain set upon his brother Abel and killed him."

—Genesis 4:8

"Noah . . . drank of the wine. . ."

—Genesis 9:18–27

Read this text before the second set of three contemplative questions at the end of this chapter. Let the words flow through your heart, mind, and soul as you consider the questions.

> *Noah, the tiller of the soil, was the first to plant a vineyard. He drank the wine and became drunk and he uncovered himself within his tent. Ham, the father of Canaan, saw his father's nakedness and told his two brothers outside. But Shem and Japheth took a cloth, placed it against both their backs, and, walking backward, they covered their father's nakedness; their faces turned the other way, so that they did not see their father's nakedness. When Noah woke up from his wine and learned what his youngest son had done to him, he said, "Cursed be Canaan; The lowest of slaves Shall be he to his brothers...."*

—Genesis 9:20–25

Knowledge gained is innocence lost, and innocence lost is paradise lost. Once Adam and Eve had eaten from the forbidden tree of knowledge, they are expelled from the Garden to live a life of wandering. God decrees that Eve is to experience pain and birthpangs[1] and Adam is to till a *"cursed"* and inhospitable ground, where *"thorns and thistles will sprout."* He will toil *"by the sweat of [his] brow"*[2]—eking out sustenance from the earth will be an arduous and miserable task. The easy life in the Garden will be no more for man and woman. Life, filled with so much promise and beauty before they had eaten from the tree, now holds only the prospect of pain and suffering, and Adam and Eve begin to understand the grave and permanent impact of their deeds.

Now clothed to cover their nudity, (their earlier innocent and pure nakedness now shameful), the first couple leaves the Garden. Soon, Eve gives birth to a son, Cain and then bears a second son, Abel. In this second generation, might things go better? Perhaps these brothers might make things right, and ease God's punishment. But this was not to be.

> *In the course of time, Cain brought an offering to the Holy One from the fruit of the soil; and Abel, for his part, brought the choicest of the firstlings of his flock. The Holy One paid heed to Abel and*

---

1. Genesis 3:16.
2. Genesis 3:17–19.

his offering, but to Cain and his offering He paid no heed. Cain was much distressed and his face fell.

—Genesis 4:3–5

Cain becomes a farmer and Abel a shepherd. With the arrival of harvest *"Cain brought an offering to the* Lord *from the fruit of the soil and Abel . . . brought the choicest of the firstlings of his flock."*[3] So far, so good. But here is the beginning of a pattern that will occur repeatedly in future generations of the Hebrew Bible—parental favoritism—and always the younger child is favored over the older.[4] Here the Ultimate Parent is God: *"The* Lord *paid heed to Abel and his offering, but to Cain and his offering He paid no heed."*

By the "sweat of his brow," Cain tills the *"cursed"* soil that God had left to his father Adam, and from this barren earth Cain brings his finest fruit as an offering to his God—and God pays no attention! But when his younger brother brings a lamb, God is pleased! Imagine Cain's turmoil, the complicated emotions of anger and rage that must have swirled in his heart! The Bible's words are understated: *"Cain was much distressed and his face fell."*[5]

And the Holy One said to Cain,
"Why are you distressed, and why is your face fallen?
Surely if you do right, there is uplift.
But if you do not do right, Sin crouches at the door;
its urge is toward you, yet you can be its master."

—Genesis 4:6–7

God seems to be mocking Cain: *"Why are you distressed, and why has you face fallen? Surely, if you do right,* you will be uplifted. *But if you do not do right, sin crouches at the door; its urge is toward you, yet you can be its master."*[6]

What a cruel Parent God seems to be! He seems to be saying to Cain: "OK, so I love your brother Abel more! So he's my favorite! Take it like a man and do right. You'll be uplifted by acting nobly! But if you resent this,

3. Genesis 4:4.

4. We shall see this pattern reoccur later in this book in the stories of Isaac and Ishmael, Jacob and Esau, and Rachel and Leah, and Joseph and his brothers.

5. Genesis 4:5.

6. Genesis 4:6–7. The non-italicized words are my own interpretive translation of שאת. The JPS TaNaKH translation is "there is uplift."

and act out in anger, '*sin crouches at the door*'—you will be just like your sinful parents, Adam and Eve. Sin's 'urge,' its temptation, is great. Sure, you're tempted to vent your anger on your brother Abel, but don't let sin get the better of you! 'You can be its master.'" Cain cannot tolerate God's words.

> *Cain said to his brother, Abel . . . and when they were in the field,*
> *Cain set upon his brother Abel and killed him.*
> *The Holy One said to Cain, "Where is your brother, Abel?"*
> *And he said, "I do not know. Am I my brother's keeper?"*

—Genesis 4:8–9

Enraged, first by God's rejection of his offering of first fruits and then by what he perceives as God's taunting of him, Cain now speaks to his brother, but we're not sure what he says. The text leaves us with an ellipsis, a blank, a frustrating mystery. We will never know what those words were!

I have always been mystified by the silence in this text. I have wondered what Cain said, whether Abel ever responded to him—did Abel simply ignore Cain, or did he respond with acceptance or hostility? I have wondered if one brother misinterpreted the other's words with an ensuing quarrel exploding between them. Sometimes words are misunderstood and rage erupts, when the conflict might have been avoided with some simple clarification. Did some crucial information got lost in what Cain was saying to Abel with each brother mistakenly assuming that he knew what the other meant, resulting in a conflict that eventually led to violence?

I once heard a terribly sad, true story about a Vietnamese man who was drafted into the army and forced to leave his pregnant wife alone at home. Weeping, they said their goodbyes, not knowing if they would ever see each other again, and the young man went off to war. After several years of great suffering in battle, the man managed to survive and eventually returned home to his wife and son.

A happy ending, one might think. But the man's son refused to recognize him as his father or to call him daddy. "My daddy is another person. He used to come to visit us every night, and every time he came my mother would talk to him a lot, for a long time, and my mother used to cry and cry; and when my mother sits down, my daddy also sits down; when my mother lies down, he also lies down; so you are not my daddy."

The man was profoundly hurt by his son's rejection and he became cold and reclusive, never smiling or showing any signs of affection to his son or to his wife. He was convinced that while he had been off fighting in the war, his wife had been having an affair with another man. He rejected her entirely.

Now, deeply humiliated, his wife suffered too. The entire family was in anguish. Things got worse, as the husband began to drink heavily, night after night, and when he returned in an inebriated state to his home he completely ignored his wife. After a time, suffering from this profound disrespect and disregard, the man's wife, in deep despair jumped into a nearby river and died.

The father was now in a complete state of depression and despair himself. He had lost the wife he had loved and who he thought had betrayed him with another man, and he was now responsible for his son, who had rejected him. Had it not been for his sense of responsibility for his son, he too, would have ended his life. Then he made a terrible discovery that illuminated the whole situation, a discovery that revealed how misunderstanding can lead to horrifying results, even to death.

One night, while caring for his son, the man lit a lamp. Suddenly, the boy exclaimed, "Here comes my father" as he pointed to the shadow created by the lamp's glow. "You know, mister, my father used to come every night like this and my mother used to talk to him a lot and she cried a lot with him, and every time she sat down, my father also sat down. Every time my mother lay down, he also lay down."[7]

A shadow! The shadow was the little boy's "father!" And all this time, the man had thought that there was a *real* man, a man with whom his wife had betrayed him! A shadow! A misunderstanding that killed his marriage, killed his wife, and almost killed him. Could this be the kind of misunderstanding that poisoned the relationship between Cain and Abel, eventually causing Cain to end his brother's life? How dangerous our words, or lack of them can be! How crucial it is to try to communicate *fully,* with open hearts with one another. *"And Cain said to Abel...."*

Nobel Prize winning author Elie Wiesel offers another interpretation: he wonders whether Cain tried to communicate with his brother Abel in some way, but that Abel ignored him. Echoing the Talmudic dictum that "there is no death without sin,"[8] Wiesel writes: "Is it possible that Abel did not pay attention to what his brother said? That Abel's mind was elsewhere? Was that his sin? His brother, rebuffed, rejected, needed to tell someone of

---

7. I thank my student Carl Woolf for first telling me this story, and for providing me with a source for it: In one of his teachings, the great Vietnamese teacher Thich Nhat Hanh taught (August 13, 1996 at Plum Village France) a version of this story.

8. Babylonian Talmud, Tractate Shabbat 55a.

his grief—and he, Abel, was not even listening! This insensitivity is what makes him guilty."[9]

Envision the scene: two brothers, each seeking to please God, one favored, one scorned. Imagine the crestfallen look on Cain's face and then his increasing pain as God tells him to accept things as they are.

I imagine Cain's trying to talk with his brother—maybe hoping for a little sympathy, maybe hoping for some comfort from the rejection he is feeling—but his brother is silent and, in Elie Wiesel's reading, turns away from him.

Rejected, misunderstood, ignored, Cain's rage must have grown wide and deep. And when rage expands in such a way, it becomes unmanageable and can turn murderous—". . . and when they were in the field, Cain set upon his brother Abel and killed him."

Death comes into the world. The first death. The first murder. Blood has seeped into the earth—its DNA has changed our world forever.

The mocking Parent's voice speaks again: *"Where is your brother, Abel?"* Cain replies, *"I do not know. Am I my brother's keeper?"*[10] God bellows at Cain: *"What have you done? Hark, your brother's blood cries out to Me from the ground! Therefore, you shall be more cursed than the ground which opened its mouth to receive your brother's blood from your hand. If you till the soil, it shall no longer yield its strength to you. You shall become a ceaseless wanderer on earth."*[11]

Poor Cain! Taunted by a Parent who favors his brother, overwhelmed by his own jealousy, yearning so much for a connection to the brother who fails to respond to him, Cain finally explodes, and commits an act of violence he probably never intended to commit. Watching his dead brother's blood seep into the cursed earth, Cain is terrified at the divine punishment that will surely come.

When the Voice speaks again to Cain, asking him where his brother is, Cain's response reflects his terror. He fears taking responsibility for Abel's fate. "I have no idea where my brother is," Cain responds to God, *"Am I my brother's keeper?"*

An impulsive response from a deeply troubled man—that is really a profound existential question: *"Am I my brother's keeper?"* Are we indeed responsible for our kin? Even when relations within our family are destructive, dysfunctional, and devastating? Do we still have an obligation to try

---

9. Elie Wiesel, quoted in *Bible History Daily*, Biblical Archaeology Society, "Cain and Abel in the Bible: *Bible Review's* Supporting Roles," by Elie Wiesel, June 1, 2015.

10. Genesis 4:9.

11. Genesis 4:10–12.

again to heal the wounds, and find pathways toward reconciliation, to dig deeper within our hearts and souls to find the love that *must* once have existed between us? Is blood thicker than water? More questions than answers and yet many of us live with such questions gnawing at our hearts, as we continue to suffer within our families' dysfunctions and the estrangements. "Am I my siblings' keeper?" we ask, "Do I have an obligation to find a pathways of peace back to them? Despite my best efforts of the past, is Torah teaching me that I must try to redouble my efforts so that love can overwhelm anguish and pain?" These are the questions that Torah compels us to ask when we read of Cain and Abel.

The tale leaves us with more questions than answers, yet its compelling queries call to us in ways that cry out like Abel's blood in the earth—something must be done: to heal our lives, to heal our families, to heal the earth itself.

After the story of Cain and Abel, we could walk away from the Bible in disillusionment. We could certainly ask why we would want to read the rest of this book about such a cruel and arbitrary God and a murderous brother. We could ask why we would want to read the stories of generation after generation in which younger children are favored over older, and parents seem oblivious to the damage done when they love some children more than others. And yet, despite their dysfunction, we keep returning to these primal stories. In Jewish tradition, we read these stories week after week and year after year, culling new meanings from the family dynamics of our ancestors.

Perhaps we feel so compelled to return to the tales of our first biblical families because they hold a mirror up to us, reflecting faces and souls like our own, telling us about people much like ourselves and reminding us of families much like our own or of people we know well. What draws us back and intrigues us so much about these stories is that the stories feel *real and authentic*—they are about passionate love and loveless marriages, about parental favoritism, about sibling rivalries. In short, these early biblical stories tell us about imperfect people in imperfect families, navigating a flawed world so much like our own. This is the world that God Him/Herself, the Ultimate Parent, has created—along with its magnificent natural beauty, a world of challenging relationships, of jealousies and rivalries, pettiness and venality, and now—with Cain—a world of violence.

> When God saw how corrupt the earth was, for all flesh had corrupted its ways on earth, God said to Noah, I have decided to put an end to all flesh, for the earth is filled with Lawlessness because of them.
>
> —Genesis 6:12–13

Enter Divine Regret. What God had planted, so He/She/It had sowed: "The Lord saw how great was man's wickedness on earth, and how every plan devised by his mind was nothing but evil all the time. And the Lord regretted that He had made man on earth and His heart was saddened."

Enter Divine Self-Denial: God understands the cosmic problem as *humankind's* corruption, not His/Her/Its own doing, so God decides to destroy the world and start all over again. How easy it would be if we could also push the "restart" button with our families and our children, but we humans don't have that luxury—only God has that chance! As human parents who inevitably make mistakes, we are challenged to learn from our errors, to find ways of healing, ways to ease past hurts and build new relationships for the future.

Enter Noah:

> *The Lord said, I will blot out from the earth the men whom I created—men together with beasts, creeping things, and birds of the sky, for I regret that I made them. But Noah found favor with the Lord.*
>
> *This is the line of Noah—Noah was a righteous man; he was blameless in his generation; Noah walked with God . . . .*

—Genesis 6:7–9

No one really knows what these words mean: what does it mean to be a righteous person in a generation of scoundrels? What does it mean to "*walk with God*"? The ancient rabbis seem to think that Noah is righteous because he was the best of a bad lot. In an ancient midrash, Rabbi Yohanan interprets the words "*in his generation*" to imply "but not in other generations." Rabbi Hanina (as a reflection on Rabbi Yohanan's comment) said: "Rabbi Yohanan's view may be illustrated by the parable of a jar of wine stored in a cellar filled with jars of vinegar. In such a place, the fragrance of the wine is sensed [because of the vinegar's fumes]; in any other place, its fragrance might not be sensed."[12] Rabbi Hanina's explanation is further clarified in the Babylonian Talmud:[13] "How much more righteous would Noah have been had he lived in a generation of righteous men."

What the rabbis are trying to say is that in a generation of scoundrels, even if Noah wasn't especially righteous, but was better than the unsavory people around him, he would have appeared to be "righteous."

We only imagine what this rabbinic discussion might have been about. Perhaps it has something to do with the fact that when God told Noah of

---

12. Genesis Rabbah 30:10.
13. Babylonian Talmud, Tractate *Sanhedrin*, 108a.

His intention to destroy the world, Noah did not speak up on behalf of his fellow human beings. Perhaps, like Cain, he didn't want to take responsibility for others. If Noah had lived in modern times, he might have ignored Albert Schweitzer's words, "You don't live in a world all your own. Your brothers are here, too." But once again, the biblical text doesn't help us out. It simply tells us that God brought the news of impending doom to Noah, and then gave Noah instructions on building an ark so that he and his family and a pair of each type of the earth's animals could survive the coming flood. Noach gave no response other than to do what he had been told and begin building: *"Noah did so, just as God commanded him, so he did"* (6:22).

I have always wondered—what would *I* do if I had prior knowledge of an impending catastrophe? What if I knew that I and my loved ones would be saved, but no one else around me would escape the calamity? I would like to think that I would warn my neighbors, so that they too could prepare for the disaster, but I cannot say with absolute confidence that I would. We human beings are often self-interested and self-preservative. We often think about our own well-being first and are not always prone to helping our neighbors, especially if we think we might put ourselves at risk. I am ashamed to say that I do not know if I would help others—I hope that my own sense of social conscience would drive me to do the right thing, but I am unsure. What would you do?

So Noah, faithful carpenter that he is, builds the ark, according to God's exact specifications. A mighty rain begins to fall and the whole earth is engulfed in raging waters that ravage the earth for forty days and nights. Then stillness comes as the ark floats upon the water—and the time of waiting begins. How agonizing to wait for the earth to dry out, to wait patiently until it was safe to walk upon the earth once again without sinking into the mud and then finally, to open the hatches of the ark and emerge into the natural light of the day!

> *And when the waters had swelled on the earth one hundred and fifty days, God remembered Noah and all the beasts and all the cattle that were with him in the ark, and God caused a wind to blow across the earth and the waters subsided. The fountains of the deep and the floodgates of the sky were stopped up and the rain from the sky was held back and the waters receded steadily from the earth.*
>
> *At the end of one hundred and fifty days the waters diminished, so that in the seventh month, the ark came to rest on the mountains of Ararat. The waters went on diminishing until the tenth*

month. In the tenth month, on the first of the month, the tops of the mountains became visible.

—Genesis 7:24—8:5

Then Noah sends out a raven and a dove to explore the earth, to ensure that the land is dry. After several forays, the dove returns with an olive leaf in its bill. Noah sends the bird out once again, and it does not return. Finally, finally! It is safe to walk upon the land!

After such a long time crammed together in the vessel, knowing that everything and everyone they knew were gone, Noah, and his family, survivors of the world's first cataclysm, finally emerge from the ark onto *terra incognita,* an unknown land, the first humans, survivors of the Great Deluge, pioneers now, given the task—ready or not—to restore a world. What an awesome, awful, and awe-filling responsibility! Imagine how tiny, terrified, and humbled Noah and his family must have felt. Imagine their grief, their anticipation, their fears, their hope . . . .

Immediately, as he uncertainly sets foot on the land, Noah, grateful for his survival, builds an altar to God, *"taking of every clean animal and of every clean bird, he offered burnt offerings on the altar"* (8:20-21). Understanding human beings' fears and frailties, God reassures Noah and his family with a promise:

> *Never again will I doom the earth because of man. . . nor will I*
> *ever again destroy every living being, as I have done.*
> *So long as the earth endures,*
> *seedtime and harvest,*
> *cold and heat,*
> *summer and winter,*
> *day and night*
> *shall not cease.*
>
> —Genesis 8:21-22

The Holy One then commands Noah and his sons: (פרו ורבו) *p'ru u-r'vu—be fruitful and multiply.*[14] Despite God's disappointment in humanity, and His understanding of human fallibility, the Holy One still has sufficient

---

14. In post-biblical, rabbinic Judaism, the first commandment to "be fruitful and multiply" was interpreted as a commandment incumbent on *male* Jews as it was understood to have been addressed to Noah and his sons (9:1, "God blessed Noah and his sons"). Therefore, according to *halakha* (Jewish law), Jewish men are required to procreate, and females are technically not required to do so. Only in the context of marriage are they obviously required to help fulfill the commandment incumbent upon their husbands.

faith in us to want us to increase in number, to bring forth life, to populate a universe, to create a new world. Perhaps we aren't that bad after all!

Nonetheless, we humans *are* imperfect—and God seems to realize this. Perhaps understanding that we will always carry within ourselves an aggressive strain, the Holy One tells Noah and his family, that they may eat meat. Unlike our ancestors in the Garden of Eden, to whom God had given only herbs, plants, and fruits to eat, the Holy One now permits us to eat meat as well.

This permission to consume meat comes with a warning: Cherish the blood! It is our life force! Do not ever think that blood is so cheap that you may shed it carelessly and without thought! *"Every creature that lives shall be yours to eat; as with the green grasses, I give you all these. You must not, however, eat flesh with its life-blood in it."*

God goes further in warning humankind. May the preciousness of *human* blood be so great to us that we were *never* to shed it: *"But for your own life-blood I will I require a reckoning; I will require it of every beast, of man too, will I require a reckoning for human life, of every man for that of his fellow man! Whoever sheds the blood of man, by man shall his blood be shed; for in His image, Did God make man"* (9:3–6).

What a complicated relationship we humans beings have with God! Not only does She grant us rights, She also imposes upon us ethical responsibilities. God teaches us that while we now have permission to eat meat, we must never devalue an animal's blood lest we end up on the "slippery slope" toward shedding human blood. We may shed an animal's blood to survive, to satisfy hunger—but we must always value the animals' blood, draining it before consuming flesh, and we should so cherish human life that shedding the blood of another person is absolutely forbidden and abominable to us.

Finally, God reiterates His promise of earth's eternity: a rainbow in the sky:

> *This is the sign that I set for a covenant between Me and you, and every living creature with you, for all ages to come. I have set My bow in the clouds, and it shall serve as a sign of the covenant between Me and the earth . . . so that the waters shall never again become a flood to destroy all flesh. When the bow is in the clouds, I will see it and remember the everlasting covenant between God and all living creatures, all flesh that is on earth.*

—Genesis 9:12–16

The rainbow is a reminder *to God* never to destroy the earth again, an audacious statement of Divine regret in which both God and humans learn about limitation. Even God's anger must be limited, and never again reach cataclysmic proportions. When we humans see a rainbow, we utter a special blessing:

בָּרוּךְ אַתָּה ה' אֱלֹהֵינוּ מֶלֶךְ הָעוֹלָם זוֹכֵר הַבְּרִית וְנֶאֱמָן בִּבְרִיתוֹ וְקַיָּם בְּמַאֲמָרוֹ

Blessed are You, Holy One, Sovereign of the World,
Who remembers the covenant, remains faithful to it,
and who is steadfast to God's own word.

With these words we bless (and remind!) God not only to recall the covenant, but also to remain loyal to it and to persist in the covenant and devoted to His own word.

This is an empowering concept for humans to understand, that the covenant is a two-way partnership, a mutual bond between the Holy One and humankind.

So, life begins again on earth. Hope is restored. And Noah, *"tiller of the soil, was the first to plant a vineyard."* A vineyard: grapes—signs of fecundity, fruitfulness, growth, sweetness, and celebration of life; the source of wine, in moderation, the most sublime of drinks; when abused, the most monstrous of libations. When the first grapes are ripe, Noah makes wine and drinks deeply, and from this first grape harvest Noah becomes rip-roaring drunk.

Why? Does Noah become drunk because he is suffering from survivor's guilt, or a deep sense of remorse that he had not stood up for his fellow human beings when he first learned about the impending flood? Now that the worst is over, and he and his family are responsible for rebuilding the world, does he wonder if he is up to the task? Does he think back to the time before the flood and wonder to himself, "If I couldn't support my fellow humans *then,* how can I possibly be worthy of rebuilding and repopulating a world *now?* Do I have the necessary skills? Am I worthy?"

The same questions arise in doomsday films and books about lost worlds and bands of survivors who are challenged to rebuild destroyed worlds. Are they morally worthy to mold a new universe? What kind of a world can we flawed human beings actually build? For those of us who live in a world that has not yet been destroyed, but who often face formidable personal challenges, these questions lie just beneath the surface of our consciousness. They are the same questions we ask ourselves: "Am I morally worthy to reshape my life? Do I have what it takes to reach my life goals while being true to myself? How do I shape a life for myself and those I love that reflects the best of who I and they are?" The core question that arises for each us is *how* we stand up to the challenges, *how* we rise to the encounters our lives bring.

Noah, in his first meeting with the new world, did not stand up well. Staggering drunk and naked in his tent, Noah falls into a stupor and is soon discovered by his youngest son, Ham, who calls out to his brothers, Shem and Japheth, who were outside the tent. To avoid gazing upon their father's nakedness, Shem and Japheth walk backwards into the tent and cover their father with a blanket, affording Noah a small measure of dignity while he sleeps off his drunken binge.

When Noah awakens and discovers what has happened, he flies into a rage and curses Ham for *"what his youngest son had done to him"* (9:24).

What had Ham done that was so wrong? The biblical text tells us only that *"Ham, the father of Canaan . . . saw his father's nakedness and told his two brothers outside"* (v. 22) No more, no less. So what actually happened there in the tent as Noah lay in his torpor? Was it that Ham had gazed upon his father's nakedness—certainly an indignity, but surely not a heinous crime? Was it that the boy told his brothers about their father's drunkenness, thus exposing Noah to shame and embarrassment? Or had something more sinister happened in the tent? What *was* Ham's great sin?

Many imaginative interpretations have been evinced about the Torah's one-line description of Ham's behavior in the tent suggesting that Ham, having seen his father's genitals for the first time, was fascinated by them and actually touched them,[15] and was therefore guilty of incest and perhaps even homosexual rape.[16] Another, much more dramatic theory offered by the ancient rabbis was that Ham actually castrated Noah.[17] Given these conclusions, Noah's harsh and extreme curse against Ham seems understandable:

> *Cursed be Canaan; the lowest of slaves shall he be to his brothers. And he said: Blessed be the* Lord, *the God of Shem, let Canaan be a slave to them. May God enlarge Japheth, and let him dwell in the tents of Shem; and let Canaan be a slave to them.*

—Genesis 9:25–27

Beyond it's immediate severity, Noah's curse on his youngest son has had grave implications for generations to come, spawning an entire racist stance that through history came to provide a moral justification for the early modern African slave trade. Ham, called in the Torah the *"father of Canaan,"* was, according to biblical genealogy, the progenitor of the Canaanite people. In later western European history, the Canaanites were believed to be "dark-skinned" people. During the era of the African slave trade

15. Cohen, *Voices from Genesis*, 55.
16. Berlin and Brettler, eds., *The Jewish Study Bible*, 26, n. for verses 22–24.
17. Genesis Rabbah 36:7.

to America, the so-called "curse of Ham" was used by some Christians as a racist justification for the enslavement of black Africans who were believed to be descendants of Ham. African slaves were called "Hamites" and were believed to have descended through Canaan and his older brothers. In the nineteenth century, advocates of slavery in the United States invoked the "curse of Ham" against abolitionist anti-slavery arguments, and effectively advanced the cause of the slave trade for generations.[18]

The story of Noah is complex and multi-dimensional. For now, let us focus on Noah's turmoil after he emerges from the ark—I am most interested in his feelings and actions at that crucial time.

Noah's first conversation with God as he emerges from the Ark

A medieval mystical text imagines what Noah might have been thinking as he stepped on dry land for the first time after the Flood. "Why were we humans created," he wonders, "if God was only going to destroy us?"

> *"Noah, the tiller of the soil, was the first to plant a vineyard. He drank of the wine and be became drunk"* (9:20–21)

> When Noah came out of the ark he opened his eyes and saw the whole world completely destroyed. He began crying for the world and said, "Master of the world! If You destroyed Your world because of human sin or human fools, then why do You create them? One or the other You should do: either do not create the human being or do not destroy the world!"[19]

After his long, sad sojourn in the ark, Noah emerges to find a silent, empty, devastated world. Only he and his family and the animals he had brought with him inhabit the planet and he understands that it is up to them to remake the world. He grieves all that had been, no matter how imperfect. Lonely, distraught, questioning the God who had saved him, Noah wonders perhaps why *he* has survived when the rest of humankind had not, remembering that time before the Flood when he failed to take the opportunity to reason with God and maybe, just maybe, have convinced God to stop the oncoming deluge.

---

18. For two examples of scholarly literature of the use of Noah's curse of Ham to advance the African slave trade, see Johnson, *The Myth of Ham*, 37 and Goldenberg, *The Curse of Ham*.

19. *Zohar: The Book of Enlightenment*, 57.

Exposure and Exile

We learn from the ancient midrashic collection Genesis Rabbah that addiction brings an inexorable movement—from inebriation to exposure to a profound internal experience of exile: *"He became drunk and he uncovered himself within his tent"* (9:21).

> *"And he was uncovered* (VA-YYITHGAL, ויתגל)[20] *within his tent."* R. Judah b. R. Simon and R. Hanan in the name of R. Samuel b. R. Isaac said: Not VA-YYAGAL (ויגל) is written but VA-YYITHGAL (ויתגל); he was the cause of exile for himself and subsequent generations. The Ten Tribes were exiled only because of wine, as it is written "Woe unto them that rise up early in the morning, that they may follow strong drink" (Isaiah 5:11).

As they often did, our ancient sages engaged in a play on words between the Hebrew word *VA-YITHGAL* (ויתגל), which means, "and he became uncovered/exposed," and *VA-YYAGAL* (ויגל), which means "and he was exiled." Noting the similarity of the two words, the rabbis commented that by becoming drunk, Noah caused himself to become exposed (his nakedness) and thus brought exile upon himself and later generations. They emphasized their point by quoting Isaiah 5:11—"Woe unto them that rise up early in the morning, that they may follow strong drink," which referred to those who overindulge in alcohol who will find themselves wallowing in *Sheol*, the biblical equivalent of an afterlife place, which is dark, gloomy, and miserable. *The teaching here, say the rabbis, is not only a general admonition against drunkenness, but a statement that such behavior leads to exposure—and exposure leads, metaphorically, and literally, to exile.* In our contemporary understanding, we define "addiction" in a more expansive way. We know that over-dependence on any substance, lifestyle, or idea can bring about a variety of "exiles": the person who drinks or eats too much or over-consumes either legal or illegal drugs can become physically and/or emotionally ill—and is thus "exiled" from his or her own body, family, and friends. The workaholic loses touch with family and friends, and is sometimes so tired and worn down that she or he is "exiled" from his or her own spirit. The person who becomes so obsessively dedicated to a political cause or idea that he or she cannot be open minded to others' views is cut off from the wonderful intellectual, emotional, and social exchange that come with open-mindedness, and becomes isolated and "exiled"; the person who cherishes material things instead of other human beings becomes an island unto him or herself, "exiled" from the

---

20. I have altered the transliteration for greater comprehension.

vibrant and vital flow of human connection. All these (and more) are forms of "drunkenness" and "addiction."[21]

Silence and Denial

It is so often true that in families touched by addiction, silence prevails. Sometimes this is the silence of denial ("it really isn't happening to us"), sometimes this is the silence of shame ("how can I admit to others that such weakness and such illness plagues me and my family?"), and sometimes this is the silence of despair that leads to paralysis ("I just don't know what to do, so I do nothing").

Contemporary feminist poet, Alicia Ostriker addresses the denial, dysfunction and destruction that so often plagues families in which alcoholism and other addictions are present. In her version of the biblical story, Ostriker tells us that Ham heroically attempted to break his older brothers' silence and denial about their father's drunkenness only to suffer Noah's wrath for his efforts.

"He became drunk and he uncovered himself within his tent." (9:21)

I thought the vineyard idea was a good one, the old man had to be kept busy somehow. Then he started drinking. Steadily. After all we had been through. The pity of it. And he would lie in his tent uncovered, naked and sweating. Father, how could I turn my back? I wanted to cover your pathetic flabby body.

I told my brothers: our father is lying naked in the tent, dead drunk. They said no. That doesn't happen in families like ours. Only gentiles are alcoholics. Shut up, they said, and quickly turned their backs. Then our father woke up and began screaming, cursing me.

You'll be black, he screamed. The sweat stood out on his forehead. You'll never get anywhere. Your children will be slaves and servants. He retched and flung himself backward shivering. That ought to teach you respect, he screamed.

—Alicia Ostriker, *The Nakedness of the Fathers*

---

21. Judaism does not condemn wine *per se*. The "fruit of the vine" is used for sanctification on the Sabbath and holy days for celebration and joy. For those who cannot tolerate wine itself, grape juice is more than acceptable. After all, the blessing is on the "fruit of the vine." What we do with it is up to us, depending on our sensitivities.

Text to Life

Amy, a mother of two teenaged children, tells of a moment of family crisis and its repercussions. It echoes Alicia Ostriker's midrash on Noah's drunkenness and the redemptive power of breaking silence:

These verses describe the shame of Noah's drunkenness, not so much in terms of its damage to himself as in the traumatic effect on his family. His son, Ham, finds Noah on the floor, passed out, naked. When Ham alerts his brothers, Shem and Japheth, they avert their eyes and cover their father. Noah curses Ham because he has witnessed his father's utter humiliation: Ham is condemned to a life of slavery, without possibility of forgiveness. Ham's enduring shame comes from observing his father, who should rightfully embody honor, robbed of all dignity. Ham is cursed forever by the stinging image of his father humiliated as a result of his own behavior.

Sadly, my own family has shared this experience of shame arising from my husband's alcoholism. Our children witnessed an episode of extreme intoxication that led to domestic violence. They saw their ordinarily moral and loving father committing an assault while in a state of drunken incoherence. Although they didn't find their father naked, they saw him being led away in handcuffs, an even more dishonorable and dehumanized condition.

I can't say if that image has left as indelible a mark in their memories as it has in my own, but the knowledge of his shame must certainly have affected them and their relationship with their father. I have a comparable image of my own father's degradation that continues to color my memories of him. Seeing my father as he was dying of cancer, getting out of bed, exposed by the hospital gown, unable to control the stool dropping on the floor behind him as he walked, corrupts the memories I hold of his accomplishments, his honor, and his powerful presence.

In Noah's story, the sons who averted their eyes are rewarded, while the son who discovered his father's shame is punished for the rest of his life. There was no parallel to this in my family's story. One of our children had the courage to call 911 [the number to report an emergency] on that awful night. The child's persistent guilt at making that call could have the effect of a curse, comparable to Ham's. However, as my husband maintains his sobriety, it's become clear that confronting his alcoholism, rather than willfully ignoring it, was the beginning of our entire family's recovery. We have been very fortunate in that we have been able not only to restore our family, but to strengthen it. My husband's sobriety, which only came about after reaching this point of despair, has earned him redemption as a husband, a father, and a human being. Rather than cursing the child who witnessed the event and made that call, he recognizes that this one act saved him and the whole family from catastrophe—and he is grateful for it.

Forgiveness has been an essential part of our family's recovery, as much as defying the destructive force of alcoholism by confronting it. Having lived through this experience, I have gained a deep understanding and appreciation of the power of forgiveness. While Noah could not forgive Ham, for me it was necessary to forgive before I could begin to heal, restore my family, and move on with my life. Forgiveness, though, was very different from averting my eyes, as Shem and Japheth did. Painful as the experience was, we can't pretend that it never happened. This was an event that dramatically changed our family and defined the person who each of is today. In order for me to forgive, it was necessary to look intently at the incident and try to understand why it happened; forgiveness then followed as a conscious decision that came hand-in-hand with acceptance.

My children know that alcoholism is a genetic trait that they may have inherited. Although it's not a sure thing, it is my hope that, having endured this painful experience without averting their eyes, they have learned about the dangerous potential of alcohol in their own lives. As with the many difficult experiences they are sure to have in their lives, they will bear scars, but the scar tissue will be tougher.

These verses leave me wondering about Noah himself. After we hear of the curse visited upon Ham, there is what looks to me as an ellipsis. We are told that Noah lived for 350 years after the flood and died at the age of 950, but we don't know if this was an isolated event or if he continued his descent into alcoholism. Did he have any recollection of the episode afterwards? Was he able to find redemption in the God who'd saved him from the flood, as members of 12-step programs would seek help from their higher power millennia later?

As our family has experienced it, alcoholism was not a single episode that we were fortunate enough to survive, but an ongoing fact of life. Our family's healing, with all the observation, intense thought, and compassion it involves, is a continuing process.

***

Bryan, a man in his mid-thirties, had been clandestinely drinking and smoking marijuana since he was fifteen. Here is his story.

What had been a way of being part of the gang, hanging out, smoking pot, and chugging cheap wine had now become a compulsion—if I didn't drink and smoke weed every day, I felt "off," unable to function during the day. Alcoholism now controlled my life. At family dinners, I would help clear the dishes and would I guzzle the last drops of wine from glasses and bottles, hoping that no one would catch me. Once, my mother walked into the kitchen and saw me as I was emptying guests' wine glasses into my mouth. I quickly wiped my mouth and we both pretended that nothing had happened. Years later, I confessed that I had felt ashamed and angry, that I had wanted to curse my mother for walking in at the that moment and catching me in the act. In my heart, I knew that *I* was in the wrong. I was humiliated. I felt like an animal picking scraps from the garbage. So why did I want to curse *her*?

In college, my drinking and pot-smoking worsened and became my main activity. My grades fell, and I began failing all my classes. Eventually I dropped out of college. My life was directionless, and all I wanted was to smoke and drink.

I had no real friends—men much younger than me took advantage of my easy personality borrowed the little money I received from my parents. I had no real home and no real purpose in life. I spent my days working at minimum-wage jobs, drifting from one to another, smoking and getting drunk in the evening and weekends.

I knew that my parents were very worried about me, but I didn't really care much about that, about them, or about himself. I knew that my parents always helped me out of the messes I had made for myself, but I still resented their interference in my life. But I stayed dependent on them for support money and periodically, when I lost my job or had an emergency, I had no choice but to turn to them for help. I had no fallback plan, no emergency money of my own, and no idea what to do when something happened that I hadn't planned for—and I never planned ahead for anything. Inside, I hated myself, and though I really loved them, I also felt a kind of hatred toward my parents and my successful sister because *they* couldn't fill the emptiness inside me. In my heart, I cursed them, I loved them, I hated them—and most of all, I felt deep shame.

During the worst years of my drinking, I knew that my parents were terrified. When I started to get sober, they said that they always feared that they would receive a call that I had bottomed out, or worse, had been seriously injured or killed in a drunk-driving accident. Finally, my drinking was so out of control that in the space of only a few weeks, I found myself four times in a hospital emergency room, first with a liver-related illness and then suffering the first stages of the DTs.[22]

My parents finally convinced me to enter a residential alcohol and drug rehabilitation treatment center. After several weeks in rehab, I moved to a sober half-way house, connected with an Alcoholics Anonymous (AA) Sponsor with whom I checked in daily, and I attended daily AA meetings. I didn't know it yet, but I was well on my way to genuine recovery. I was lucky. I have stayed sober for five years now—but I have also lost a lot along the way. I never really made close friends, I lost my connection to art, which was a major part of my life. I hope I can reconnect to it—the artistic spark that fed me and was the only real light in my life has been stilled for now, but I hope that, like an ember, it can be brought back to life as a warming fire.

I still feel pretty lost. All those years of drugs and drinking may have damaged my brain some. I often don't think as quickly or as sharply as I would like, and sometimes I don't remember things very well. I still haven't found my place or my career and I haven't found a "special" woman to love and who loves me. I'm pretty lonely. Turning back to drinking is a daily temptation for me, and, while I resist mightily, I succeed in resisting most, but not all of the time.

Sometimes, like Noah in the Bible, I still want to curse those who discovered me in my drunken state, but my more rational mind knows better. I know that if my parents had not finally accepted that I was an alcoholic and realized how desperate I was, I would be dead now. I don't want to die. I have found a

---

22. DTs = *delirium tremens,* also known as the "shaking frenzy"—shivers, sweating, heart palpitations, and trembling that accompany withdrawal from alcohol.

> newborn faith, each day I choose life with all its temptations and uncertainties. And I pray that I can hold back the curses that I have brought on myself.

Exploring the Text Within

Find a quiet and comfortable place to sit in contemplative silence with the above teachings and with the following questions about you and your life's experience. You may choose to focus on one question or sit with several. Ask yourself: what do the biblical text and these teachings mean to me in my life?

The Holy One paid heed to Abel and his offering, but to Cain and his offering He paid no heed.

(Genesis 4:4–5)

> Can I recall a time when I have felt ignored or disregarded by a parent or someone else I loved, and from whom I craved approval?

Noah, the tiller of the soil, was the first to plant a vineyard. He drank of the wine and he became drunk.

(Genesis 9:20–21)

> Can I recall a time when I have wondered why *I* have been blessed when others have not, when I have experienced "survivor's guilt"?
>
> Have I tried to soothe my guilt by overindulging—in wine, in drugs, in food, in overconsumption of another kind?

He became drunk and he uncovered himself within his tent

(Genesis 9:21)

> Can I recall a time when I or someone I love have fallen into the clutches of *addiction* of any kind and have become *exposed* to emotional, physical, or spiritual exile?

Chapter 4

Lech Lecha I

Exploring a New World

"Take yourself and go forth . . ."
—Genesis 12:1–5

"Make journeys. Attempt them. There is nothing else."

"There is a time for departure, even when there is no certain place to go."
—Tennesee Williams

The Lord said to Abram, "Go forth [Take yourself, Go to yourself . . .] from your native land, from the place of your birth, and from your father's house to the land that I will show you.

I will make of you a great nation.

And I will bless you;

I will make your name great, and you shall be a blessing.

I will bless those who bless you and curse him that curses you;

and all the families of the earth shall bless themselves by you."

—Genesis 12:1–3

At the end of the story of Noah, we are introduced to a long genealogy that links Noah through several generations all the way to Abram the first patriarch of what is to become the Israelite—and later, the Jewish—people. In this genealogy, we are also introduced to Abram's wife, Sarai. And so the story of the first generations of the Israelite people begins. Later, Abram and Sarai receive new names, Abraham and Sarah (see chapter 6 below) (Gen 17:5, 15). But at this stage, still named Abram and Sarai, they are about to set out on the journey of their lives.

The Holy One calls out to Abram and said:

> *"Lech lecha—Go forth* [Take yourself, Go to yourself . . .] *from your native land, from the place of your birth, and from your father's house to the land that I will show you.*
> *I will make of you a great nation.*
> *And I will bless you;*
> *I will make your name great, and you shall be a blessing.*
> *I will bless those who bless you and curse him that curses you;*
> *And all the families of the earth shall bless themselves by you."*
>
> *Abram went forth as the* LORD *had commanded him and Lot went with him. Abram was seventy-five years old when he left Haran. Abram took his wife Sarai and his brother's son Lot and all the wealth that they had amassed, and the persons that they had acquired in Haran; and they set out for the land of Canaan.*
> —Genesis 12:1–5

The Hebrew words that begin God's call to Abram, *Lech lecha* (12:1), have intrigued interpreters for millennia, because they can be translated in a number of ways: go forth, go to yourself, go by yourself, or take your whole self. Both emphatic and redundant, *lech* is the masculine imperative, "Go!" and *lechá* is the masculine preposition, "to/for you." Thus, interpreters discern both a play on the words' similar sounds (*lech* and *lecha*) and a play with the preposition, and ask: is it *to*? is it *for*? Let's look at five different versions of this rabbinic "play" on the words:

1. A late-eighteenth-century Hassidic master, Reb Levi Yitzchak of Berdichev,[1] explained God's charge to Abram, *lech lechá*, as "Go *to* yourself."

---

1. Levi Yitzchak of Berdichev also known as the *Berdichever* (1740–1809) was a Hassidic leader who was popularly known as *Hasanegor*—or the "defense attorney" for the Jewish people, because he often interceded with God on behalf of the people. He had a reputation for great gentleness and compassion for every Jew and is especially famous for a time when he put God on trial. In this speech, known as *A din Toyre mit Gott* (A Trial of Torah with God), Levi Yitzchak reflects the ancient tradition of sacred arguing with God described on p. 16, footnote 16 when he demands a stop to all the sufferings that God has brought on the Jewish people: *"I, Levi Yitzchak, son of Sarah*

"*Every place that a person goes, he goes to the root of his soul.*" The journey is the place that one needs to be. It is not some ultimate goal that is important. "It is the challenge of being on the "way"; . . . [it] is the challenge of attending to the moment and the place I occupy *now*. That moment and that place has something I need *and* something I need to take care of."

Have you ever looked back at events in your life and wondered why things have happened to you in a certain way, or why you met specific people at unexpected moments in your life? Has it ever occurred to you that things were just *meant* to happen that way, or that you were *meant* to meet just that person at that time in your life because something changed in your life or because that chance meeting made all the difference as your life unfolded? Reb Levi Yitzchak is telling us that the *journey* of our lives, not our lives' destination, is exactly where we need to be—because *it is on the journey that we discover ourselves*. It seems that the most important journeys we take are the ones that lead us to profound discoveries, and that this was understood not only by Hassidic rabbis like Levi Yitzchak, but also by philosophers who lived long before them.

As early as the first century C.E., Philo Judeus of Alexandria, a Jewish philosopher and theologian, wrote that Abram's emigration from his homeland to the unknown place that God promised to show him was "one of soul rather than body, for the heavenly love overpowered his desire for mortal things." Philo emphasized that Abram's departure from his birthplace was a result of his *discovery of* God and his rejection of the idolatrous ways of his native land. Abram's soul, Philo taught, yearned for the spiritual perfection that he instinctively knew the Holy One would bestow upon him as he set out on his journey: "*. . . opening the soul's eye* as though after a profound sleep, and beginning to see the pure beam instead of the deep darkness, he [Abram] followed the ray and discerned what he had not beheld before, a character and pilot presiding over the world and directing in safety his own work, assuming the charge . . . of that work and of all such parts of it as are worthy of the divine care."[2] In this way, Philo explained, Abram's soul cleaved to the divine *pilot*, and the first biblical patriarch went forth to the root of his own soul.

---

of Berdichev say, 'From my stand I will not waver, and from my place I shall not move until there be an end to all this sorrow and suffering!'" What is most powerful in Levi Yitzchak's stand is that immediately after these words, he begins the Mourners' Kaddish (the prayer for the dead), reflecting his faith, articulated so well in Nobel Prize winner Elie Wiesel's words, "For the Jew, it is possible to argue against God, even indict and convict God, but not to live without God."

2. In Birnbaum, "On the Life of Abraham," 939 and 940–41.

2. Samson Raphael Hirsch, a nineteenth-century German rabbi and founder of modern Orthodoxy, suggests that the Hebrew words *lech lecha* mean *"Go by yourself"*: "Abraham appears merely as an individual who is told to "dare to be alone . . . ." It was Abraham's task to isolate himself and to walk alone with God."[3] Sometimes aloneness is the circumstance that brings *insight, a new state of being, or a turn in a new direction.*

In the Torah, we see many moments when important people are alone—and dramatic and often transformative stories begin. For example, Jacob is alone as he fearfully flees his brother Esau's revenge after having stolen his older brother's birthright and paternal blessing. After a lonely night with his dreams, Jacob awakens to the epiphany that *"God is in this place and I, i did not know it."*[4] This *insight* ("in-sight") initiates a spiritual journey for Jacob that culminates twenty years later when Jacob dreams again as he anticipates reuniting with Esau. Our text tells us that *" Jacob was left alone"*[5] in great fear and trepidation on the eve of his encounter with his older brother. During this solitary night, Jacob wrestles with an angel (or a man—the text is unclear) and receives a new name—Israel—the one who *"has striven with beings divine and human" and has survived."*[6] This new name is to change Jacob's status and *state of being* forever—the private man, the *pater familias*—the father of a tribe, Jacob, now given the name *Israel*, has become the father of the people. (For a more complete telling, see chapter 11 below.)

And yet another example of transformative aloneness: early in the Book of Exodus, we see an example of a *turn in a new direction*, when Moses stands at a burning bush he notices in the wilderness. Watching the bush carefully, Moses discovers that the bush is not consumed by the fire, and from the bush a mysterious Voice emerges—the Voice of God—telling Moses that he must return to Egypt to liberate the Israelite people. Moses, who has fled from Egypt after having killed a slave master who had viciously beaten an Israelite slave, heeds God's commandment and returns to the land of Israelite bondage to become his people's liberator and initiate the great exodus from that land. Alone in the desert, Moses has heard the Voice of God, has understood the divine call, and has *turned in a new direction* that will change his life and the life of the entire Israelite people.

3. *The Pentateuch,* translated by Hirsch, and excerpts from Oratz, ed., *The Hirsch Commentary,* 61.

4. Genesis 28:16.

5. Genesis 32:25.

6. Genesis 32:29.

Perhaps aloneness is precisely that condition of the mind, soul, and heart that allows a human being to *hear* most keenly. Perhaps it is that profound place in which silence prevails, in which the din of external voices has no dominion. Perhaps, as Rabbi Rami Shapiro has commented, "silence is the language of the soul" in which transformation can truly take place. Perhaps Abraham indeed could go forth *by himself*, as Rabbi Samson Raphael Hirsch suggests, even in the company of an entourage of his wife, Sarai, servants, and livestock, in the solitude of his soul—and in so doing, he could become open to new perspectives, become a new person (indeed the patriarch of a new people), and turn in new directions.

3. A nineteenth-century Hassidic rabbi, Rabbi Mordechai Yosef Leiner of Isbitza (also known as the Ishbitzer Rebbe), interprets *lech lecha* as "go forth," which means to your *authentic* self, for it is true that all of the world's concerns [i.e., distractions] should not be called *life*—for the essence of life you will discover within yourself."[7] This interpretation is a profound understanding of Torah's words. The Holy One is telling Abram, "take your self—your *whole* self, your truest self—on this new journey," on this great adventure into a land where questions abound and answers are still a mystery. Perhaps what God was saying to Abram was that he could not set out on this adventure in a half-hearted way, that he had to bring *all* of who he was—his noble and beautiful side and his shadow side with him on the journey. Perhaps God was saying that *any truly significant journey, any journey worth embarking upon, demands our full presence, our most profound honesty, the fullness of who we are.*

As I noted in my Introduction, God instructs the Israelites to love Him with "all your heart(s), with all your soul, and with all your might" (*v'ahavta et Adonai Eloheicha b'chol l'vavchá, b'chol nafshechá, u-v'chol me'odécha*). Judaism's ancient sages remind us that when we love the Holy One, with all our hearts (plural), we bring our entire selves into the loving relationship—the part of us that is represented by the *yetzer tov*, our natural human inclination for good, and also the part of us that is represented by the *yetzer rah*, our also-very-human inclination for evil. We love with our nobility and our gentleness, with our sweet souls and our generosity of spirit, and we also love with our baseness and our aggression, with our nastiness and our pettiness.

Thus, Abram (later Abraham)—this complex, multi-faceted, noble and ignoble, imperfect man—is the one who must embark on the journey. Later in this same Torah portion, we witness Abram's nobility (as when he argues with God to save the innocent people of Sodom and Gomorrah) and

---

7. Mordechai, *Living Waters*.

his cowardly side (as when, in order to protect himself, he introduces Sarai [later Sarah] to the Egyptians as his sister, not his wife).[8] Abram acts both courageously and timidly—but, true to the complex man he is, he brings his *whole self* along in his travels.

4. And still another perspective on *Lech lecha*: In the nineteenth century, the Hassidic master, Reb Yehudah Aryeh Leib Alter,[9] who was also known by the title of his most famous work, the *Sefat Emet* (The Language of Truth), taught that the first person imperative *lech* comes from the Hebrew verb *lalechet*—to walk.

> The human being is called a walker, always having to go from one [spiritual] rung to another. For habit makes things seem natural, and this sense of "nature" hides the inner light.... That is why God "renews, in God's goodness, each day, the work of Creation," so that we are not overpowered by the sense of nature (habit). This is the burning castle, this world of nature and all that passes through it. Even though all of nature came to be only through the transcendent single point of life, it becomes stamped with the imprint of nature (the ordinary). Therefore, the Blessed Holy One renews each day the work of Creation.
>
> The person has to search and seek out this renewal, "to watch My doorways each day" (Prov 8:34)....
>
> [This is the meaning of *lech lecha:*] "Get you out of your land"—a person should always keep walking.
>
> "To [that which] I will show you"—always some new attainment. This is why the human being is called a walker. Whoever stands still is not renewed, for nature holds that person fast. The angels above are beyond nature; they can be said to "stand". But the human being has to keep walking.[10]

5. In our own time, Rabbi Arthur Green, who has written a commentary on the *Sefat Emet*, writes:

> Thank you, Lord, for all that nervous energy. Life as an angel might have been easier—standing still to do Your bidding. But it is our walking, our ever climbing (and sometimes falling!) from rung to rung that makes us human. Despite all the

---

8. Genesis 12:10–20.

9. Rabbi Yehudah Leib Alter (1847–1905), the *Sefat Emet*, was the leader of the Gerer Hassidim (the Hassim from the town of Ger, in Poland), and was therefore also known as the Gerer Rebbe.

10. Leib, *The Language of Truth*, 22. (Green translation).

struggle and pain that go along with growing, we wouldn't have it any other way."[11]

As the biblical text continues, God offers Abram a promise: *I will make your name great, and you shall be a blessing* (12:2).

In Genesis Rabbah, Rabbi Berakiah commented on a verse from Song of Songs (1:3)

> "Thine ointments have a goodly fragrance." What did Abraham resemble? A vial of myrrh closed with a tight-fitting lid and lying in a corner, so that its fragrance was not disseminated. Similarly, the Holy One, blessed be He, said to Abraham, "Travel from place to place, and your name will become great in the world."[12]

Rabbi Berakiah compares Abram to a sealed vial of precious perfume that God wants to share with the world. The Holy One commands Abram to "go forth" in order that Abram's *fragrance*, his special gifts—spiritual, intellectual, and personal—might be shared with a world that needs him. This is a profound message. *Each of us has gifts we might share with the world.* The question is: *will we?*

Text to Life

> When I was ten years old, I lived in Mexico City. My parents, who were art lovers, often sought out young new artists. Among them was a twenty-eight-year-old painter named Leonardo Nierman.
>
> My parents and I once visited Mr. Nierman's studio and I was mesmerized by his paintings—resplendent with subtle lines and bold colors and abstract views of the cosmos, the heavens and earth in various stages of creation, a swan-like bird occasionally peeked through the clouds, or a thin slice of a newly born moon hovered in the firmament. A flash of lightning, a hint of sunlight, a stream of water so vivid that one could almost hear it, would emerge out from Nierman's wood-based oil works—and classical music surrounded us on all sides.
>
> Mr. Nierman welcomed us warmly, paying special attention to me, for it was rare for a ten-year-old to visit his studio. Gently taking my hand, he guided me from painting to painting, explaining his feelings and thoughts and his creation process. I

---

11. In Leib, *The Language of Truth*, 23. (Green translation).
12. Genesis Rabbah 34:2.

felt as if I were in an enchanted land, with a magician who could conjure up such wondrous images. Leonardo and my parents became good friends, and we were blessed to have several of his paintings grace the walls of our home.

A year after our first visit to Leonardo's studio, I asked for one of his paintings for my birthday, and I received a small work in oil on wood, filled with movement, almost like a magnificent dance, all articulated in abstract form. Leonardo had named this wondrous painting, "Listening to Stravinsky," after the famous early-twentieth-century Russian composer Igor Stravinsky, whose musically innovative style excited him. Nierman told me that he had been listening to Stravinsky's "Firebird" while painting, and that some of the quieter parts of his painting came from listening to the firebird's stirring and that the flourishes of color that seemed like dance to me emerged from the similar flourishes in Stravinsky's work. I was thrilled and enchanted. Then, Leonardo told me the story of his own emergence as an artist.

From early childhood, Leonardo had played the violin. Well-known in Mexico as a prodigy, he began performing in concert halls at a very early age Nierman seemed well on his way to a stellar international career as a violin soloist, when he heard a recording by the famed violinist Yehudi Menuhin. Realizing that his own talents paled in comparison to Menuhin's, Nierman put down his violin, and never played professionally again. And as he set his violin in its case, he picked up a paint brush and the world was blessed with his artistic genius.

I am reminded of the *midrash* about the biblical patriarch Abraham, who is compared to a tightly closed vial of perfume. Had Abraham not followed God's command to *"take yourself and go forth,"* his unique contribution would never have come out into the world. Similarly, when Leonardo Nierman set down his violin and picked up his paintbrush, a new and unique *aroma* blessed the world, as it still does in our time, more than half a century since he first painted. I cannot imagine the world without his work.

How much poorer we would be without it.

LGB

Martin, a rabbi in New England, writes about a time in his life when he felt like Abraham called to "go forth" from the land that he knew to a new and unfamiliar place that held promise for him. This is his story.

Several times in my life I have felt a sense of *Lech lecha*—that I had to leave the place where I was comfortably living and pick up and try to change my life. There's a Hebrew expression—*m'shaneh makom, m'shaneh mazal* ("change your location, change your luck/fortune")—that I first heard in a popular Israeli rock song by the band *Kaveret* (aka *Poogy*) called "*Yo—Ya*." I was living in Northport, New York about 100 yards up the road from the harbor where I learned to swim in the summer of my fourth year. I loved the water, Northport's proximity to Manhattan, the combination of culture and nature that Northport afforded, the friendships that I had developed over the years in New York, having spent most of my life there.

In my mid-forties, I had been writing songs for a few years and I had been getting quite a bit of interest in my tunes down in Nashville. I visited in Tennessee a number of times and was told often that if I seriously wanted my songs to be recorded and ultimately heard I would have to relocate to Nashville to fully absorb the music as it was done there. I became convinced, but the decision to move was wrenching. I loved living in Northport; I loved the house, the location, everything about it. But I wasn't writing songs only for my own pleasure; I wanted to communicate with other people and to try to get my words and music out there. I decided I had no choice but to pick up and make the journey southward.

While settling things in New York, I prepared myself emotionally and practically for my move. I found someone to rent my house, found an apartment in Nashville within walking distance of the synagogue I would be attending, found employment teaching in Hebrew schools for two synagogues, and did a yard sale at my house. From the time I decided I had to move and for the six months it actually took me to depart, I began to mourn leaving Northport and the house.

The house was originally my parents' summer cottage purchased when I was four years old, and so many of my life's pivotal experiences had happened there. I had made lifelong friendships from my summers as a kid there, I had first begun to write there, I lost my virginity there. During the thirteen years I lived in Manhattan in the West Village, I would often go to Northport to escape the city. I eventually moved to Northport at the age of thirty-seven and five years later renovated the house, putting all of the resources I had into that project. The place was small, but perfect for me. So leaving my home was very, very difficult. I was, in a very deep sense, like the biblical Abraham, leaving my homeland and all that was familiar to me. I spent a lot of time packing up the house, perhaps unconsciously delaying my departure to inhale its aura to take with me. Friends would come from the city to help me pack or to say goodbye for who knows how long. Preparing for my departure became a long ritual. Finally, moving day came. The huge moving truck had great difficulty getting up the small street I lived on, but they managed to squeeze in.

So much in my life was about to change. I was scared, but also excited. Transitions are not easy for me. My new tenants in Northport were very considerate of my feelings, which were very close to the surface. I'm not very good at keeping my emotions a secret. I tend to verbalize them. (I wonder if Abraham experienced such feelings as he left *his* home!).

Finally the day came for me to get in the car and say goodbye. I kissed the beautiful florid mezuzah on the front door and drove off. I stayed at a friend's house still on Long Island that night and then drove about 700 miles to my brother's home in Monroe, North Carolina. The following day I drove to Nashville. About seventy-two hours later, the movers delivered my belongings. I did some unpacking, but left a lot of boxes in the living room where I sat to write. Every day I would sit in the corner of the living room in a chair and write—working on songs preceded by writing in my journal. Elements of my past were sitting in boxes all around me. I was thinking over the trajectory of my life as I wrote in my journal. I was now forty-five years old, not quite Abraham's age, but certainly no longer an adolescent. I reviewed my life year by year from about the age of seventeen or eighteen until that moment in time—and I noticed that I recalled three major elements of my life when remembering each year: who (if anyone) I was involved with romantically, what I had written, and where I had travelled. I tried to write a number of hours every day because there was no other way to justify this major upheaval in my life.

Ironically, the seeds for my eventual return to Huntington three years later were sewn just before I left home, but I had no clue at the time. I had met someone back in Huntington a few months before leaving—and we eventually began a long-distance relationship the first summer I was in Nashville.

Other seeds were sewn in Nashville: someone I dated briefly early in my time there told a local rabbi that I was very

> involved in Kabbalah (Jewish mysticism) and the rabbi invited me to lead meditation *minyanim* (prayer services) and teach Kabbalah. These activities eventually took me down a spiritual road some fourteen years later to becoming a rabbi.
>
> A long journey from a beloved home in Northport, New York to the capital of country music in Nashville Tennessee—a journey of self-discovery that led me away from some primal aspects of myself and back again, with a new self-knowledge and maybe a deeper spiritual grounding. God tells Abraham the He shall bless him. In my journey I have been deeply blessed with a life partner, my wife, whom I love deeply, and my son, who is the heart of my life—all this came from my *Lech lecha* trek, away from home to an unknown land, and back again to a new and more expansive homeland.

Exploring the Text Within

Find a quiet and comfortable place to sit in contemplative silence with the above teachings and with the following questions about you and your life's experience. You may choose to focus on one question or sit with several. Ask yourself: what do the biblical text and these teachings mean to me in my life?

> The Holy One said to Abram: "Go forth from your native land and from your father's house to the land that I will show you."
>
> (Genesis 12:1)

> Every place that a person goes, he goes to the root of his soul. "Go by yourself." This is one journey that must be made alone. . . . Any journey worth taking demands our full presence, our most profound honesty
>
> (Rabbi Levi Yitzchak of Berdichev)

> Can I recall a time when I have taken a lone journey and I have been fully present, fully honest with myself, and I have gone to the core of my soul?

[T]he human being has to keep walking.... Thank you, Lord, for all that nervous energy. Life as an angel might have been easier.... But it is our walking, our ever climbing (and sometimes falling!)... that makes us human. Despite all the struggle and pain that go along with growing, we wouldn't have it any other way.

(Rabbi Arthur Green)

Can I recall a time when I wanted to stand still, to keep the comfortable *status quo*, but my spirit demanded change, and my soul knew that I must keep walking life's path, come what may?

What did Abraham resemble? A vial of myrrh closed with a tight-fitting lid and lying in a corner, so that its fragrance was not disseminated. Similarly, the Holy One, blessed be He, said to Abraham, "Travel from place to place, and thy name will become great in the world...."

(Genesis Rabbah 34:21)

Do I have gifts within me, sealed as in a tight vial of perfume that I want to reveal and share with the world?

Chapter 5
Lech Lecha II

Infertility and Sorrow

"Sarai, Abram's wife, had borne him no children."
—Genesis 16:1–16

Sarai, Abram's wife, had borne him no children. She had an Egyptian maidservant whose name was Hagar. And Sarai said to Abram, "Look, the Lord *has kept me from bearing. Consort with my maid; perhaps I shall have a son through her." And Abram heeded Sarai's request. So Sarai, Abram's wife, took her maid—Hagar the Egyptian—after Abram had dwelt in the Land of Canaan ten years—and gave her to her husband as a concubine. He cohabited with Hagar and she conceived; and when she saw that she conceived, her mistress was lowered in her esteem.*

—Genesis 16:1–5

After God's call to Abram to set forth from his homeland to an unknown land of promised blessings, the patriarch, his wife Sarai, Abram's nephew Lot, and their whole entourage embark on a great journey and travel southward, eventually reaching Canaan where they scout out the land. Ironically, the promised blessings of land and children are at this stage unfulfilled for Abram and Sarai.

A short while after settling in Canaan, famine comes upon them and they are forced to leave their new home, and journey further southward into prosperous Egypt in search of food. So far, their adventure into the promised land has been anything but blessed.

After some misadventures in Egypt, they eventually return to Canaan where Abram and Lot part ways, with Lot and his family settling in Sodom and Gomorrah, and Abram, Sarai and their people settling near the terebinths of Mamre.[1]

By this time, both Abram and Sarai are old and have not been blessed with children. Their childlessness saddens the couple and leaves them emotionally and practically impoverished. Emotionally, they are bereft, unfulfilled and left without the chance to nurture and raise little ones. Practically, they have no offspring who will, as Abram and Sarai grow old, help support them and the tribe. For Abram, the stigma of being a man without sons stings, for he is unable to fulfill his obligation as set out earlier to Noah and his sons: *"be fruitful and multiply and fill the earth."*[2]

For Sarai, the shame of being a barren, childless woman stings even more sharply than for her husband—a woman's raison d'être, her reason for being in biblical society, is to procreate, to bring forth new life to the tribe. To be unable to do so is a humiliation, and renders her worthless.

Sarai, now long past childbearing age, recognizing her husband's need for an heir, makes an agonizing decision. She will enable him to procreate by offering her Egyptian maidservant Hagar as a surrogate wife to Abram. How wrenching a moment this must be for Sarai—to give her husband over to another woman, and a subservient one at that!

Sarai, however, is not acting altogether altruistically. In their ancient culture, any child birthed by a slave is officially considered to be the child of her mistress. Therefore, culturally and legally, a baby borne by Hagar would be considered Sarai's baby. *"Consort with my maid,"* Sarai says to Abram, *"perhaps I shall have a son through her."* (16:2)

In the contemporary context, adoption could have been an alternative route that Sarai could have taken. Indeed, in biblical times, the birth mother would sit on the lap of the "adoptive mother" (mistress) as she gave birth and as the baby was born, she/he would be given to the mistress. In our world, where so many babies are in need of loving homes, what a felicitous alternative this might be! But sadly for Sarai, things did not turn out as she expected. As soon as Hagar conceives, *"her mistress was lowered in her esteem"* (16:4) and Hagar has no intention of turning her baby over to Sarai.

---

1. Located half way between the West Bank cities of Hebron and Halhul, which is five kilometers north of Hebron.
2. Genesis 9:1.

In due time, Hagar gives birth to a boy. Abram named the baby Ishmael ("God hears" or "God has heard"). Sarai watched silently and in aching frustration as Hagar assumes what should have been *her* maternal role. Hagar nurses and cares for Ishmael and never gives the baby over to Sarai's care. Sarai, who has yielded for her husband's sake (and for her own too), remains with empty arms and an aching heart, watching as the baby is cradled at Hagar's breast.

"*Sarai, Abram's wife, had borne him no children.*" (16:1)

Sarai whole being yearns for a child. For so many years she and Abram had tried to conceive, and yet no child had grown in her womb. Now, old, frustrated and sad, she aches to hold a baby in her arms, to love a little one and nurture it to adulthood. But there is more at stake than simply her emotions. In a world in which so many pregnancies ended in miscarriage and so many women died in childbirth, bringing forth new life was an imperative for survival. Sarai has failed to accomplish her primary task as a woman in her society—to procreate. Thus, the pain of her infertility, emotionally excruciating as it was, also topples her on the tribal totem pole, from a woman of stature to the status of a barren woman, useless in a survival-oriented world. In her culture, Sarai logically sees herself as a failure, and would no doubt be viewed as such by others. Like Sarai, many of us feel that we are failures if we haven't produced what our society expects of us. In Sarai's world she was expected to procreate. In our world, we are expected to "produce." We gain high status through wealth, productivity, political power, scientific discovery, cultural influence, and fame. If we do not achieve in these conventional ways, we are prone to consider ourselves less than worthwhile. We yearn for significance; we yearn to be known as creative, generative.

The Hebrew Bible, however, expresses the idea that *every human soul is precious and of intrinsic worth to God*, whether or not she or he has procreated biologically: "Let not the barren one say: 'Behold I am a dry tree.' . . . I will give them in My house and in My walls a monument and a name, better than sons and daughters; an everlasting name I will give him, which will not be discontinued."[3]

What does an "everlasting name" (*yad vashem*) mean? It means *a reputation, a monument to the sum of one's deeds during one's lifetime—these are considered one's progeny.*

---

3. Isaiah 56:4–5. While the text says literally "eunuchs," instead of "barren," given later, rabbinic Judaism's conclusion that the obligation to procreate was incumbent only upon men (RaMBaM–Maimonides, *Ishut* [Laws of Marriage] 15:2 and *Even Ha-Ezer* [The Stone of Help] 1:13, part of the law book *Arba'ah Turim* [Four Columns] by Jacob ben Asher [late thirteenth, early fourteenth century], which deals with the laws concerning women), we may extrapolate that the sentiment applied to both women and men.

Rabbi Shlomo ben Yitzchak, also known as *RaSHI*, the greatest Torah scholar of medieval northern Europe, once wrote that "the many generations [progeny] of the righteous are good deeds." Later Jewish tradition also teaches that if we teach Torah to others' children, it is as if we have given birth to them. This is based on an interpretation of the words from the book of Deuteronomy 6:7, "And you shall teach them [i.e., God's commandments] to your children." Here our understanding of Torah is much more expansive, encompassing all Jewish and general learning—and it includes teaching to children and adults. The very act of teaching is a kind of midwifery, a birthing of new ideas and wider horizons. In the Jewish context, *RaSHI* and the Talmud explain, regarding Deuteronomy 6:7,

> "These are your disciples. We find everywhere that disciples are termed "sons [children]" as it is said: "You are children to the Lord your God" (Deut. 14:1).... So too, we find that Hezekiah taught Torah to all Israel and called them children, as it is said: "My sons, now do not forget" (II Chronicles 29:11). And just as disciples are called "children," as it is said, "You are children of the Lord your God" so too, the teacher is called "father [parent]" (RaSHI, Deuteronomy 6:7). "Anyone who teaches the son of his fellow person Torah, Scripture considers him as if he gave birth to him. How do we know this? Because the Torah says, "These are the generations of Aaron and Moses" (Numbers 3:1).[4]

An early biblical example of a non-biological kind of *giving birth* is in the story of Abram and Sarai when they first left Haran for Canaan. Metaphorically, they bore many children, even though they had not yet had any children of their own. There is an often ignored line in Genesis 12:5. "Abram took his wife Sarai and his brother's son Lot, and all the wealth that they had amassed and the persons that they had acquired in Haran; and they set out for the land of Canaan." The English does not do justice to the text in Hebrew, which says "the souls that they had *made* [not, 'acquired']" and brought to the God of Israel. In later midrash, we read: "*And The Souls That They Had Made:* [This] refers to the proselytes that they had made. That is to teach you that he who brings a Gentile near to God, it is as though he created him. Said Rav Huna: Abraham converted the men and Sarah the women."[5] Later, in the

---

4. A reminder: The Hebrew language is not inflected and thus translates a word like *banim*, which could be translated as "children," as *"sons,"* and always defaults to the masculine form. Nonetheless, we can legitimately think of these statements as referring to both genders—children and parents, both fathers and mothers. Indeed, in the Bible itself (Proverbs 1:8), we read clearly the statement, "do not forsake the Torah (teaching) of your mother."

5. Genesis Rabbah 39:14.

Babylonian Talmud, we read, "One who brings a person to Torah is regarded as having given birth to him or her."[6]

> *And Sarai said to Abram: "Look, the* LORD *has kept me from bearing. Consort with my maid; Perhaps I shall have a son through her."*
>
> —Genesis 16:2

After years of yearning, Sarai finally yields, and offers her slave woman Hagar to Abram so that he might sire a child, and Sarai says, *"perhaps I shall have a son through her."* The Hebrew of this sentence is particularly powerful. Once again, Torah offers us a wordplay: *"ulai ibaneh mimenah."* Here, *ibaneh* means literally, "I will be built up, as in: Perhaps *my status will be raised up* through Hagar," for when Hagar gives birth (as a surrogate for Sarai), Sarai will become *em b'Yisrael*—a mother in Israel, a matriarch—and she will now hold a revered status among the people. In stark contrast, as a childless woman, she was viewed *"as if [she] were dead and demolished."*[7] Even more poignantly, the Hebrew word *ibaneh* echoes the word *ben*—son—so that this sentence might also be translated as "Perhaps I will have a son through her [Hagar]. Sarai's standing as a woman, her whole life as a mother, and her place within her culture—how her husband and her kin will relate to her—now depend entirely on Hagar's surrogacy and on the outcome of the pregnancy. Sarai is entirely dependent on Hagar.

How the roles have reversed! Mistress becomes enslaved to bondswoman! Sarai, assuming that she will soon receive her glorious status as matriarch of our people, is patient throughout Hagar's pregnancy, eagerly awaiting the baby's birth. But to her great dismay, as soon as Hagar conceived, *"her mistress was lowered in her esteem"* (16:4). How agonizing for Sarai! It must have been cold there in Hagar's shadow.[8]

Let us think more expansively about this difficult situation. What happens when one's primary status, reputation, or prestige is dependent on another? What happens to one emotionally and spiritually when one spouse depends too much on the other's position for reflected glory? What happens to parents when they try (perhaps unconsciously) to live out their own unrealized dreams through their children's "success"? And what happens to their children? *Living vicariously is not truly living. It is the illusion of living,*

---

6. BT Sanhedrin 99a.

7. Genesis Rabbah 45:2. See also Genesis 30:1 where Rachel said to Jacob, "Give me children, or I shall die."

8. I am alluding to the song, "The Wing Beneath My Wings," Jeff Silber and Larry Hensley, composers.

but when one reaches out to touch the "life" we think we see, *it is a chimera, a mirage, with little substance.* Such is Sarai's life after Hagar's disdain. Rather than being "built up" through Hagar, Sarai implodes in frustration and fury.

> *Then Sarai treated her harshly and she* [Hagar] *ran away from her.*
>
> —Genesis 16:6

Imagine Sarai's sorrow! Imagine her rage, born from the depths of her pain. Like pouring salt on an open wound, nubile Hagar now mocks her mistress. We can imagine the words that cross between them, omitted by the Torah, but vivid in our thoughts:

> *Hagar:* "Look at me, you old crone! I conceived immediately! You tried for years and failed! You are old and arid as the desert sands! Your god has locked your womb! This is my baby and Abram will honor me, not you, as the child's mother! I will nurse the baby! Your breasts are like dried up prunes! How I pity you!"
>
> *Sarai:* "Silence! I demand silence! You are my slave! You shall do as *I* say! You are just a vessel! You are carrying my baby! You are big and bloated and you will suffer the pangs of birth for me! I will be this baby's mother! Don't you dare speak to me in such an insolent manner!"

Whatever words were exchanged between the two women, Torah tells us that Hagar *"ran away"* from Sarai. Perhaps she did indeed fear that Abram would punish her for insulting his wife; perhaps she just couldn't abide being abused by Sarai any longer. Whatever her reasons, a divine angel—perhaps an "in-sight"—comes to Hagar and tells her, *"Go back to your mistress, and submit to her harsh treatment. . . . I will greatly increase your offspring and they shall be too many to count"* (16:10).

We certainly cringe at Sarai's treatment of Hagar. After all, as a bondwoman, Hagar involuntarily becomes a surrogate mother for Sarai. She was simply used as a sexual object, an instrument of Sarai's desire for a child. There is no doubt that she must have felt oppressed, abused, and angry. In this context, her mockery of Sarai is an understandable response for an exploited woman.

Yet Sarai deserves compassion as well. Years of longing to be a mother have turned desire into despair, and now that she is so close to having a baby to hold and love and nurture, Hagar's scorn (emerging from her own pain at being so egregiously exploited) is especially searing to Sarai's soul.

Sarai's ache is deepened by Abram's lack of understanding and support. Calling out to Abram, Sarai cries: *"The wrong done me is your fault!*

I myself put my maid in your bosom; now that she sees that she is pregnant, I am lowered in her esteem. The Lord decide between you and me!" (16:5). Sarai pleads with her husband to understand her plight, to stand up for her against the arrogant maidservant, to advocate for her with God to assert that she, Sarai, is first in his heart.

The ancient rabbis of Genesis Rabbah empathize with Sarai. On the biblical verse The Wrong Done To Me Is Your Fault! (16:5)

> Rabbi Judan explained in Rabbi Judah's name "You wrong me with words, since you hear me insulted [by Hagar] yet you are silent." Rabbi Berakiah explained it in Rabbi Abba's name: "I have a grievance against you. For imagine two men incarcerated in prison, and as the king passes one of them cries out, execute justice for me! The king orders him to be released, whereupon his fellow prisoner says to him, 'I have a grievance against you, for had you said, Execute justice for us, he would have released me just as he has released you; but now that you said, execute justice for me, he released you but not me.' Similarly, had you said, 'We go childless,' then as He [God] gave you a child so would He have given me. He gave you a child but not me."[9]

Sarai seeks loyalty and advocacy from the man she has dutifully followed from their homeland in Ur of the Chaldees into the unknown land of Canaan, down into Egypt, and back again into Canaan. But Abram's response is far from tender or steadfast: *"Abram said to Sarai, your maid is in your hands. Deal with her as you think right"* (16:6).

If one were giving Abram the benefit of the doubt, his reply to Sarai may be interpreted as respectful—"she's *your* maid, *you* make the decision." Or, one might conclude that Abram is indifferent; this is a squabble between women—"*you* decide, Sarai, this doesn't concern me."

Or, as American poet, Mindy Rinkewich suggests, this entire situation is symbolic of the victimization of both Sarai and Hagar, who find themselves in an untenable trap. Sarai, because of her infertility in a society that demands fecundity, is victimized by her need of Hagar as a surrogate, Hagar is victimized because of her status as a slave, forced into becoming an unwilling surrogate—and Abram reaps the reward, a child, preferably a son. For the women, there is no escape from their victimization:

> . . . We still would have had that big fight
>
> If not over a child
>
> It would have been my authority

---

9. Genesis Rabbah 45:5.

>   or her privileges
>
>   or my jealousy
>
>   or hers.
>
>   Abraham still would have yelled:
>
>   —You bitches, be quiet, I tell you!
>
>   —Can't a man have a moment of peace?
>
>   Had I done this, that, or the other
>
>   The tunnel was sealed at both ends from the start.[10]

I have been a teacher for almost forty years. I have seen young minds open to new ideas and to new perspectives about life. I have seen horizons widen for my students, sometimes in transformational ways. Each time this happens, I experience the thrill of giving birth to new humans who are left changed by the learning I have been honored and blessed to convey to them. Though I am a mother to a daughter, I have never physically given birth, and yet I have never felt the loss of that experience. Each day as I enter a classroom, each time a student tells me that her mind has been opened, each time a pupil reminds me of the importance of my teaching, I feel as if I have borne that person—young or old, they are all my children.

Generativity comes in myriad forms: birthing new souls and ideas through teaching, caring, writing, social activism, movement building, and creating art of all kinds. We are capable of enlivening the world in so many ways—through consistent kindness and daily gentleness, and nurturing authentic relationships, and caring for the earth. Bringing forth new fertility manifests in many ways—nurturing the young, dancing with a shy teenager, encouraging a young adult, honoring elders, celebrating different kinds of families, growing old gracefully, bringing forth new wisdom, sage-ing in our age-ing.[11] All this makes the world a more fecund, fertile, and fabulous place!

Text to Life

> Bella, a social worker and therapist in a large East Coast city, reflects on birthing:

---

10. Rinkewich, "Sarah: Cheshbon Nefesh," 10.

11. This wonderful phrase, "from aging to sage-ing" was coined by Rabbi Zalman Schachter Shalom, of blessed memory, my beloved teacher and friend, father/founder of the Jewish Renewal movement. See his many books, especially, *From Age-ing to Sage-ing: A Profound New Vision of Growing Older.*

Birthing comes in many forms. I was single and unmarried, of childbearing age, yet I felt a deep wound within me, because I didn't anticipate that I would have a chance to give birth to, or parent children.

A feminist, I belonged to several Jewish women's groups. As we shared our stories, I realized that we were, in some profound way, giving birth to ourselves anew. I sensed that we were birthing a new Judaism, as new forms and expressions of Judaism emerged from us. We felt ourselves to be transforming Judaism itself as we explored new ways of understanding Torah, shaping innovative Jewish liturgy, creating inclusive and expansive God-language, writing new *midrashim*, and generating a bold Jewish feminist theology.

As we listened and heard each other into speech and personal transformation, we created communities in which we could be whole as straight, lesbian, bisexuals, single, and married Jewish women. We were mothers and women who did not parent children. We were breaking out of traditional female models and creating new intimacy constellations, new concepts (and conceptions) of families because the word "family" seemed insufficient. There was enormous creativity. We were changing the world!

I remember vividly learning and singing *"Lechi Lach"* by Debbie Friedman of blessed memory, in which the call to Abram to *go forth* to a new uncharted land—felt like a call directly to *us*. We experienced *ourselves* being called to *go forth* to create a new Judaism—with new perspectives on the Jewish present and future, and new explorations of history in which Jewish women were truly present and central. We understood that a Jewish faith for our times was emerging *through us*, and that *we* were the birth canal for this faith. My own sense of generativity and creativity was deeply informed by these experiences, which came to be "imaged" by me as a way of birthing souls in the non-biological sense.

In my professional life as a therapist, and as I personally struggled with my own questions about childbearing, my life within the Jewish women's movement gave expression to the generative "maternal" within me. My Jewish women friends and I knew that the Judaism to which we were giving birth would forever transform Jewish women's (and men's) lives into the next centuries and millennia. What blessed and holy *chutzpah* we allowed ourselves!

> Today, when I meet younger Jewish women whose lives I know would not have been possible without Jewish feminism, I experience them as both my sisters *and* my daughters—I belong to a generation of women who were *imahot b'Yisrael*—mothers birthing a new Israel.
>
> ---
>
> Across the millennia, the term "the children of Abraham" has taken on a metaphoric meaning—the name "Isaac" has become identified with the Jewish people and the nation-state of Israel. And "Ishmael" now denotes Arab peoples, especially Palestinians, yearning for a nation-state of their own. The struggle between Sarai and Hagar now connotes the so-called "Middle East conflict," Hagar symbolizing the Palestinian refugees, Sarai representing the dominant mistress, Israel.
>
> It is not my intention to delve into contemporary politics, but rather to touch upon the pathos in this story in its contemporary symbolism, and to approach the powerful healing potential and efficacy of empathy. *What might have happened so long ago if Sarai and Hagar, despite their parallel victimizations, had been able to transcend their pain and anger and reach out to each other? What might have happened if, despite their respective anguish, they had been able to approach one another, as women often do? What might have happened if the two women had been able to work together to co-parent little Ishmael? What might have happened if, instead of enmity between the two women, empathy had won out?*
>
> LGB
>
> ---
>
> Contemporary cantor and composer Linda Hirschhorn has captured these wondrous possibilities in her song, "Sarah and Hagar:"[12]
>
> I am calling you Oh Sarah
>
> this is your sister Hagar
>
> calling through the centuries
>
> to reach you from afar
>
> Here is my son Ishmael
>
> your sister's son alive

---

12. ©Linda Hirschhorn, "Sarah and Hagar." See also a similar expression of this wondrous possibility given musical expression in chapter 9 in my "Isaac and Ishmael."

> we share the sons of Abraham
>
> two peoples one tribe
>
> Oh yes I am your Sarah, I remember you Hagar
>
> your voice comes through the distance
>
> a cry upon my heart
>
> It was I who cast you out in fear and jealousy
>
> yet your vision survived the wilderness
>
> to reach your destiny
>
> But it wasn't till my Isaac lay under the knife
>
> that I recognized your peril, the danger to your life
>
> I tremble now Hagar, for our peril's still the same
>
> we will not survive as strangers
>
> we must speak each other's name
>
> We must tell each others' stories, make each other strong
>
> and sing the dream of ancient lands where both of us belong
>
> Oh let us hear the prayers where spirit first was sown
>
> that all of our children, may call this land their own

In this contemporary context, I invite you to employ the same contemplative process that I suggest throughout this book in the *"Exploring the Text Within"* questions. You might imagine your life as a relatively still pond into which you gently toss stones (your actions and self-initiated life experiences). These stones create circular ripples in the water. The water is the world, the circular ripples are ever-expanding circles, that symbolize you, your family, your closest community, your town, your country, and ultimately, the last circle merges into the world, the water. You might want to sit in silence for some time and ask yourself:

> How might I be an agent of peace
>
> —for myself?
>
> —for my family?
>
> —for my closest community?
>
> —and beyond?

Exploring the Text Within

Find a quiet and comfortable place to sit in contemplative silence with the above teachings and with the following questions about you and your life's experience. You may choose to focus on one questions or sit with several. Ask yourself: what do the biblical text and these teachings mean to me in my life?

> I will give them in My house and in My walls as a monument and a name, better than sons and daughters, an everlasting name I will give him, which will not be discounted.
> (Isaiah 56:5)

A monument and a name, an "everlasting name" (*shem olam*) mean a reputation, a testimony to the sum of one's deeds during a lifetime—these are considered one's progeny—they are, as the text tells us, even "better than sons or daughters." So any forms of generativity, so many ways to enliven the world, so many ways to bring forth new life!

What is my *yad va-shem* and *shem olam*? (my life's monument and my everlasting name or reputation?)

In my life, what is *my* generativity?

How do I enliven the world?

How do I bring forth new life?

(Here I suggest that depending on what you are feeling at a particular time, you choose either Sarai's or Hagar's or Abram's question. At another time, you might choose to reflect on a different question.)

Sarai's and Hagar's Question:

Can I recall a time in my life when I have treated another harshly either because I myself have been in deep pain or have felt powerless?

Abram's Question:

Can I recall a time in my life when I have felt so caught in the middle between people I love that I have been unable to respond with empathy or respect to anyone?

Chapter 6

Lech Lecha III

Hagar Flees

Then Sarai treated her [Hagar] harshly, and she ran away from her. An angel of the LORD *found her by a spring of water in the wilderness . . . and said, "Hagar, slave of Sarai, where have you come from and where are you going?" And she said, "I am running away from my mistress Sarai." And the angel of the Lord said to her "Go back to your mistress and submit to her harsh treatment." And the angel of the* LORD *said to her, "I will greatly increase your offspring and they shall be too many to count. . . . Behold you are with child and shall bear a son. You shall call him Ishmael, for the Lord has paid heed to your suffering."*

—Genesis 16:6–11

Much has happened in Sarai and Abram's lives since Abram sired Ishmael with Sarai's Egyptian maidservant Hagar. Sarai remains deeply anguished at Hagar's disdain and her lost chance to mother the child Hagar carried in her womb as a surrogate. Watching Hagar every day nurse and nurture the infant Ishmael, Sarai's anguish eventually turns into rage, and she mistreats Hagar harshly, causing Hagar to run away into the desert. A divine angel[1] finds Hagar there by a spring of water and instructs her to return to her mistress, adding a promise that *"I will greatly increase your*

---

1. Contrary to popular belief, Judaism includes within it a well-developed angelology. See, for example: Isaacs *Ascending Jacob's Ladder*; Jung, *Fallen Angels in Jewish, Christian and Mohammedan Literature*; Margolies, *A Gathering of Angels*; Shapiro, *The Angelic Way*; and Sullivan, *Wrestling with Angels*.

offspring, and they shall be too many to count" (Gen 16:10). The angel assures Hagar that her son "will dwell alongside all of his kinsmen."

Hagar names the divine being *El-roi*—"God who sees me"—and calls the spring *Beer-lahai-roi*—"the well of the Living One who sees me." Then, reluctantly, hopefully, Hagar returns to serve Sarai, but still holds on to Ishmael as *her* son.

Beer-lahai-roi—"the well of the Living One who sees me." When Hagar feels the presence of God's angel, she experiences a theophany, a palpable and comforting feeling that God (represented by the angel) is with her. For the first time since she is involuntarily taken to be Sarai's surrogate, Hagar truly feels *seen* for exactly who she is—a young woman who has never had a chance to be truly free. She finds the strength and self-esteem to return to Sarai, as the angel instructed. Hagar *knows* in her heart and soul that God is watching over her and Ishmael and that they will ultimately be safe.

What an amazing feeling it must have been for Hagar to feel *seen*, to be known by God in her authenticity! All her life she has been used by others—as a slave and maidservant, and then as a surrogate for Sarai, expected to give birth to, and nurse Sarai's baby, wean him, and then hand him over to Sarai. Mistreated and disregarded, she is helpless and hopeless. Her only moment of self-assertion comes when she refuses to give up the baby she conceived with Abram.

After her sudden and wondrous realization of God's Presence and companionship with her at the well, Hagar is revived by spiritual as well as physical waters. Strengthened in her faith in God, she is ready to face new challenges. It is almost as if her encounter with God's angel has given Hagar a new clarity about her life's purpose—almost as if the well's life-giving waters have not only quenched her physical thirst, but have also helped her discern that her survival, for her own sake, *and for her son's sake*, is part of a destiny greater than herself. For this destiny, Hagar is now able to brave great challenges, including Sarai's cruelty and, ultimately, even Abraham's abandonment.

Linguistically, the biblical text illumines a fascinating connection between the word *be'er* (בְּאֵר)—well of water—and the word *barur* (בָּרוּר)—clarity, clarification, or discernment. Both words come from a cluster of words—באר בור ברר ברא ברה—*be'er, bor, berer, bara, barah*—that "are obviously related in form and meaning. For some curious reason, all the root-verbs deal with either clearly declaring statements or else purifying items, while the derived nouns all have to do with water wells and pits and such."[2]

Thus, the linguistic connection gives us a wonderful symbolic clue: Hagar's epiphany about the presence of God occurs at a well of living

---

2. See "*Beer-lahai-roi* meaning | *Beer-lahai-roi* etymology"—http://www.abarim-publications.com/Meaning/BeerLahaiRoy.html#.VFhzwoeisd9.

waters—*Be'er l'hai*—the well of the Living [One] *Ro'i* who sees me. Water and clarity—*be'er* (בְּאֵר, well) and *beirur* (בֵּרוּר, clarity or discernment) are joined in this beautiful marriage of language and symbolism.

James D. Rapp has captured this sublime kind of "seeing" beautifully in his poem, "Hagar on the Run (Genesis 16)":[3]

> I didn't ask to be a slave.
> Who would ask to be a slave?
> I didn't ask to be sent away
> As "maidservant" in the entourage
> Of a foreign woman I'd never known.
> I didn't ask to be a surrogate
> For a Hebrew woman
> Desperate to have a son;
> To be "given" to her man to raise up one
> That *she* could call *her own*.
> I didn't ask to lie alone tonight,
> Sheltered by the darkness,
> From Sarah's tongue and lash,
> Sheltering, in my body,
> One for whom I didn't ask.
> But you have found me, God who sees,
> And tell me I must cease to run from Sara's tongue,
> Must turn again and bear *for Abram,* Ishmael, his son.
> And you promise *me* unnumbered "sons"
> Although I didn't ask for even one.
> Because you sought me, God who sees,
> I return to be, for Abram, a bearer of *his* seed.
> You promised, and Your promise I believe,
> That the son I didn't ask for, nonetheless will be
> A child of Abram, co-inheritor with Abram's seed.

Hagar returns to Sarai, with clarity, courage, fear (and perhaps some hope) in her heart. Sadly, the enmity between the two women continues unabated.

---

3. In Rapp, *Sandals*, 32. Used with permission.

Text to Life

> Samira is a fifteen-year-old girl who was taken against her will from her home in Africa and brought to the United States to work as a virtual slave in the home of a diplomatic family.
>
> Through heroic efforts of law enforcement and social service agencies, Samira was rescued, given asylum in the United States and is now working to learn English and going to school. She is sheltered appropriately and like Hagar, through the love and care offered by a foster family, she has seen the face(s) of the living God who has truly "seen" her.

Exploring the Text Within

Find a quiet and comfortable place to sit in contemplative silence with the above teachings and with the following questions about you and your life's experience. You may choose to focus on one question or sit with several. Ask yourself: what do the biblical text and these teachings mean to me in my life?

What a blessing it is to be "seen" for what we truly are in our wholness, in our brokenness, in our authenticity, as Hagar was seen by God at Be'er lahai-roi.

> Can I recall a time when I have felt truly "seen" by another in my full authenticity?

Sometimes a course of action becomes clear, even if it isn't what we want.

> Can I recall a time when I have felt utterly alone with a deep challenge and then felt absolute clarity as to how to go forward?

Hagar never asked to be a slave or a surrogate...

> Can I recall a time when I have felt I had no choice but to endure a situation I had neither asked for nor wanted?

Chapter 7

Vayera I

Jealousy and Discord

Sarah saw the son whom Hagar the Egyptian had borne to Abraham playing. She said to Abraham, "Cast out that slave woman and her son, for the son of that slave shall not share in the inheritance with my son Isaac."

—Genesis 21:9–10 (Vayera 1)

Abram, now ninety-nine years old, experiences a profound moment of reconnection with God, as the Holy One speaks to him.[1] "I am El Shaddai. Walk in My ways and be blameless and I will establish My covenant between Me and you and I will make you exceedingly numerous" (17:1–2). With this covenant comes a new name for Abram—Abraham—the father of many, and God changes Sarai's name, too, to Sarah ("princess"), indicating that along with her husband, she will become the matriarch of many generations. As a physical sign of the covenant, Abraham is commanded by God to circumcise himself and all the menfolk of his tribe, and he obeys. The circumcision is a spiritual sign of the covenant and is symbolized in the changing of the couple's names—each has a ה (*hey*, a letter that signifies God's name) added to their names. Now, they come to know that they will be a source of greater godly blessing, including parenting a child.

---

1. Numbers in the Hebrew Bible are perplexing. Certainly Abram couldn't have been ninety-nine years old in 365-day "years." It is more likely that he was ninety-nine *seasons* old. In the biblical land of Israel, there were (climatically) really three seasons—fall (a pleasant autumnal time followed by a late, slightly colder time), spring, and summer. Thus, if Abram was ninety-nine seasons old, he might have been about thirty-three years old, of advanced age for a man in biblical times.

Two powerful signs of identity have now become part of the Abrahamic covenant: a blood ritual through male circumcision and the giving of symbolically important names. It is clear that throughout the Hebrew Bible, names are intentionally given to individuals to be emblematic of the lives they will live. For example, David, Israel's second king, who brought victory and peace to the people, means "beloved." Certainly, he must have been beloved to God, who enabled him to be so victorious in battle! Similarly, his son Solomon—whose name in Hebrew derives from the word *shalom* or *shlemut*—peace or fulfillment—reflects the time of peace and prosperity of his reign. There are literally hundreds of names with such symbolism in the Hebrew text.[2]

After his circumcision, God tells Abraham that Sarai, now forever to be called Sarah, will soon become pregnant and will be blessed with a child of her own. What an amazing gift this is to be to her! A child of her old age! Abraham, astounded by this God-given news, falls to the ground in laughter: *"Can a child be born to a man a hundred years old or can Sarah bear a child at ninety?"* (17:17). God assures Abraham that the amazing news is indeed true: *"God said, 'nevertheless Sarah your wife shall bear you a son, and you shall name him Isaac, and I will maintain My covenant with him as an everlasting covenant for his offspring to come'"* (17:18–19). Note the symbolism of the baby's name: Abraham and Sarah's infant son will be called Isaac—*Yitzchak* in Hebrew, meaning "laughter," echoing Abraham's laughter upon hearing the news of his forthcoming birth, and reflecting the laughter and joy that this baby will bring to Sarah, who has for so long yearned to hold her own baby in her arms, to nurture, to play with, to raise with loving care. Sarah will experience no greater joy, no deeper laughter than that which the birth of Isaac will bring to her.

The family drama continues. Now settled near the terebinths of Mamre, and recovering from his own circumcision, Abraham is sitting at the entrance to his tent in the heat of the day.

> Looking up, he saw three men standing near him. As soon as he saw them, he ran from the entrance of the tent to greet them, and bowing to the ground, he said, "My lords, if it please you, do not go past your servant. Let a little water be brought; bathe your feet

---

2. The importance of the meaning of names may be seen in the earliest Christian tradition. For example, Jesus, a Jew, was known in Hebrew as *Yeshua*, which means "redeemer" or "savior." Certainly this is no coincidence. Because of the meaning of his name, one wonders whether this was his original name or the appellation given to him, once he gained a following and once his followers came to believe that he was indeed a savior.

> *and recline under the tree. And let me fetch a morsel of bread that you may refresh yourselves; then go on."*

—Genesis 18:2–5

In these few verses, we catch a glimpse of a scene of typical "Middle Eastern hospitality," practiced even millennia ago! Strangers pass by. It is hot and dusty. Water is immediately brought to clean their dusty feet, and to quench their thirst caused by the hot sun. Food is offered to sate their hunger from difficult desert travel.

Abraham is a gracious host. He *"ran"* from the entrance of his tent to serve his guests! In Judaism, there is a concept called *zerizut*—an eagerness to perform God's commandments—and certainly kindness and hospitality are among them. Abraham's act of heartfelt hospitality is more than a simple expression of local custom. Coming immediately after the establishment of his new covenant with God, his acts indicate a deeper connection to what will become Israelite and then Jewish tradition—a holistic sense that our behavior—*in all areas of life*—is a reflection of the breadth, depth, and quality of our covenantal relationship with the Holy One. If indeed Abraham is going to be a true and faithful "son of the covenant," he must not sit idly by when he sees weary travelers passing by. He must be eager to serve them; he must hurry to assist, and he must do so with an open and gracious heart. Thus Abraham's guests are well served, not only because Abraham's personality dictates that they be so entertained, but also because it is now part of his religious *obligation* to attend to their needs, not because he must, but because he wants to, as a way of deepening his own covenantal life.

After a sumptuous meal, the men ask after Sarah:

> *"Where is your wife Sarah?" And he [Abraham] replied, "There in the tent." Then one [of the men] said, "I will return to you next year and your wife Sarah shall have a son!" Sarah was listening at the entrance of the tent, which was behind him. Now Sarah and Abraham were advanced in years; Sarah had stopped having the periods of women. And Sarah laughed to herself, saying "I am withered, am I to have enjoyment—with my husband so old?" Then the* Lord *said to Abraham, "Why did Sarah laugh, saying 'Shall I in truth bear a child, old as I am?' Is anything too wondrous for the* Lord*? I will return to you at the same season next year, and Sarah shall have a son." Sarah lied, saying, "I did not laugh," for she was frightened. But He replied, "You did laugh."*

—Genesis 18:9–15

Once again, laughter comes, this time in the form of skepticism—and God (in the form of the man—who might just be an angel!)[3] reprimands Abraham and Sarah—have faith, the Holy One says, God's ways are mysterious, and no miracle is too great for God to accomplish. (This vignette in the Torah reminds me of a dear friend, Lisa, who suffered infertility for decades. She was in her late forties and her husband was in his early fifties and they had essentially given up on ever having children. When her period was two months late, she simply assumed that she was entering into early menopause. Eight weeks later, and after enduring morning sickness (!), Lisa discovered to her great surprise and immense joy that she was pregnant.

Lisa and Howard's son, Isaac (no coincidence in his name!), is now a tall, handsome young man, his parents' delight, who often brings laughter, gladness, and pleasure to their lives. "We felt as if we were reliving Abraham and Sarah's story," Lisa told me. "If anyone had come and told *me* at age forty-seven that I would bear a baby, *I would have laughed them out of the room.* Will wonders never cease?"

This interlude, from Genesis 17:1—18:15, a mere forty-verses, offers us much to ponder. Here we learn about the depth of laughter and human joy, about human skepticism (Abraham and Sarah's) in the face of improbable odds, and about the possibilities of new beginnings in older age. Any one of these themes could be the topic of deep reflection and so many lovely questions for contemplation arise:

- When was the last time I experienced true, deep laughter, the kind that starts in my belly and reverberates throughout my whole body, heart and soul? How did that laughter make me feel? Were there any lasting effects?

- Do I tend to be a skeptical person? When I am told about possibilities that seem improbable, do I generally gravitate to an attitude of doubt and disbelief, or am I more open to faith and potential?

- What are the opportunities that might await me in my elder years? Like Abraham and Sarah, can these years, too, be a time of new beginnings and generativity?

---

3. Often angels are described as men in the Hebrew Bible, though their actions are clearly far more mysterious (and sometimes mystical) than mere mortals. See, for example, Jacob wrestling with the "man" (*ish*) in a long night of struggle, and awakening to be given a new name, "Israel," by God. The nighttime struggle is clearly far more profound than a simple wrestling match. Indeed, it sets Jacob/Israel on a trajectory toward leadership as he evolves into the role of the *pater familias*—father of the family and leader of the whole people Israel.

Torah offers us so many possibilities for imaginative reflection—if we only allow our hearts and our minds to expand and open to these possibilities.

But back to our story! After the "man's" happy announcement to Abraham and Sarah, he and his two companions set out toward Sodom, Lot's home. Abraham walks along with them for a while to see them off."[4] (See chapter 8 for the continuing story.)

> *Early next morning, Abraham took some bread and a skin of water, and gave them to Hagar. He placed them over her shoulder, together with the child, and sent her away. And she wandered about in the wilderness of Beer-Sheba. When the water was gone from the skin, she left the child under one of the bushes, and went and sat down at a distance, a bowshot away, for she thought, "Let me not look on as the child dies." And sitting thus afar, she burst into tears. God heard the cry of the boy, and an angel of God called to Hagar from heaven and said to her, "What troubles you, Hagar? Fear not, for God has heeded the cry of the boy where he is. Come, lift up the boy and hold him by the hand, for I will make a great nation of him." Then God opened her eyes and she saw a well of water. She went and filled the skin with water, and let the boy drink. God was with the boy and he grew up.*
>
> —Genesis 21:14–20

Much has happened in Sarah and Abraham's lives since Abraham sired Ishmael with Sarah's Egyptian maidservant Hagar. Sarah remains deeply anguished at Hagar's disdain and her lost chance to mother the child Hagar carried in her womb as a surrogate.

After years of bitterness, and after the birth of her long-yearned-for son of her old age, Isaac, Sarah no longer can abide Hagar and Ishmael's presence. It is just too painful for her to see Abraham's love for his rough-and-tumble son, Ishmael, and watch the lad playing with his baby half-brother, *her* son, tender Isaac.

One day, the moment that "breaks the camel's back" comes. Finally having had more than enough of Hagar and Ishmael, "*Sarah saw the son whom Hagar the Egyptian had borne to Abraham* playing. She said to Abraham, 'Cast out that slave woman and her son, for the son of that slave shall not share in the inheritance with my son Isaac'" (21:9–10).

---

4. Genesis 18:16.

"Playing?" *This* is the reason for permanently banishing the Egyptian maidservant and her son? How can it be? The word in Hebrew for what the older boy was doing is מצחק, which can be translated as laughing at, laughing with, laughingly playing (that is, just having fun) or mocking.

The ancient rabbis, however, give the word "playing" far more sinister connotations and attribute to Ishmael more evil motivations than simply innocently playing with his little brother. For example, Rabbi Simeon bar Yohai, a great sage of the first century C.E., summarizes several sages' views:

- Rabbi Akiba used to interpret this to [Ishmael's] shame. Thus Rabbi Akiba lectured: *"And Sarah saw the son of Hagar the Egyptian, whom she had borne to Abraham, making sport* [i.e., 'playing']*"*—Now, "making sport" refers to nought else but immorality, as in the verse, *"The Hebrew slave, whom you brought into our house, came to me to dally* [i.e., make sport; 'play'] *with me"* (Gen 39:17).[5] Thus this teaches that Sarah saw Ishmael ravish maidens, seduce them, and dishonor them.

- Rabbi Ishmael[6] taught: "The term 'sport' [once again, meaning 'playing'] refers to idolatry. . . . This teaches that Sarah saw Ishmael build altars, catch locusts [which were ritually unclean animals for Jews], and sacrifice them."

- Rabbi Eleazar said: "The term 'sport' ['playing'] refers to bloodshed . . . ."

- Rabbi Azariah said in Rabbi Levi's name: "Ishmael said to Isaac, 'Let us go and see our portions in the field.' Then Ishmael would take a bow and arrows and shoot them in Isaac's direction, while pretending to be playing. Thus it is written, [one who gets involved in someone else's quarrels is] like a madman scattering deadly firebrands, arrows, is one who cheats his fellow, and says, 'I was only joking.'"[7]

- Finally, Rabbi Simeon bar Yohai reveals his own view: "This term 'sport' [mockery, playing] refers to inheritance. For when our father Isaac was born, all rejoiced, whereupon Ishmael said to them, 'You are fools, for I am the firstborn and I receive a double portion.' You may

---

5. Jewish Publication Society TaNaKH translation—words in brackets are mine to explain that they are synonyms for "playing" and the Soncino Genesis Rabbah translation as "making sport." The incident referred to here is when the unnamed wife of Potiphar, counselor to the Egyptian Pharaoh, tries to seduce Joseph, and then blames Joseph, claiming that he attacked *her!*

6. Not to be confused with the biblical Ishmael!

7. Jewish Publication Society TaNaKH translation. Proverbs 26:18–19. I inserted the bracketed words come from the preceding verse to make the context clear.

infer this from Sarah's protest to Abraham: 'For the son of this bondwoman shall not be here with my son, with Isaac.'"[8]

One wonders what the source of these awful charges against Ishmael are, since in the biblical text, we are given absolutely no indication that Ishmael bears any bad feelings toward Isaac. The only hint at anything untoward is in *Sarah's reaction to Ishmael "playing" with Isaac*. Thus, we can only speculate that anything "bad" going on is happening purely in Sarah's imagination. This reminds me of a parent who favors one child over another and sees that child as the "good one" and the other as the "bad one" in the family. While such parental favoritism often happens in nuclear families where there have been no divorces or remarriages, it also often occurs in blended families with step-children. While Abraham, Sarah, and Hagar's situation is not quite equivalent to the contemporary blended family, there are certainly several parallels and similarities:

- Ishmael is a kind of step-son to Sarah. Worse yet, he is the boy *she* had hoped to nurture as his mother in the original surrogacy plan with Hagar.
- Abraham's loyalties are divided between his first-born son Ishmael and Isaac and he is caught between two women (Sarah and Hagar) who are vying for his attentions.
- The two women relate differently to each boy, who certainly cannot avoid feeling the tension between the two women and their respective attitudes towards them.
- Knowing about Abraham's affection for Ishmael, Sarah fears that he will bequeath half his assets to his older son, leaving *her* son Isaac with half. Since she considers Isaac the rightful heir to *all* of Abraham's wealth, she sees Ishmael as a competitor not only for Abraham's affection but also for his property. Ishmael must be banished, she believes, lest he *steal* Isaac's rightful inheritance. How often material possessions are the sources of family discord!

All these circumstances evoke images from a television soap opera or reality show! How familiar the situation seems to many of us from our own family lives!

Abraham is deeply distressed by Sarah's demand. He loves both Ishmael and Isaac. He knows that God has told him to *"Listen to her voice! Do as she says, for it is through Isaac that offspring shall be continued for you"* (21:12), so he knows that he will obey Sarah. Nonetheless, Abraham's heart is breaking.

---

8. This entire series of *midrashim* comes from Genesis (*Bereishit*) Rabbah 53:11.

He no doubt asks himself why he must give up Ishmael to fulfill Isaac's destiny. What an excruciating sacrifice this is—for both father *and* both sons. A father loses a son and the brothers lose each other, only to reunite when they bury their father years later! Abraham is a man caught "between a rock and a hard place"—either he disobeys Sarah (and thereby God) or he loses Ishmael. With great sadness, Abraham chooses to remain a faithful servant of God and adhere to his wife's demands. Two brothers are torn from one another, a father is bereft—the family dysfunction deepens.

Sometimes I wonder about the tragedies that occur when parents' dramas are played out to the profound detriment of their children. They and subsequent generations are caught in between, victim of their parents' and grandparents' hostilities. Estrangements occur, siblings are separated—family feuds last decades, even to the point that over generations the original reasons for the feuds are long forgotten, though bitterness and family rupture stubbornly persist.

And life moves on, though Abraham is grieving. Given his unhappiness about sending Ishmael away, Abraham's actions seem particularly callous—*one* skin of water and a scant amount of bread for a long desert journey? Surely mother and child will die out there in the wilderness! But Abraham is a man of faith who has been assured by his God that Ishmael will survive and thrive *"As for Ishmael, I have heeded you. I hereby bless him. I will make him fertile and exceedingly numerous. He shall be the father of twelve chieftains and I will make of him a great nation"* (17:20). So, despite his sorrow, Abraham sends his first-born son and Hagar out into the wilderness, perhaps believing in his soul that God will rescue them.

> *Early next morning, Abraham took some bread and a skin of water, and gave them to Hagar. He placed them over her shoulder, together with the child, and sent her away. And she wandered about in the wilderness of Beer-Sheba. When the water was gone from the skin, she left the child under one of the bushes, and went and sat down at a distance, a bowshot away, for she thought, "Let me not look on as the child dies." And sitting thus afar, she burst into tears. God heard the cry of the boy, and an angel of God called to Hagar from heaven and said to her, "What troubles you, Hagar? Fear not, for God has heeded the cry of the boy where he is. Come, lift up the boy and hold him by the hand, for I will make a great nation of him." Then God opened her eyes and she saw a well of water. She went and filled the skin with water, and let the boy drink. God was with the boy and he grew up.*
>
> —Genesis 21:14–20

Here once again, as in chapter 6, Hagar's first encounter with an angel of God, she experiences a moment of clarity. We again encounter the juxtaposition of a well, *be'er* (באר well)—clear water. This time, Hagar's own clarity about Ishmael's destiny and her own led Hagar in a new direction. Rabbi Charles Sherman's perspective helps us understand:

> The well was always there, but Hagar has been so consumed with her own fear that she had failed to notice. Had she managed to break through her fear a bit earlier, she might have seen the well earlier and embarked much sooner on her journey to healing and renewal. It took something else—in this case, an angel of God—to say, "Hagar, look up, it's right in front of you!" Negative emotions are extremely seductive, making us feel like we are victims. They can smother us, preventing all healing. Most of us don't have angels of God tapping us on the shoulder and pointing the way. But that's okay; gratitude can serve as that angelic voice, pulling us out of our current misery. By directing our minds to feeling thankful, we allow ourselves to see reality in a startlingly new way, finding solutions in our everyday lives that have been there all along.[9]

It has been said that sometimes one can transform one's life by a very slight turn in a new direction, that a turn of just one degree can make all the difference. It all depends on one's perspective and attitude. When confronted with life's challenges, each of us has choice. We can look upon what faces us with an attitude of pessimism (the proverbial glass half empty) or optimism (the glass as half full). Initially Hagar's attitude was fatalistic—"Let me not look on as the child [Ishmael] dies"—but then, she hears a divine voice, and suddenly, she *sees* a well of water. As Rabbi Sherman has noted, the well of water "has been there all along." Hagar simply had to turn her head (i.e., *change her attitude*) but one degree—and there it was with its life-saving water!

Text to Life

> In a university class I taught on *midrash,* my students and I explored the stories of Genesis, delving in depth into the biblical characters' family relationships. At semester's end, I assigned each student to choose one story from Genesis and write a *midrash* of their own.

---

9. Sherman, *The Broken and the Whole,* 175.

One student, Miles, delivered a paper that moved me deeply. "I am Ishmael," the paper began. Miles wrote in the first person *as Ishmael*, about his distress and grief at having been cast out from the only home he knew by his father Abraham. He wrote of his early years, when his father loved him so, and used to walk with him in the fields, both of them shepherding their flocks together, and hunting for animals for meat. "My father was so proud of my hunting skills, and he praised my strength and my athleticism," Miles wrote (in the voice of Ishmael).

"But then one day, he cast me and my mother aside when his other wife, Sarah, not *my* mother Hagar, gave birth to a little baby boy. Now *that* baby, Isaac, was the apple of my father's eye. Now, my father Abraham spent all his time with the baby—and I seemed to disappear from the picture. 'Father, Father,' I cried out—'notice me, pay attention to *me*, your eldest son, just as you did when I was younger! I miss you! I *need* you.' But my pleas fell on deaf ears. I became a cypher, lost to my father."

After I had finished reading Miles' paper, I sat for a long time in my office wondering what to do. It was clear to me that this academic assignment had become much more to my student and that either Miles was a brilliant writer of fiction or that the piece was autobiographical.

I invited Miles to my office and asked him whether his *midrash* had any basis in his own life. Miles immediately began to cry—certainly an unusual reaction for a young male college student. As his story tumbled out, it was clear that the story of Abraham, Sarah, Hagar, Ishmael, and Isaac had deeply struck a nerve for Miles as his own divorced father had remarried and had, in the past three years, sired a son with his second wife.

Clearly, Miles had experienced his father's infatuation with his baby son as a kind of abandonment, a turning away from him, his first-born. Miles' pain had turned into anger and the anger had led to an estrangement. He had ceased to communicate with his father, despite repeated attempts at contact by his dad.

A few days after my conversation with Miles, I received a call from the Dean of the College, who inquired about my teaching relationship with Miles. Apparently my young student was failing all his classes except mine, in which he was receiving an excellent grade. When I related my conversation with Miles to the Dean, he told me that he knew of the estrangement between father and son, because Miles' father had been calling the College seeking assistance in communicating with his son, who refused to speak with him. Knowing that in addition to serving as a professor I was also a rabbi with some pastoral experience, the Dean sought my assistance in bringing father and son together.

I invited Miles back to my office and told him about my conversation with the Dean and asked him if he would agree to meet with his father in my office with my presence as a kind of "go-between." I explained that his father was very worried about him, and that his estrangement from his dad couldn't continue forever.

Miles agreed to speak with his father, but only in my presence. The following Sunday, Miles' father flew into town and the three of us met in my office on campus. First, I gave Miles' dad a copy of Miles' *midrash* and asked him to read it. Miles and I sat in silence as we watched him read.

By the end of his reading, Miles' dad was in tears. "I didn't know," he said, responding fully to the metaphor the *midrash* offered. "I never meant to abandon you, Miles. I was just so excited about the baby's birth. I honestly didn't realize what I was doing. I love you so much, and I am so terribly sorry."

Miles' father's heartfelt apology began a tearful, angry, loving, honest conversation that lasted for several hours in my office on that Sunday afternoon. I didn't need to say much. I simply provided a safe *container* in which father and son could safely talk with one another. Two men, a modern-day *Abraham* and *Ishmael* finally found the language of love they needed to heal a wound that in the biblical story was never healed. Baby *Isaac*, miles away in another city, blissfully unaware of the drama unfolding, later could become the adored baby brother that Miles, as an only child, had always wanted. Father and son walked out of my office that afternoon, certainly not fully healed, but on their way. I am always in awe of the power of a biblical story to transform lives.

LGB

Exploring the Text Within

Find a quiet and comfortable place to sit in contemplative silence with the above teachings and with the following questions about you and your life's experience. You may choose to focus on one question or sit with several. Ask yourself: what do the biblical text and these teachings mean to me in my life?

What a curse it is to be innocently branded as "bad" because of the enmity and bitterness of others, as Ishmael was condemned by Sarah. So many unfortunate people are predestined to live lives of disadvantage because of circumstances of their birth—their skin color, poverty, where they were born, and more.

> Can I recall a time when I have felt that I could do no right with certain people, that from the beginning I was identified as a "black sheep"?

What a sorrow it is to be caught in the middle of a painful circumstance, subject to the emotional demands of someone we love, as Abraham was caught in being obliged to heed to Sarah's demand to banish Hagar and Ishmael.

> Can I recall a time when I have felt caught in the middle of a painful circumstance in my family or with others, feeling compelled to do something I did not want to do?

What a blessing it is to be able, with just a small change in attitude, to turn in a new and better direction towards healing and even transformation.

> Can I recall a time when I have turned in a new, better, and more healing direction by changing my attitude or perspective?

Chapter 8

Vayera II

Sin, Consequences, and Grief

> "*Flee for your life! Do not look behind you,
> nor stop anywhere in the Plain . . . .*"
> —Genesis 19:17

> "*Lot's wife looked back, and thereupon
> turned into a pillar of salt.*"
> —Genesis 19:26

> "*Flee for your life! Do not look behind you, nor stop anywhere in the Plain*"; . . . *Lot's wife looked back, and thereupon turned into a pillar of salt.*
> —Genesis 19:17, 26

While the tragic story of Hagar and Ishmael unfolds, other dramatic events are taking place in Abraham and Sarah's extended family. After their sojourn in Egypt during a famine in Canaan, Abraham and Sarah and his nephew Lot had parted ways. Abraham's part of the tribe settled at the terebinths of Mamre and Lot's family settled in the city of Sodom, on the plain of the Dead Sea, about two or three days' trek from Abraham's home near the city of Hebron.[1]

We turn now toward Sodom and Gomorrah and the reputedly evil people who lived in these towns. In the text we can catch a glimpse of God's

---

1. Today, driving time between Mamre and where biblical Sodom was located would be about thirty to forty-five minutes.

"mind." It is almost as if we see God as a character at the edge of a stage sharing his thoughts with us in a loud whisper:

> *Shall I hide from Abraham what I am about to do? . . . The outrage of Sodom and Gomorrah is so great, and their sin is so grave. I will go down to see whether they have acted altogether according to the outcry that has reached Me; if not, I will take note.*

—Genesis 18:17, 20–21

Then, magically "the LORD" morphs back into the three angels/men who come to Sodom (v. 22). The visiting strangers arrive at Lot's house and experience the great "outrage" of the city: a "gross violation of the conventions of hospitality" and sexual depravity.[2] What a contrast to Abraham and Sarah's tent—a haven of hospitality!

> *They had not yet lain down, when the townspeople, the men of Sodom, young and old—all the people to the last man—gathered about the house. And they shouted to Lot and said to him, "Where are the men who came to you tonight? Bring them out to us, that we may be intimate with them." So Lot went out to them to the entrance, shut the door behind him, and said: "I beg you, my friends, do not commit such a wrong."*

—Genesis 19:4–7

At this point, as he tries to protect his guests, Lot sins terribly. He offers his two virgin daughters to the unruly mob in place of the men.[3] (One might wonder why Lot is ultimately saved from the destruction in Sodom—but that's another story!) The crowd, however, rejects Lot's offer, preferring to assault the strangers, and tries violently to smash Lot's door down to get to the strangers. The angels/men strike the violent throng

---

2. Adele Berlin and Marc Zvi Brettler, eds., *The Jewish Study Bible*, 41—comment to verses 4–5. While in common parlance, the word "sodomy" is defined as sexual acts between males (homosexuality), the sexual sins of the men of Sodom do not fall into the category of what contemporary society has come to understand as loving, committed male homosexual relationships. Rather, the biblical Sodomites are interested in raping the strangers (the angels/men who have arrived after having visited with Abraham and Sarah)—thus "sodomy" in this context might be defined as xenophobia combined with violent sexual attack.

3. Perhaps this story is an object lesson about how one sin leads to another. Or, perhaps, it is simply a reflection of the very lowly status of women in biblical society, in which men's welfare is more important than women's: Lot is more concerned with his male guests' well-being than with his own daughters' safety. All of this is lamentably echoed in a variety of biblical stories. See, for example, the story of Dinah, Jacob's daughter (Genesis 34) during which Jacob seems more concerned about his own well-being than with his daughter's (34:30).

with a *"blinding light"* (v. 11) and the hooligans are forced to disperse. The angels/men hurriedly inform Lot and his family of God's plan to destroy Sodom and tell Lot to go to the homes of his two married daughters and warn them of the impending doom, and tell them to pack up so that they may escape the city before the destruction begins. Lot does as the angels/men have advised him, but when he tells his daughters and sons-in-law of what is about to happen, they ignore his warnings:

> *So Lot went out and spoke to his sons-in-laws who had married his daughters and said, "Up, get out of this place, for the* LORD *is about to destroy the city." But he seemed to his sons-in-law as one who laughs.*
>
> —*Genesis 19:14*

(Note again the use of the same root for laughter [*tzachak*—צחק]. It is an echo of all the laughter mentioned in this Torah portion.)

An ancient *midrash* suggests that Lot's sons-in-laws are too arrogant to listen to their father-in-law because they can only see the prosperity and comfort of the wealthy city of Sodom: "They [the sons-in-law] said to him [Lot]: 'Organs and cymbals are in the land and the land is to be overthrown!?'"[4] Lot's foolish sons-in-laws simply cannot believe that the town that seemed so strong and prosperous to them could be destroyed. Certain that they will be safe in their comfortable town, they will not pack up and leave. Life seems good right where they are.

And so the destruction begins.

> *As dawn broke, the angels urged Lot on, saying, "Up, take your wife and your two remaining daughters, lest you be swept away because of the iniquity of the city." Still he delayed.*
>
> —*Genesis 19:15–16*[5]

Why is Lot delaying? He has already experienced the violence of an angry mob trying to knock down the doors of his home, his daughters

---

4. Genesis Rabbah 50:9.

5. An interesting side note: In the Hebrew, the word for *"he delayed"* is יתמהמה/ *yitmahmey'a* and the Torah trope (cantillation mark) is a rare *shalshelet*. This trope mark is mentioned regarding Joseph's vacillation regarding Potiphar's wife's sexual advances in chapter 16. As in that instance, which indicates Joseph's ambivalence as to whether to accept Mrs. Potiphar's advances, here too, Lot is ambivalent: Should he warn his sinning sons-in-law? Should he persist in insisting that they take his daughters and run, or should he not? Therefore, "he delayed." The cantillation accentuates Lot's vacillation—a wonderful example of how the chanting itself elucidates and dramatizes the text, bringing a poignant moment even more alive.

and sons-in-laws have mocked his warnings, and the city is on the edge of utter devastation—what is Lot waiting for? He can't seem to tear himself away from Sodom. Maybe he is lamenting his daughters, hoping that they will change their minds, or maybe he just can't seem to leave what was *home* to him.

Sometimes it is wrenchingly difficult to leave one's home, even if it is an unhappy place. It is all we know—and sometimes we cannot imagine setting down roots anywhere else. Perhaps the familiar, even in the midst of impending doom, felt safer to Lot than the unknown ahead of him. Rabbi Alan Cook points out that "sometimes what is behind us seems more comforting than that which lies ahead. Change may appear distasteful; it involves learning new tasks, adjusting to a new way of doing things. The landscape that stretches out before us may appear foreign and frightening, compared to the one that is already familiar . . . ."[6]

Lot's own actions reveal that he is at best, a weak man and at worst, that he is like his neighbors, an evil man (remember how he offered his virgin daughters to the mob). Maybe he really *did* belong among the sinners who were about to be destroyed! Perhaps he wondered why *he* was being spared, while others, undeserving of such a terrible fate, would soon die. We can't really know, but, for some inexplicable reason, Lot's life is saved—one of those mysteries of life, when the less deserving benefit and some, perhaps more deserving, suffer.[7]

Events take on a life of their own, as God's will unfolds. Lot *must* move on.

> *So the men* [the angels] *seized his* [Lot's] *hand, and the hands of his wife and his two daughters—and the* LORD's *mercy on him—and brought him out and left him outside the city. When they had brought them outside, one* [angel] *said, Flee for your life! Do not look behind you, nor stop anywhere in the Plain; flee to the hills, lest you be swept away!*
>
> —Genesis 19:16–17

Lot, his wife (nameless in the biblical text, but called *Idit* or *Irit* in some Talmudic-era and medieval *midrashim*),[8] and two unmarried daughters

---

6. Rabbi Alan Cook, in Person, ed., *Voices of Torah*, 46–47.

7. This is the great dilemma of the biblical Book of Job, which is addressed in numerous books on theodicy ("the problem of evil"). A contemporary treatment of this subject is in Rabbi Harold Kushner's best-selling book, *When Bad Things Happen to Good People*.

8. There are several *midrashim* that suggest that Lot's wife's name was derived from *gematria* (Hebrew numerology), or that her punishment for looking back was not specifically for looking at *the city of Sodom*, but that the *sin* was that in looking back, she inadvertently caught a glimpse of God, whose Presence (in the form of the *Shechinah*,

have now escaped the doomed city of Sodom, but stop along the way. *"Don't look back,"* the angels have warned them. But *"Lot's wife looked back and thereupon turned into a pillar of salt."*

Idit or Irit—what could the authors of the Midrash wish to communicate with later generations by proposing these two names?

IDIT—עדית—may be derived from the Hebrew root, *eyd* (עד), meaning "witness."

IRIT—עירית—may be derived from the Hebrew root, *eyr* (ער), meaning "awake."

Perhaps these two variations of possible names for Lot's wife teach us one very deep lesson—that Lot's wife stands in silent witness (*IDIT*——עדית—עד) and profound, awakened awareness (*IRIT*—ער—עירית) of the grave, even cataclysmic consequences, of terrible sin.

But there is more. A dear Israeli friend, Ben-Ami, told me once of his feelings at the death of his son: "It is like a life sentence of grieving," he said to me. Perhaps Mother Idit (from the Hebrew word עד—*ed*—as in *l'olam va-ed—forever and ever*) stands as a symbol of the "life sentence," a grieving a parent feels when their child dies. Perhaps she is now a life prisoner. And perhaps Mother Irit is also a life prisoner. As a mother, Irit stands in aching awareness (ער) of the sorrow of the moment. Perhaps she is grieving on the deepest level possible for her two married daughters who are now dead, pulverized in the fiery tempest of the destruction of Sodom.

As a mother, I cannot even begin to imagine the agony of losing my child at all, and especially in such a brutal and violent manner. Perhaps Idit (witness), watching the annihilation of her own babies, Irit (the awake one), acutely aware of the worst kind of pain—that of losing a child, is grieving and saturated with her own salty tears, and she becomes paralyzed in her own profound and immutable sorrow—figuratively and literally, a pillar of salt.

IDIT/IRIT LOOKS BACK

My daughters,

My precious sweetnesses,

My babies!

God's female and imminent aspect) was actually *in* the town as the agent of destruction). Since actually *seeing* either the *Kadosh Baruch Hu* (the male aspect of God) or the *Shechinah* is forbidden, Idit/Irit was punished by being turned into a pillar of salt for *this* reason, not because she looked back at the city itself. These interpretations are offered by *Pirkei d'Rabbi Eliezer,* attributed to the second-century C.E. sage, Eliezer ben Hyrcanus with later additions, and *RaMBaN* (Rabbi Moses ben Nachman, also known as Nachmanides) in the thirteenth century.

I carried them as Lot's seed,

tiny seeds

growing big in my womb,

I suckled them, my milk

sweet on their lips,

filling their little bellies.

And then they grew—

And I comforted them

when the first cramps came,

when their first blood

seeped from between their legs.

I told them

now your own babies will come!

Not to be. Not to be.

The fiery maelstrom!

Wind whipping the blistering air,

searing my eyes,

cracking my heart,

clouding my eyes,

salty tears, salty tears.

If only to save them, if only . . .

Not to be. Not to be.

Is it You, Shechinah,

Agent of such devastation?

But You, too, are a mother!

If only to save them, if only . . .

Not to be. Not to be.

Don't look behind you!

Run away! Don't look!

I turn back.

My babies!

Grown women now—

and yet, my babies.

Salty tears, salty tears,

my body slowing.
I cannot leave this place.
I cannot leave my daughters.
I cannot leave—even if it is a plain of
ashes.
But what of my two daughters,
hearts still beating?
O, my daughters,
I am stilled now.
Halted now—
a petrified column of sorrow.
No future.
Only ashen, grieving
Memory.

Lot's wife remains petrified, yet we must ask the compelling question: must *all* grieving parents, even in their "life sentences," remain perennially petrified? In his comments about change, Rabbi Cook points out clearly that "It is undeniably important to remain conscious of our past. But we must not get mired in it."[9] For the sake of surviving children and spouses, *and for their own sake,* bereaved parents must move on, holding on to cherished memories, continuing in active and alive ways to honor their deceased children's lives; and the tears will come from time to time. Salt is a life-giving substance, it balances our bodies—without a sufficient amount of sodium in our bodies, we become ill, and yet with too much of it within us, we become diseased and dis-eased. Our tears' salt helps us to balance memory, life, death, and movement into the future. We can live through our grieving *without becoming petrified.*

In Hebrew *gematria* (numerology), the imperative for the word "remember" is *zachor* (זכר). It equals 227. Another word with the same numerical equivalent is *bracha*—blessing (ברכה). Traditionally, when a human being has passed from this world, we say "May his/her *memory* be for a *blessing.*" Indeed—the tears we shed, the salt of grieving, the precious memories—are all blessings. And the tears are also tears of blessed healing that allow us to move on with our memories as guides for the next steps in our lives.

---

9. Rabbi Alan Cook, in Person, ed., *Voices of Torah,* 46–47.

Text to Life

Years ago, I had a conversation with the father of my schoolmate Lena about "being comfortable in America." All I knew about Mr. Gruen was that he was born in Germany before the Second World War. He seemed to be a very serious man who rarely smiled or laughed. I had mentioned that as an American, I felt very comfortable in my native country. Mr. Gruen sighed at my words and said "Never feel *too* comfortable anywhere, dear. My family was wealthy and very *comfortable* in Berlin. And then one night in November 1938 the Nazis attacked Jewish businesses, buildings, and synagogues all over Germany and Austria and thousands were destroyed—the 'Night of the Broken Glass,' *Kristallnacht* it was called. That was the beginning of the end for the Jews of my *comfortable* homeland, where my family had lived for generations. My parents refused to leave Germany, despite the pleas of relatives here in America. 'This is the land of Beethoven, Mahler, and Goethe,' they said. 'We are safe here.' Perhaps to my parents, the familiar, even on the eve of impending doom, felt safer than the unknown. To change one's place (geographically or emotionally), even in the face of the most compelling of circumstances, is very hard to do. I don't know. In the end, I am the only one of my family who survived the Holocaust. Never be *too* comfortable, dear."

While I have never lived my life in fear of the kind of oppression or danger that Mr. Gruen experienced, I have always heeded his words never to be too comfortable or too complacent anywhere. Just as there are kind angels around every corner, ready to assist us, and care for us, there are (sadly) forces in the world that place dangers in front of us. Judaism teaches that every human being's nature is made up of two inclinations: the *yetzer tov*—our inclination toward the good, and the *yetzer rah*—our inclination toward evil. Our lives are a constant struggle to enable our good natures to dominate our bad. Thankfully, we usually succeed in bringing forth the best of who we are. Nonetheless, I believe that while we should always celebrate "the better angels of our nature" it is always wise to stay aware of the demons that lurk in every society. Lot's two married daughters' and their husbands' ultimate fate resulted from their own complacency and their own inability to recognize the *rah*—the evil that resided in their midst.

Text to Life

Here is a true story about when grief petrifies—and when it might be liberated:

Heftzibah was a survivor of the Holocaust, who managed to make her way to Israel. There she married, gave birth to two daughters, and lived into very old age. When Heftzibah died a few years ago she was mourned by her daughters, grandchildren, and great-grandchildren.

Heftzibah was a sad and depressed woman, never allowing herself to fully rejoice at family celebrations or to enjoy the blessings of the life with which she was blessed after the Holocaust. A religious and pious woman, Heftzibah was always plagued with "survivor's guilt," and could not delight in the simple pleasures of life. "Why did *I* survive," she wondered, "when so many others perished?" Heftzibah always wondered why God had let her live when brilliant scholars, scientists, and artists had died at the hands of the Nazis. After all, she was an uneducated woman, of use to no one!

A few years before she died, a family friend was standing near Heftzibah at the Bat Mitzvah celebration of one of her great-granddaughters. The friend said to Heftzibah, "Do you see all these young people, your grandchildren and great-grandchildren?" "Yes," Heftzibah replied.

"Well," said the friend," "Just think, if you hadn't survived the Holocaust, none of these beautiful young people would ever had been born!"

Suddenly Heftzibah's face lit up in understanding. She had for the first time perceived God's purpose and meaning for her existence. From that day on, Heftzibah was a happy woman, certain of her place in God's vast plan for the universe. And from that day on, Heftzibah lived with joy and delight, a smile adorning her beautiful wrinkle-etched face. Heftzibah had gained wisdom and, as it written in the biblical book of Proverbs, "She [Wisdom] will bring you honor if you embrace her. She will adorn your head with a wreath of grace [and] crown you with a diadem of glory" (Proverbs 4:9).[10] Heftzibah's life and survival had meaning indeed—and it shone on the faces of each and every one of her grandchildren and great-grandchildren!

LGB

---

10. I am grateful to my sister, Ilana Berner, for telling me this story.

Exploring the Text Within

Find a quiet and comfortable place to sit in contemplative silence with the above teachings and with the following questions about you and your life's experience. You may choose to focus on one question or sit with several. Ask yourself: what do the biblical text and these teachings mean to me in my life?

> *So Lot went out and spoke to his sons-in-laws who had married his daughters and said, "Up, get out of this place, for the LORD is about to destroy the city." But he seemed to his sons-in-law as one who jests.*

(Genesis 19:14)

> Can I recall a time when I did not heed a warning because I felt safe and comfortable, only to discover later that I would have been wise to heed the alert?

> *As dawn broke, the angels urged Lot on, saying, "Up, take your wife and your two remaining daughters, lest you be swept away because of the iniquity of the city." Still he delayed.*

(Genesis 19:15–16)

> Can I recall a time when I resisted change, even though I knew that change might be good for me?

> *Lot's wife looked back.*

(Genesis 19:26)

> Can I recall a time when I remained in my memories of a sad past and felt stuck—or even paralyzed—there?
>
> Have I been able to release myself from the grip the past had on me?

Chapter 9

Vayera III

Sacrifice, Fear, and Trembling

Some time afterward,[1] *God put Abraham to the test.*

—Genesis 22:1–2

Some time afterward—after Isaac's birth, after Hagar and Ishmael's banishment, after Sodom and Gomorrah have been destroyed, Abraham faces a new challenge—the most terrifying and formidable of his life. God says: take your son, your favorite one, the one you love, and sacrifice him, give him to Me as a burnt offering! Kill your beloved son—all for *Me*! Show Me that you have unshakable faith, Abraham! Show Me that your loyalty and faith come first, above and beyond all else, even your sweet boy."

God understands the extremity of the decree, knowing that the order will wrench Abraham's heart. Nonetheless God commands. And so the text itself and an ancient *midrash* both tell us that even God says "please." *Kach na*—"*please* take your son . . .":

> Rabbi Simeon bar Abba said: "The word *na* can imply only entreaty.
>
> The matter may be illustrated by the parable of a king of flesh and blood who had to face many wars, in all of which he had one mighty warrior who invariably achieved victory. In the course of time, he faced a war [that was] particularly severe. The king said to the mighty warrior, I beg you, stand with me in this war, that mortals should not say, the earlier wars were of no substance."[2]

---

1. After the expulsion of Hagar and Ishmael into the wilderness.
2. Quoted in *Sefer Ha-Aggadah* (trans. Braude), no. 45, 39–40.

Indeed, the ancient rabbis truly knew how God's order to Abraham must have been for the old man. In trying to explain why God did not simply say "Please take your son, Isaac to the Land of Moriah" but instead said *"[Please] Take your son, your favored one, Isaac, whom you love, and go to the land of Moriah,"* one rabbi writes "Why did God drag out his command to such length?" The rabbis answer is simple and empathic: "So that Abraham's mind might not be stunned [by such a heartwrenching demand]."[3]

Nonetheless, even if (as the *midrash* suggests) God appreciates the gravity of His command, what a *horrifying* moment this must have been for Abraham! It is almost enough for us now to throw down the book and say, "No! No more! These stories are too awful, too terrifying! This God is too demanding and too narcissistic for me. I *will* not cleave to such a God."

I can accept the temptation to reject such a God. And I won't even argue for faith and loyalty to the Divine. I can only declare, for myself, with absolute faith, that the story is offered *precisely* to pose for us the most profound moral dilemma and question: when do we stand up against demands that seem ethically and morally reprehensible and say, "No, not this time!" and when do we obey? Did Abraham pass God's test, or did he fail miserably?

Sages and scholars have been debating this very question for millennia, and my modest attempt to raise the question here could not suffice to do justice to the debate—so just a few thoughts:

For deeply faith-filled individuals, "argument" with God may come out in what might seem a half-hearted manner to a less devout person. Let's look at one example. In the late eleventh century, one of the greatest rabbis of northern Europe, Rabbi Shlomo ben Yitzchak, also known as RaSHI, offered his interpretation of God's words to Abraham, "Take your son, your favored one, Isaac, whom you love."

RaSHI asserted that there was actually a two-way conversation taking place between God and Abraham. Imagine, RaSHI suggested, that the conversation went something like this:

> God: *Take your son*
>
> Abraham: *Which one? I have two sons—Ishmael and Isaac.*
>
> God: *Your favored son.*
>
> Abraham: *But I love them both equally!*
>
> God: *The one whom you love.*
>
> Abraham: *But I love them both!*
>
> God: *Isaac.*

---

3. Quoted in *Sefer Ha-Aggadah* (trans. Braude), no. 45, 39–40.

This seemingly mild, almost *informational* conversation between God and Abraham might be seen by some as a simple conversation, but by others as a powerfully charged interchange: Abraham is a father desperately trying to convince God that the command he has just been given should be reversed. According to RaSHI, he *is arguing* with God in the way he best knows how. He is saying to God: "You can't ask me to do this, God! I have two sons! I have no favorite. I love them both! Don't ask me to sacrifice either one!" In fact, Abraham has already reluctantly "sacrificed" his older son Ishmael by casting him out into the wilderness with his mother Hagar (21:14. See chapter 5 above).

If we accept RaSHI's interpretation, we see that in the end, Abraham comes to realize that his arguments will not prevail and that at this dreadful moment, he must make his decision. Will he show his faith in the God who sent him to an unknown land, the God who has blessed him with two sons, the God who *promised* him progeny as numerous as the stars and an endless, blessed future? Will he cast his fate and his son's destiny with God and continue to *believe* that God will not force him to complete the terrifying task? Will he steadfastly adhere to his faith that he will receive God's blessing and his son will be saved? Abraham chooses to remain faithful—even *after* he has argued. He chooses to pray for God's blessing, to hope with all his heart for a happy outcome.

Here the words of the late Nobel Prize winner Elie Wiesel resonate profoundly for me. Even in yearning to God, Wiesel finds that he is praying to that very same God:

> I want to blaspheme and I can't quite manage it. I go up against Him. I shake my fist. I froth with rage, but it's still a way of telling Him that He's there, that He exists, that He's never the same twice, that denial itself is an offering to His grandeur. The shout becomes a prayer in spite of me.[4]

Perhaps, however, Abraham's faith has gone far beyond the deep faith of protest turned into prayer and obedience as Elie Wiesel's words suggest. Perhaps Abraham has become "God-intoxicated."[5] Perhaps his faith had escalated to the point that he has become a man of *too much* faith, intent on carrying out God's command at all costs.

---

4. I am grateful to my friend and colleague Rabbi Ilyse Kramer for our conversations about arguing with God and for the texts that she shared with me. Elie Wiesel's words are found in *The Town Beyond the Wall*.

5. A description of Abraham I first learned from my colleague, Rabbi Joy Levitt in an unpublished *midrash* in which she depicts Isaac's savior not as God but as Sarah masquerading as God. (See below.)

In the biblical text, just as Abraham raises his hand to slay his son, an angel of God calls out to him, not once, but *twice*. It is almost as if Abraham is so mesmerized, so determined to execute the command that the angel is forced to shake him out of his stupor, saying to Abraham, *"Do not raise your hand against the boy, or do anything to him"* (22:10–12).

An ancient *midrash* from Leviticus Rabbah[6] more than hints at Abraham's zeal when asking why the angel referred to Abraham's *hand* and not the knife. The *midrash* poses the question—why didn't the angel say, *"Do not raise your knife against the boy . . ."*? The author of the *midrash* answers that the knife had been dissolved completely by the angel's tears and when Abraham realized that he no longer had a knife in his hand, he began to figure out other ways to slaughter Isaac:

> Said Abraham: Perhaps (this happened because the lad) is not fit to be a sacrificial gift. May I strangle him, may I burn him, shall I cut him up in pieces before You? God said to him [Abraham]: *"Lay not your hand!"* Abraham said to Him [God]: "In that event, I have come here in vain. Let me bruise him, let me extract some blood from him, let me remove from him one drop of blood!" Said He [God] to him [Abraham]: "Don't you do anything to him, don't you bruise him."

What a scene! According to the *midrash*, Abraham, in a frenzy, is dismayed that he cannot complete the sacrifice! Instead of being profoundly relieved that his son has been saved, Abraham wants to continue and finish the job! It seems to matter more to Abraham that his son is eligible for sacred martyrdom than that his life has been spared! He is completely unable to pause to reflect on what he is doing; he is in the throes of overwhelming fanaticism and utter insanity. If it weren't for the intervention of the Divine via the angel, Abraham might well have slaughtered Isaac.

What a twisted moment the *midrash* conjures. Perhaps it is warning us of the ugly, incredibly destructive potential of zealotry and fervor taken to its most extreme lengths. Perhaps the *midrash* and the story of the binding of Isaac are meant to wake us up to consider oh so carefully the impact of our choices, and what happens when, intentionally or not, we make decisions that powerfully affect those we love, decisions that have the potential to rupture relationships irreversibly.

Let us consider two examples of family rupture as we return to Abraham's small family—Sarah and Abraham and the Egyptian maidservant Hagar, and the two boys, Ishmael and Isaac.

---

6. Leviticus Rabbah 20:2.

First, recall the moment when Abraham agreed to banish Hagar and their son Ishmael into the wilderness, equipping them with only one container of water, which would certainly not suffice for a long desert journey. In effect, Abraham was condemning Hagar and her son to death—and it was only through divine intervention that Hagar and Ishmael were saved. Though some *midrashim* suggest that Abraham regretted his actions and tried to visit with Ishmael and re-establish a relationship with his elder son, the biblical text never tells us about any reunion between father and son. Abraham's connection to Ishmael was ruptured irrevocably.

Second, after the crucial moment on the mountain when Isaac is rescued from death by God's angel, we notice a remarkable omission in the text. That phrase, repeated twice in the nineteen verses of the text—*"the two of them walked on together"*—as Abraham and Isaac trekked toward the mountain is missing! During the three solemn days' hike to Mount Moriah, there is a kind of grim unity between Abraham and Isaac. Even when Isaac realizes that there is wood and fire for the offering but no sacrificial animal and he asks his father about it, he accepts his father's answer and once again *"the two walk on together"* (22:8).

The great sage RaSHI, who I mentioned earlier, suggested that "Abraham, who was aware that he was going to slay his son, walked along with the same willingness and joy as Isaac who had no idea of the matter."[7] RaSHI continues by saying that once Isaac has asked his father where the lamb is for the sacrifice and Abraham responded that God will provide the animal, "Isaac then understood that he was travelling to be slain." Nonetheless, *"the two of them went on together"*—with the same *ready* heart.[8]

At the episode's end, however, when Isaac arises from the altar, whole in body, but certainly broken in spirit after the trauma of having been bound on a stone altar with flames licking at his body and his father's hand with a knife aimed at his jugular vein, father and son do *not* walk on together. How could they possibly have been united, at peace with one another, after such a horrific experience? How could Isaac even look at his father after what Abraham had just done to him? A poignant *midrash* speaks to this dramatic moment: "If two people are walking and one is filled with sorrow and the other is not, then the one who is filled with sorrow will not be able to walk at the pace of the one who is not. Rather, he or she will remain behind because of his or her sorrow."[9] Isaac is emotionally and spiritually traumatized, deeply wounded and hobbled by the pain of

---

7. Pentateuch with Rashi's Commentary on Genesis 22:6.
8. Pentateuch with Rashi's Commentary on Genesis 22:8.
9. Rabbi Avraham Yisroel Rosenthal, *KeMotze Shalal Rav al HaTorah*, no. 138.

what he has endured. He walks slowly, his heart aching. Abraham, in contrast, is joyful (according to RaSHI's interpretation). His son has survived, he himself has proven his faith in God. It is a time to celebrate. He must have walked briskly. Little does Abraham know that he has caused a great schism, so blind is he to his son's grief.[10]

At this point in our tragic saga, we read nothing at all about Isaac. He has disappeared from the text. Immediately after the binding, we read only of Abraham: "Abraham then returned to his servants, and they departed together to Beer-sheba and Abraham stayed in Beer-sheba" (22:19). Our biblical text never again mentions Abraham and Isaac being together; father and son are estranged.

Isaac is next mentioned by Abraham when, now widowed and very elderly, he instructs his servant to find a proper wife for Isaac (24:4). Isaac himself reappears in Genesis 24:62 where he has just returned *"from the vicinity of Beer-lahai-roi for he was settled in the region of the Negev."* It would seem that after his near-death experience at his father's hand, Isaac traveled away from Abraham's encampment toward the place where Hagar and his older brother Ishmael had experienced the miracle of the "spring of the living God who sees me" (*Beer-lahai-roi*). Perhaps Isaac, like Hagar needed to be truly "seen" in a way that his father Abraham was unable to see him, or perhaps he sought to reestablish a bond of fraternal kinship with his brother Ishmael. In either case, Isaac moved far away from his father.

The estrangement between Isaac and his father is deep. The great patriarch's family is now completely torn asunder. His first son, Ishmael is somewhere out in the wilderness, abandoned. His second son, beloved child of his old age, has gone off in a different direction after his near-death experience. Abraham leaves the scene alone—and the text doesn't even mention Sarah, who, *midrash* tells us, has gone off to search for her son Isaac. Everyone is gone—and Sarah will soon die. What a horrific emotional toll Abraham's actions have taken on the whole family!

And indeed, returning to the beginning of our saga, where *was* Sarah when Abraham took her son into the mountains? Our text doesn't mention her. We read that on the morning after Abraham heard God's command, Abraham awoke "early" (22:3), *"saddled his ass, and took with him two of his servants and his son Isaac."* Why so early? Was he eager to get on with the journey, or did he not want to wake Sarah, lest she discover his plan? Though we will never know, because the text gives us no hint, we can wonder and speculate. If I were Sarah, mother of a beloved child of my old age,

---

10. I am indebted to Morateinu Alissa Thomas-Newborn, spiritual leader of B'nai David-Judea Congregation in Los Angeles, California for the Rosenthal source and these insights. *Jewish Journal*, September 18, 2015.

mother of the son I yearned for for so long, I would protest vociferously. I would cry "no!" Perhaps I would even have thrown myself in Abraham's way and try to stop him from embarking on this deadly journey. The text is eerily silent—and we see that Abraham not only does not consult Sarah about God's command—he keeps it a secret from her.

We learn that Abraham and Isaac's journey takes three days for it is *"on the third day [that] Abraham looked up and saw the place* [of sacrifice] *from afar"* (22:4). Three days journey, plodding slowly to the mountain, to the place of slaughter, a journey of thousands of steps to what will be a dreadful moment of wood and fire and a boy bound to an altar like an innocent lamb—and all the while, for three excruciatingly long days, Sarah sits alone in her tent, wondering what has become of her son.

The next thing we read about Sarah is that she has died! Can silence and secrets kill? Several ancient *midrashim* tell us about Sarah's death. One simply says that the report of her demise "comes close to the passage" about the binding of Isaac.[11] Two others are more elaborate. A first-century C.E. sage[12] reported that Samael (who was believed to be the angel of death) approached Sarah and told her that Abraham had seized the boy and that despite Isaac's resistance, his father had succeeded in sacrificing him. Samael describes the scene to Sarah in vivid detail—and Sarah wept bitterly and died of grief.[13]

A much more detailed *midrashic* subplot is recounted in the obscure apocryphal Book of Jasher, which is mentioned in the Hebrew Bible.[14] After attempting to thwart Abraham's plan to obey God's command, Satan turned to Sarah, appearing to her "in the figure of an old man very humble and meek." Here are the dramatic words of this *midrashic* text:

77. And he [Satan] said unto her [Sarah]: "Do you not know all the work that Abraham has made with your only son this day? For he took Isaac and built an altar, and killed him and brought him up as a sacrifice upon the altar, and Isaac cried and wept before his father, but he [Abraham] did not look at him [Isaac] and he did not have compassion over him . . . ."

78. And Sarah lifted up her voice and cried out bitterly on account of her son, and she threw herself upon the ground and she cast dust upon

---

11. Genesis Rabbah 58:5.

12. *Pirke d'Rabbi Eliezer*, understood to have originated with Rabbi Eliezer ben Hyrcanus in the first century C.E.

13. *Pirke d'Rabbi Eliezer*, 32.

14. See, for example, 2 Samuel 1:18 and Joshua 10:13.

her head, and she said, "O my son, Isaac, my son, O that I had this day died instead of you!"

79. And she continued to weep and said, "It grieves me for you, O my son, my son Isaac. O that I had died in your place." And she still continued to weep, and said: "It grieves me for you since I have reared you and have brought you up; now my joy is turned into mourning for you. I, who yearned for you, and cried and prayed to God until I bore you at ninety years old. And now you have served this day for the knife and the fire to be made as an offering!"

80. "But I console myself with you, my son, in its being the word of the LORD, for you did perform the word of your God, for who can transgress the word of our God, in whose hands is the soul of every living creature?"

81. "Thou art just, O LORD our God, for all Your works are good and righteous. For I also rejoice in Your word which You did command, and while my eyes weep, my heart rejoices."

82. And Sarah lay her head upon the bosom of one of her handmaids, and she became as still as a stone.

83. She afterward rose up and went about making inquiries till she came up to Hebron and she inquired of all those she met walking in the road, and no one could tell her what had happened to her son.

84. And she came with her maid servants and men servants to Kiryath-arba, which is Hebron, and she asked concerning her son, and she remained there while she sent some of her servants to seek where Abraham had gone with Isaac;[15] they went to seek him in the house of Shem and Eber, and they could not find him, and they sought him throughout the land and he was not there.

85. And behold, Satan came to Sarah in the shape of an old man, and he came and stood before her, and he said to her: "I spoke falsely to you, for Abraham did not kill his son and he is not dead; and when she heard the word her joy was so exceedingly violent on account of her son that her soul went out through joy; she died and was gathered to her people.[16]

What a terrifying tale! Those of us who are parents can only imagine the terror in Sarah's heart as she awaits the return of her beloved son—three

---

15. Presumably with Isaac's body for burial.
16. *Sefer Ha-Yashar* (book of Jasher) ch. 23:76–86.

days to the mountain, and three days' return—six days she awaits Isaac in vain. Six agonizing days. And finally, either from grief or relief, Sarah dies. The spiral of Abraham's actions has reached its nadir—death is its result—not the sacred sacrifice of the beloved son, but the tragic demise of Isaac's devoted mother.

How might *Sarah* have acted had the Divine Voice spoken to *her?* Sarah, take your son, your only son, the one whom you love and take him to the place that I will show you—and bind him to a mound of stone and wood and fire and sacrifice him to Me so that you may show Me your absolute loyalty and fidelity and faith. After all the pain and suffering and yearning for a child to love and nurture, would Sarah have responded as Abraham did?

Rabbi Joy Levitt offers this thought-provoking late twentieth-century *midrash*:[17]

Where Was Sarah?

Although the text reveals nothing of Sarah's presence, perhaps she was there in disguise. Perhaps, Sarah woke up as Abraham was preparing to leave and asked where he was going. Perhaps he told her to go back to sleep. And perhaps she tried and couldn't, and glanced over to see Abraham waking Isaac and getting him dressed. Perhaps, as they were leaving the tent, she decided to follow them—at a respectable distance, you understand.

Perhaps she watched as they climbed the mountain, and she heard her son ask what was going on and she heard Abraham's response and became more and more worried. After all, this God thing was really Abraham's thing—not hers—although here she was with a son in her old age. . . . [D]idn't Abraham tell her to relax, it would work out?

So she kept following them, watching with increasing fear as Abraham built the altar, laid the wood, and bound her son, her only son, the son whom she loved, on the altar above the wood.

As Abraham put out his hand and took the knife, Sarah made an immediate, instinctive decision. Calling out from behind the cliff where she was hiding, she screamed, "Abraham! Abraham!" And Abraham, intoxicated with his Godly mission, responded as he tended to do: "Here I am." Realizing that, in the early morning fog, Abraham hadn't recognized her, she

---

17. Rabbi Joy Levitt, Unpublished *midrash* that emerged from a class in women's *midrash*. Used with permission.

continued, making it up as she went along. "Do not lay thy hands upon that child; do nothing to him, for now I know that you are a God-fearing man, in that you have not withheld your son, your only son, from me."

Just as Sarah was deciding that she had gone too far, pretending to be God and all, she saw a ram in the thicket nearby and she jumped to get out of its way. The ram, confused, was caught in the brushwood by its horns. And Abraham took the ram and offered it up as a burnt offering in place of their son.

And perhaps Sarah watched in quiet relief and resignation, knowing that her son was safe and that her husband, well, he was God-intoxicated. But perhaps the voice of God, at least in this case, at this moment, was that of a mother.

Text to Life

> I recall a time millennia removed from that moment when Abraham began that tortuous walk to the mountain with his son Isaac. It is 1973. I am living in Jerusalem. It is October 6th and the day is Yom Kippur, the Day of Atonement—the most solemn day of the Jewish calendar. Millions of Israeli Jews are in synagogue, fasting and praying, recalling their misdeeds of the year that has passed and looking ahead to the new year with conviction and determination to do better. With heartfelt sincerity, they pray the ancient words, chant the ancient melodies, and look into the inner rooms of their souls to try to cleanse the places that need cleansing, heal the places that need healing, and, with hope and optimism, look to the future. I am a young, secular Jewish woman and I am not in synagogue. The religious life is not yet part of my consciousness. I have spent the morning of this crisp Autumn day hiking in the hills of Judea, and I have just come home. I am about to sit down to lunch—eating on Yom Kippur—a sacred day of fasting!! A blasphemy for the millions who are in synagogue! Suddenly air raid sirens blared out their frightening wail in the city streets. The Yom Kippur War had begun as a Syrian-Egyptian coalition attacked the State of Israel.[18]

---

18. Varying degrees of support for Egypt and Syria in their attack on Israel also came from Jordan, Iraq, Algeria, Saudi Arabia, Libya, Kuwait, Morocco, Tunisia, Lebanon, Sudan, Cuba and North Korea.

During the ensuing days, I witnessed the modern-day re-enactment of parents sending their sons "to the mountain" as offerings—this time not for God but for their country, the State of Israel. I even recall speaking to friends and neighbors who spoke about *"Akedat Yitzchak,"*—the binding (or sacrifice) of Isaac—and how they felt that the ancient demand to sacrifice their sons for the *cause* of their homeland was incumbent upon them. Many of those young "Isaacs" did not return from the war—more than 2,800 young men and women were killed.[19]

This book is not the place to argue Middle East politics. What I write of here is a heart memory—how a biblical story and modern-day reality become intertwined. For the Israelis I knew in 1973, the story of Abraham and Isaac on the mountain was all too real, but at that time in Israel's history, the question of arguing whether to respond to the call to defend Israel was less salient than it might be in the minds of some soldiers today. The thicket of Middle East politics today has made the question of service, defense of governmental policies and territories far more complex than it was in 1973. Nonetheless, for me at least, combined with my most ardent prayer for peace and solutions to the quagmire of Israel's place in the political arena of the area, there is no question in my mind that in answering the call, even today, to defend the land and the people of Israel, my answer would be an unequivocal "yes."

And with that conviction to answer the call, comes the following song—a meditation on Abraham's two sons, *after* their father's death—in the context of the present-day Middle East conundrum. It is my way of weaving the biblical story and contemporary realities. It is a prayer beyond words, a prayer beyond song. It is a cry wailed in the aching heart of every mother, and every father—Jewish, Muslim, or Christian—who has lost a child to this horrendous, bloody and insane conflict.[20]

LGB

---

19. I am reminded of the stark poem by Israeli poet Aliza Shenhar with its military metaphors: "The loudspeaker screamed/'Take your only one/the one who you love.' And the altar is destroyed/Wood of the burnt offering is scattered.... The knife is shining in the wadi/In the light of the moon/of mid-border./The white angel, the one/who always cries/'Please don't lay a hand'/is on leave."

20. ©1989 "Isaac and Ishmael" See Appendix B for musical notation.

Isaac and Ishmael

ISAAC AND ISHMAEL

*Shalom aleichem, aleichem shalom, shalom
Shalom aleichem, aleichem shalom.*

I. *Sh'mi Yitzchak, ayeh achi, ayeh achi?*
   Sh'mi Yitzchak, ayeh achi Yishmael?
   My name is Isaac, where's my brother?
   Where's my brother?
   My name is Isaac, where's my brother Ishmael?

Salaam aleikum, aleikum salaam, salaam, salaam aleikum, aleikum salaam

II. *Ismi Isma'il, wayn achi, wayn achi?*
    Ismi Isma'il, wayn achi, Is-hak?
    My name is Ishmael, where's my brother?
    Where's my brother?
    My name is Ishmael, where's my brother Isaac?

Shalom aleichem, aleichem shalom, shalom, shalom aleichem, aleichem shalom.

III. Born on the same Land
     Guided by the same God's hand
     We were torn apart,
     And it broke our father's heart.
     I was bound on the altar.
     You were left to wander.
     Both of us sacrificed,
     And it broke our father's heart.

Salaam aleikum, aleikum salaam, salaam, salaam aleikum, aleikum salaam.

IV. When our father Abraham died,
    We laid him down, you and I.
    Then our brother's bonds were broken,
    And it broke our father's heart.
    Our children's children don't know why
    They must fight and kill and die.
    We are slaughtering each other—
    It breaks our father's heart.

> *Shalom aleichem, aleichem shalom, shalom, shalom aleichem, aleichem shalom.*
>
> V. O Isaac—I dream of you in the desert sands!
> O Ishmael—I dream of you in the hills!
> O Ishmael—can we share our father's Land?
> O Isaac—can our mothers, too, be friends again?
>
> *Salaam aleikum, aleichem shalom, salaam, shalom aleichem, aleikum salaam.*
>
> O Isaac—can we live free at last?
> O Ishmael—with justice in the land?
> We are brothers—can we live in peace again?
> O Abraham, father—can we heal your broken heart?
>
> *Salaam aleikum, aleichem shalom, salaam, shalom aleichem, aleikum salaam.*

Exploring the Text Within

Find a quiet and comfortable place to sit in contemplative silence with the above teachings and with the following questions about you and your life's experience. You may choose to focus on one question or sit with several. Ask yourself: what do the biblical text and these teachings mean to me in my life?

> Some time afterward, God put Abraham to the test. He said to him, "Abraham," and he said, "Here I am."

> Can I recall a time when I was faced with a formidable, even terrifying challenge, and I didn't know what to do?

> Some time afterward, God put Abraham to the test. He said to him, "Abraham," and he said, "Here I am."

> Can I recall a time when I became so obsessed with a task or goal that I couldn't let go, even when wise advisors or my inner voice told me to change course?

Some time afterward, God put Abraham to the test. He said to him, "Abraham," and he said, "Here I am."

> Can I recall a time when my own obsession blinded me to the pain of another and deafened me to another's cry?

Chapter 10

Chayei Sarah

Death, Burial, and New Love

> "Sarah's lifetime [literally: these are the lives of Sarah]—the span of Sarah's life—came to one hundred and twenty-seven years.[1] Sarah died in Kiriath-arba, now Hebron . . ."
>
> —Genesis 23:1

After the terrifying events of Isaac's near-sacrifice, father and son go their separate ways. Isaac is now estranged from his father. How can he even look his father in the eye after what his father had done to him? Mother Sarah, desperately awaiting her son's return, finds herself becoming increasingly frightened when he doesn't return. Abraham had left with Isaac early in the morning before she had awakened. She found their encampment empty—now more than a week has gone by and there was no sign of either Abraham or Isaac.

Folklore tells us that as Sarah awaited her son's return, Satan visited her:

> At that time, Satan went to Sarah and appeared to her in the guise of Isaac. When she saw him, she said to him: "My son, what has your father done to you?" He answers her: "My father took me up hill and down dale, up to the top of a certain mountain, he built an altar, arranged the wood, bound me on top of it, he took the knife to slaughter me, and if God had not said, 'Don't stretch out your hand,' I would already have been slaughtered." He did not finish telling the story before she died.[2]

---

1. Sarah's age seems unrealistic if we calculate in 365-day contemporary year blocks. See p. 89, footnote 1.

2. Midrash Tanchuma Vayera 23.

This legend describes Sarah's death and hints at a moral lesson as well. The nineteenth-century Danish philosopher Søren Kierkegaard, in writing about the complex story of Abraham and Isaac, concludes that even though Abraham knew that to sacrifice his son would be unethical, it would be right to do so as an expression of ultimate faith in God. Given the terrible choice between faith in God and his son, Abraham chose God—and God, in the end, stayed Abraham's hand and returned him to the ethical—and saved Isaac's life.[3] In Sarah's eyes, however, Abraham's choice is grotesque. How *could* Abraham bring his own son to sacrifice?! Sarah never abandons the ethical choice. She was, in Kierkegaard's words, "bound to the ethical."[4] She was so horrified by Abraham's act that she died of a broken heart at the very thought. Utterly disillusioned with her husband and devastated by the loss of her cherished son, Sarah could no longer live with Abraham and without Isaac.

Here a new Torah portion called *Chayei Sarah* begins recounting Sarah's death and Abraham's search for an honorable place to bury her. "*Chayei Sarah*"—translated as "Sarah's lifetime" or, more literally, "Sarah's lives" (note the plural). The literal translation renders the Hebrew "*chayim*"—life—more accurately, as it is a plural noun even when meant in the singular. In truth, this plural noun reflects reality for all of us—*for don't we each live many "lives"?* Don't we each pass through different seasons of life, with the manifold experiences of every stage, each so different as we grow, mature and encounter what life throws at us. Certainly this was true for Sarah.

First, she lived the life of a young woman in Ur of the Chaldees where her name was Sarai, and then she married Abram. Then, in her *second* life, she embarked on the great adventure southward into an unknown land, Canaan, envisioned only in Abram's dreams, the land to which God told him to go (Genesis 12). As a young, strong woman, she was ready to leave the safety of home for the adventure of traveling to a new place with new challenges.

Still later, in her *third* life, with Abram she goes down into Egypt to seek food when a famine strikes Canaan (12:10–20). Here she is hungry and vulnerable, subject to the dangers of being a beautiful woman in a foreign culture (12:11–20).

After returning to Canaan from Egypt, as we have seen, she lived her *fourth* life—suffering with infertility and yearning for a child. In this life, she courageously offered her Egyptian maidservant, Hagar, to Abram so that he might sire a child.

---

3. Søren Kierkegaard, *Fear and Trembling*.

4. Kierkegaard, *Fear and Trembling*. See also Rabbi Rona Shapiro, "Woman's Life, Woman's Truth," in Goldstein, ed., *The Women's Torah Commentary*, 71.

This is a tormented and selfish time in Sarai's life. Tormented by her inability to become pregnant, she acts with complete disregard for Hagar's feelings or welfare. True to the culture of her time, as Hagar's mistress, Sarai uses Hagar as an instrument of her will, a tool through which (rather than through "whom") she might achieve her goal of attaining a child for Abram and herself. In her culture, as mistress of the tribe, the baby who would emerge from Hagar's womb would be considered to be *Sarai's* child, and Hagar would be viewed merely as a surrogate mother, not the infant's "real" mother. She would be considered simply as the vessel in which the child had grown for nine months. Hagar's emotions were unimportant. Sarai's expectations were that *her* maternal position and needs would be fulfilled with the baby's birth (Genesis 16). She dreamed of loving and nurturing the baby, whom Abram named Ishmael, and gaining the honored status of *mother* in her society.

But this was not to be. Hagar claimed the baby as her own—and Sarai, in this "fourth" life feels even more acutely her loss, her barrenness, her emptiness. A while after she loses Ishmael to Hagar, God tells Abram that he and Sarai will indeed have a child of their own and the Holy One changes their names—from Abram to Abraham ("father of many"), from Sarai to Sarah ("princess," understood to be "mother of nations") (17:5, 15). Incredulous that such a thing can happen at their advanced ages, both Abraham and Sarah laugh bitterly, even after they have received their new names.

Finally, in a miraculous *fifth* life, Sarah actually *does* become pregnant and gives birth to baby Isaac, who brings her truly joyous laughter (Genesis 21). What a life Sarah has lived! Then, just as the rabbinic legend tells us, Sarah experiences a momentary *sixth* life as a bereaved mother, thinking that Isaac has been slaughtered, in the instant before she dies. So many "lives"; what a wealth of experiences! Indeed, these are the "lives" of Sarah.

And now Sarah's time on earth is over—and Abraham mourns her. He sets out to find the best of burial places for his beloved, the woman who followed him everywhere, even at her own peril, who offered her servant to him so that *he* could sire children, and who late in life brought him his second son, the source of their greatest joy, the fruit of their deepest laughter, Isaac.

> . . . *and Abraham proceeded to mourn for Sarah and to bewail her.*[5]
>
> —Genesis 23:2

---

5. The ancient sages say that to "bewail" someone is to eulogize them, as Abraham did for Sarah.

Abraham searches for the choicest of burial plots for Sarah—he wants to find a place that all who visit will revere. It is important to Abraham that his purchase of the burial site is legal and publicly witnessed, so that there will be no doubt that he is the legitimate owner. He negotiates the price and in the presence of many witnesses, he pays for the Cave of Machpelah and its surrounding acreage.

Two ancient *midrashim* tell us that Abraham and Sarah and son Isaac were not only divinely destined to be buried in the Cave of Machpelah, but that the place held the aura of pristine innocence—an attribute he sought to lift up about his wife and indeed about himself.

The first story tells us that

> Prior to Abraham, there were many who wanted to be buried there, but could not enter the place because of a fire emanating from it. The fire was put there by the ministering angels who were guarding the place. When Abraham came, he entered and bought the place.[6]

It is as if God (via the medium of the angels) was waiting just for Abraham to come and claim his rightful possession of the cave!).

The second tale tells us that.

> Rabbi Rehumai said: God Himself created Adam and God Himself took care of Adam at his death. No one knew of Adam's burial place until Abraham came, entered the cave and saw him. As Abraham entered, the place was filled with the scent of the Garden of Eden and the voice of the ministering angels saying: "Adam is buried here. Abraham and Isaac will be prepared for this place." Abraham saw the lit candle and went out. At that moment he developed a desire for the place.[7]

If we consider Abraham's desire for the Cave of Machpelah on a purely literal level, we could simply conclude that he was selecting the best real estate around, but there might be a deeper meaning here. Perhaps Abraham wants a place that evokes the Divine Will and the purity of the Garden of Eden—both of which he would associate with Sarah, and hope for himself.

What might be stirring within Abraham? Perhaps he is experiencing guilt pangs for almost killing Isaac! Perhaps he is realizing that his zeal in bringing Isaac to the mountain was misguided. Perhaps he was coming to understand that when "God put [him] to the test" (Genesis 22), he had actually failed—perhaps God had hoped that he would shake his fist at heaven

---

6. Pirkei d'Rabbi Eliezer ch. 36.
7. Zohar: Ruth: 79, 4.

and say, "No! I will not sacrifice my son—not even for You, my beloved God!" Perhaps by ensuring that he, too, would be buried in the Cave of Machpelah, he hoped that exoneration for his own sin against his son Isaac might come when he died. Perhaps God would forgive him for having failed this most profound of theological choices—to choose the love of one's child over the love of God. Perhaps Abraham believed that the cave's special aroma meant that even Adam and Eve had been forgiven for *their* sin in the Garden, since they had been given the honor of having been buried in the Cave of Machpelah. Perhaps Abraham reasoned that if *they* could be forgiven, then maybe he, too, could be blessed with God's pardon. Perhaps by selecting the Machpelah Cave, Abraham hoped to accomplish two goals—first, to attain the best possible grave for Sarah, and second to find a place where his own troubled conscience could rest in peace.

> *Abraham was now old, advanced in years, and the* Lord *blessed Abraham in all things.*
>
> —Genesis 24:1

Years after Sarah's death, Abraham sees his own death approaching. Torah does not tell us of any reunion with his son Isaac since that fateful day on the mountain. Nonetheless, Abraham still wants to ensure that Isaac will be well cared for once he died. He sends his servant to find a suitable Israelite wife for Isaac. This wife, Abraham tells his servant, must be found in his ancestral homeland to the north among his *"father's house"* (24:7) *"Then the servant took ten of his master's camels and set out, taking with him all the bounty of his master, and he made his way to Aram-naharaiim, to the city of Nahor"* (24:10). There the servant seeks to find a kind and lovely young woman, who will naturally demonstrate her generosity of spirit:

> *And he [the servant] said, "O* Lord, *God of my master Abraham, grant me good fortune this day, and deal graciously with my master Abraham: Here I stand by the spring as the daughters of the townsmen come out to draw water; let the maiden to whom I say, 'Please lower your jar that I may drink,' and who replies, 'Drink, and I will also water your camels'—let her be the one whom You have decreed for Your servant Isaac. Thereby shall I know that You have dealt graciously with my master."*
>
> —Genesis 24:12–14

The servant's prayer is answered:

> *He had scarcely finished speaking, when Rebekah . . . came out with a jar on her shoulder on her shoulder. The maiden was very*

> *beautiful, a virgin whom no man had known. She went down to the spring, filled her jar, and came up. The servant ran toward her and said, "Please let me sip a little water from your jar." "Drink, my lord," she said, and she quickly lowered her jar upon her hand and let him drink. When she had let him drink his fill, she said, "I will also draw for your camels until they finish drinking." Quickly emptying her jar into the trough, she ran back to the well to draw, and she drew for all his camels.*
>
> —Genesis 24:15–20

Abraham's servant is elated. He has found a wife for Isaac, beautiful, a virgin, and kind as well! He inquires whether there might be lodging in her family's home for him and the camels—and she replies that indeed there is a place for him: "'There is plenty of straw and feed at home, and also room to spend the night' . . . [and] the maiden ran and told all this to her mother's household." (24:25, 28).

So—what have we learned so far about Rebekah? In addition to her beauty, we discover that she is strong. It takes considerable strength to "go down" to a spring multiple times to draw water for ten camels—and that she does so "quickly" and with enthusiasm. We also learn that she is hospitable—she does not hesitate to invite him to stay with her family and to bring his ten camels along with him.

Once Abraham's servant asks for Rebekah's hand in marriage to Isaac and agreement is reached, it becomes apparent that the bride-to-be is an independent-minded young woman. When Abraham's servant wants Rebekah to depart immediately with Isaac to return to Canaan (despite her family's request that she remain for ten days to prepare for the journey), the family leaves the decision in Rebekah's hands:

> *And they said, "Let us call the girl and ask for her reply." They called Rebekah and said to her, "Will you go with this man?" And she said, "I will." So they sent off their sister Rebekah and her nurse along with Abraham's servant and his men. And they blessed Rebekah and said to her,*
>
> *"O sister!*
> *May you grow into thousands of myriads;*
> *may your offspring seize the gates of their foes."*
>
> —Genesis 24:57–60

The moment has come for Rebekah and Isaac to meet.

> Isaac went out walking in the field toward evening, and looking up, he saw camels approaching. Raising her eyes, Rebekah saw Isaac. She alighted [literally: "fell"[8]] from the camel and said to the servant, "Who is that man walking in the field toward us?" And the servant said, "That is my master." So she took her veil and covered herself.

Does Rebekah fall off her camel in dismay? Does she see the wounded Isaac, still traumatized from his time on the mountain when his father held a knife to his neck to slaughter him? Or does she see a young man, subdued by the grief of his mother's death? Does she slip off her camel because she felt compassion and love for this man walking toward her? Is it love at first sight? We will never know for sure, but the text hints at a mutual tenderness between Isaac and Rebekah, who seem to come together at a moment when their personalities fit together like two pieces of a puzzle. Isaac is in deep need of comfort and care and Rebekah, the stronger, has the capacity (and perhaps the desire) to comfort and bring forth her power gently and softly:

> The servant told Isaac all the things that he had done. Isaac then brought her into the tent of his mother Sarah and he took Rebekah as his wife. Isaac loved her, and thus found comfort after his mother's death.

—Genesis 24:66–67

There are few places in which the Torah speaks of love between a couple. Here, in this moment between Isaac and Rebekah and in their nascent relationship we can feel the love, we can palpably feel the poignancy of the moment—Isaac is wounded from the terror of the mountain and grieving his mother's death, Rebekah willingly comforts him—and Isaac comes to life again.

A wonderful *midrash* speaks to the beauty of Rebekah's coming into Isaac's life:

> As long as Sarah lived, a cloud [of the Divine Presence] hung over her tent; when she died, that cloud disappeared; but when Rebekah came, it returned. As long as Sarah lived, her doors were wide open; at her death that liberality ceased; but when Rebekah came, that openhandedness returned. As long as Sarah lived, there was a blessing on her dough and the lamp used to burn from the evening of the Sabbath until the evening of

---

8. A *midrash* asserts that Rebekah's falling off her camel should not be viewed negatively, and links the "fall" to Psalm 37:24: "Though he fall, he shall not be utterly cast down."

the following Sabbath; when she died, these ceased, but when Rebekah came, they returned. And so when he [Isaac] saw her following in his mother's footsteps, separating her challah in cleanness and handling her dough in cleanness, straightway, "and Isaac brought her into the tent" (Genesis 24:67).[9]

Text to Life

> Peter and Talia met in a kibbutz in the northern Negev of Israel. Peter was a thin young man, with sad eyes and a gentle smile. He had immigrated to Israel, fleeing the repressive regime of Nicolae Ceausescu, who was ultimately toppled from power in Romania in 1989. Peter had suffered in Romania. His parents had been labeled political dissidents and imprisoned by Ceausescu. He never saw them again. He himself had been twice arrested and had been beaten brutally.
>
> Talia was a beauty and was much sought after by the young men on the kibbutz, and everywhere she went. In addition to her physical beauty, Talia was known to be a very kind young woman. She had grown up in the healthy atmosphere of the kibbutz, in a loving family, among friends who surrounded her, in a community that helped her to feel safe and secure.
>
> Soon Peter and Talia became a couple. Kibbutz members wondered about the odd pairing. Peter seemed so frail, wounded by his youth in Romania. He seemed needy and dependent, and Talia was so strong and many thought she "could do better for herself." But somehow Talia sensed that perhaps *because* of what Peter had experienced in his life, he would be a kind and gentle person, a man who would appreciate her love and reciprocate well. She nurtured Peter, knowing that he could heal from the past.
>
> Three years after meeting, Talia and Peter married, and like Rebecca and Isaac, Talia continued to care for Peter, loving him with the innate kindness that was in her, lightening his soul, brightening his world. Little by little, Peter began to heal. Talia and Peter became parents to two sons and a daughter. Peter was able to transcend his woundedness and become a wonderful and loving father to his children. In some profound way, Talia (like in the biblical story of Rebecca and Isaac) was the medium through whom the healing took place, and just as the broken

---

9. Genesis Rabbah 60:16.

> Isaac became whole again with Rebecca's help, so too, the broken Peter became whole again with Talia's gentle nurturing.
>
> Peter and Talia have three grown children now and some grandchildren too. They have a very happy marriage and the wounds of the past have healed.

Exploring the Text Within

Find a quiet and comfortable place to sit in contemplative silence with the above teachings and with the following questions about you and your life's experience. You may choose to focus on one question or sit with several. Ask yourself: what do the biblical text and these teachings mean to me in my life?

> *Sarah's lifetime* [literally: these are the lives of Sarah]—*the span of Sarah's life—came to one hundred and twenty-seven years.* (Genesis 23:1)

> How many *lives* have I lived?
>
> Can I recall moments, feelings, and people from my different lives?
>
> What life-long effects have my different *lives* had on me?

> *. . . and Abraham proceeded to mourn for Sarah and to bewail her.* (Genesis 23:2)

> When I have grieved, how deeply have I entered into my grief?
>
> Which emotions have I faced and which have I avoided?

> *Isaac then brought her into the tent of his mother Sarah, and he took Rebecca as his wife. Isaac loved her, and thus found comfort after his mother's death.*
>
> (Genesis 24:67)

> Have you ever been blessed to be lovingly comforted by another?
>
> Have you generously comforted another during a vulnerable time in their life?

Chapter 11
Toldot
Sibling Rivalry

"When the boys grew up, Esau became a skillful hunter, a man of the outdoors, but Jacob was a mild man who stayed in the camp. Isaac favored Esau because he had a taste for game; but Rebekah favored Jacob."

—Genesis 25:27–28

Isaac, now married to Rebekah, has settled down. Abraham had remarried after Sarah's death and had sired several more children. As he prepares for his death, he "willed all that he owned to Isaac" and gave gifts to his concubines' children while he was still living (25:5–6). He died at a ripe old age and Isaac and Ishmael came together to bury their father beside Sarah at the Cave of Machpelah.

As a new Torah portion begins, we find Isaac and Rebekah trying to build a family with Rebekah struggling to become pregnant. Unlike his father Abraham, who was satisfied with using Hagar the Egyptian as a surrogate, Isaac's deep love for Rebekah stops him from cohabiting with a maidservant or concubine. Isaac prays to God that his beloved Rebekah might bear a child. His sincere and loving prayers are answered when Rebekah feels the life of *two* babies growing in her womb!

After a particularly difficult pregnancy, Rebekah delivers twin boys. "*The first one emerged red, like a hairy mantle all over; so they named him Esau.*[1] *Then his brother emerged, holding on to the heel of Esau, so they named him Jacob*"[2] (25:25–26).

1. Synonym of *Seir*, which is a word play on *se'ar* which means "hair."
2. This is a word play on *ekev*, which means "heel."

> *When the boys grew up, Esau became a skillful hunter, a man of the outdoors, but Jacob was a mild man who stayed in the camp. Isaac favored Esau because he had a taste for game; but Rebekah favored Jacob.*
>
> —Genesis 25: 27–28

Once again we encounter parental favoritism—that familial curse that seems to plague the early biblical generations.

- Even God the Parent is guilty of favoritism: Remember Cain and Abel? God accepted Abel's offering but rejected Cain's—and that ends in Cain's jealous murder of Abel.
- Abraham loved both his sons equally, but Sarah favored Isaac and demanded that Ishmael be banished.
- And now, Esau and Jacob. Isaac favors Esau *"because he has a taste for game."* Rebekah's love for Jacob seems more natural. There are no reasons. She loves Jacob simply because he was her son. But then, why doesn't she favor Esau as well? No reasons are offered in the biblical text, though in *midrash* the rabbis speculate that Jacob loves study and Esau gravitates more to idolatrous worship.[3]

When Isaac met Rebekah, he seemed wounded and subdued, comforted by his new wife in his mother Sarah's tent. Isaac is a quiet, passive man—at least, since that moment on the mountain when his father held a knife to his neck. Was Isaac's confidence taken from him by the shock of his near-death experience? Perhaps Isaac loves Esau more *because Esau is his exact opposite.* In Esau, perhaps he sees what he might have become—strong, manly, a hunter, a man of the field. Isaac may not wish to identify with Jacob, the *"mild man who stayed in the camp."* Is Jacob whom Isaac knows himself to be more akin to, but wishes he were not, and this is why he rejects Jacob and favors Esau?

And Rebekah? Why does she love Jacob, who is described as a *"mild man who stayed in the camp"*? (25:27). Does Jacob remind her of the husband she loves, of Isaac, that tender, subdued man she had met in the field, the man whose visage from afar caused her to fall off her camel and decide that her destiny was to care lovingly for him?

Perhaps also, just like Isaac, who sees and loves his opposite, Rebekah loves and sees *her* opposite in Jacob. In the previous chapter, we saw how strong Rebekah is, how she was able to water ten camels, by running up and down to a spring. She is almost more masculine in her strength. Indeed, in

---

3. See Genesis Rabbah 63:10.

the Torah scroll, there is an unusual phenomenon in which when Rebekah is referred to as a maiden, a נערה/*na'arah*, the text also has written next to *na'arah* the word נער/*na'ar* which means "lad." This calligraphic technique is known as *kere u'ketiv*—which indicates that what it is written in the text as *na'ar* (lad) should actually be read aloud as *na'arah* (lass).

Rachel Brodie points out that "Rebecca may have been physiologically and emotionally more a *na'ar* [lad] while presenting to the world the image of (making people "read" her as) a *na'arah*."[4] Could Rebekah, so strong, perhaps even as strong as a man, feel more protective toward Jacob, her gentle son, the one who is so different from the "macho" hunter Esau?

Of course, we can only speculate about these parental preferences— but what we *do* know is that the family was divided—twins who are at odds with one another, mother and father divided in their preferences for their sons. The same family dysfunction that plagued the generation of Isaac's parents, Abraham and Sarah, continues in this generation.

> *Esau came in from the open, famished. And Esau said to Jacob, "Give me some of that red stuff to gulp down, for I am famished. . . ." Jacob said, "First sell me your birthright." And Esau said, "I am at the point of death, so of what use is my birthright to me?" But Jacob said, "Swear to me first." So he swore to him, and sold his birthright to Jacob. Jacob then gave Esau bread and lentil stew; he ate and drank, and he rose and went away. Thus did Esau spurn the birthright.*

—Genesis 25: 29–34

Imagine the scene: big, husky Esau comes in from the field. Ravenous, he thinks of nothing but food, so when Jacob asks *to buy* his birthright, Esau doesn't care about it at all, and gives it away—all for a piping hot bowl of red lentil soup. Does Jacob really steal the birthright or is Esau so cavalier that he simply relinquishes it without thought or care?

For millennia, Jews have been taught that Jacob had stolen Esau's birthright, but this doesn't appear to be the case. After all, Jacob asks Esau to *sell* him the birthright. At this point, there is no deception on Jacob's part. He sees that his brother doesn't seem to care about or see the importance of his birthright—an older son's right to inherit his father's property upon his father's death.

Despite his physical strength, perhaps Esau is really a simple man, interested in his carnal pleasures. When he is hungry, he is hungry, and cares little about anything else. Worldly material matters like inheritance don't

---

4. For a fascinating perspective on Rebekah's strength, and her breaking of stereotypical gender roles, see Brodie, "When Gender Varies," 34–37.

seem to matter to him—he simply wants to satisfy his physical cravings. In this sense, we might see Esau as a naïve and rather unmaterialistic man, less concerned with property than fulfilling his primal needs.[5]

We might view Esau's disinterest in material possessions favorably— Esau simply wants to live a good, honest life, earning his livelihood as a hunter, in the natural world, which he loves, competing with no one, not even his younger brother. But there is an inherent competition between the brothers—a competition initiated by Jacob, more hungry for power than Esau is for food.

Jacob is wily. He knows that with his father's birthright (an inheritance of property) comes an "innermost" paternal blessing (27:19), a benediction of heart and soul. How complicated this all is! Could the *power* that Jacob yearns for be his father's affection, a love he has never felt, because of Isaac's preference for Esau? *This* is the curse of parental favoritism—when a parent favors one child over another, the child who is left out inevitably feels a yearning, a craving for the blessing of love—which comes, in Jacob's case, from Isaac's innermost birthright blessing. If Jacob cannot attain this the natural way, that is given freely by a parent to a child, then he feels he must get it by any means he can—even stealing it.

> *When Isaac was old and his eyes were too dim to see, he called his older son Esau and said to him, "My son," He answered, "Here I am." And he said, "I am old now and I do not know how soon I may die. Take your gear, your quiver and bow, and go out into the open and hunt me some game. Then prepare a dish for me such as I like, and bring it to me to eat, so that I may give you my innermost blessing before I die."*
>
> —Genesis 27:1–4

Rebecca has overheard Isaac asking Esau to hunt for game and cook up a tasty meal of venison for him. She tells her favorite son, Jacob: "*Now, my son, listen carefully as I instruct you. Go to the flock and fetch me two choice kids, and I will make of them a dish for your father, such as he likes. Then* [you, Jacob], *take it to your father to eat, that he may bless you before he dies*" (27:8–10). Rebecca wants to help Jacob wrest away the birthright blessing from Esau and ensure that he, the younger by only a few seconds,

---

5. The ancient rabbis who write of Esau are less charitable to him. Even in utero, they declared, Esau was more interested in idolatry than Torah learning (see Genesis Rabbah 63:6) and that once he completed his formal education at age thirteen, he gravitated to "shrines of idolatry" rather than "houses of study" like his more admirable twin, Jacob (see Genesis Rabbah 63:10).

receive it.[6] Jacob, willing to go along with his mother's suggestion, worries that his father will see right through their trickery even though Isaac is old and blind: *"But my brother Esau is a hairy man and I am smooth-skinned. If my father touches me, I shall appear to him as a trickster and bring upon myself a curse, not a blessing"* (27:11–13).

Mother Rebecca has thought of everything. *"Rebecca then took the best clothes of her older son Esau, which were there in the house and had her younger son Jacob put them on; and she covered his hands and the hairless part of his neck with the skins of the kids. Then she put in the hands of her son Jacob the dish and the bread she had prepared"* (27:15–17).

Jacob is now ready to go forward and trick his elderly and blind father.

> *He went to his father and said, "Father." And he said, "Yes, which of my sons are you?" Jacob said to his father, "I am Esau, your first-born; I have done as you told me. Pray sit up and eat my game, that you may give me your innermost blessing."*
>
> —Genesis 27:18–19

Suspicious from the beginning, Isaac wonders how Esau has managed to hunt the game and cook it up so quickly and asks "Esau" about this. Jacob answers in somewhat cryptic way, perhaps giving a hint to the older man of his true identity: *"Because the Lord your God granted me good fortune"* (27:20). This is an answer, but not really an answer!

Isaac's suspicions are not eased and he asks Esau to come closer *"so that I may feel you, my son—whether you are really my son Esau or not"* (27:21). When Jacob draws closer, and Isaac feels him, he says, *"The voice is the voice of Jacob, yet the hands are the hands of Esau"* (27:22).

Perhaps Isaac has also picked up on a subtler clue of Jacob's deception. When Jacob answered about the quickness of bringing the goat stew, he said *"Because the Lord your God granted me good fortune,"* not *"Because the Lord my God granted me good fortune."* Jacob doesn't even cleave to his father's God! He doesn't even show his father that he believes in the God to whom Isaac is so devoted! Is *this* the son to whom Isaac will give his innermost blessing? And yet, Isaac proceeds to do something very puzzling: Isaac eats Jacob/"Esau's" stew, he asks Jacob/"Esau" to kiss him, he smells his clothing, and *then* he offers him his innermost birthright blessing!

Is this the wishful blessing of a father who hopes that *through* the blessing Jacob will become a believer in the God to whom Isaac is so

---

6. From the boys' youth, parental favoritism cursed the family: "When the boys grew up, Esau became a skillful hunter, a man of the outdoors, but Jacob was a mild man who stayed in the camp. Isaac favored Esau because he had a taste for game, but Rebekah favored Jacob" (26:27–28).

devoted? Is this the plaintive blessing of a loving father who prays that his son will find a way to this God? Is this the devoted father who, despite his knowledge of the deception, still has a sense, an intuition, that Jacob will become a great and devoted man, the Father of a People? Is this a father who is taking a leap of faith by blessing *this* son?

My own sense is that indeed Isaac is all that. Like many parents, he sees his son going in a direction that pains him deeply—and yet still he hopes; still he has faith—and so he blesses his child, with wounded optimism, yet optimism nonetheless:

I am reminded of the French author Antoine de St. Exupery's observation that "it is only with the heart that one can see rightly; what is essential is invisible to the eye."[7] And so, the not-so-blind Isaac finally blesses Jacob:

> *May God give you*
> *of the dew of heaven and the fat of the earth,*
>   *abundance of new grain and wine.*
> *Let peoples serve you,*
>   *and nations bow to you;*
> *be master over your brothers,*
>   *and let your mother's sons bow to you.*
> *Cursed be they who curse you,*
>   *blessed be they who bless you.*
>
> —Genesis 27:28–29

Jacob, now in possession of both the birthright and Isaac's blessing of the soul, leaves his father.

But is the blessing genuine or is it, as Peter Pitzele describes it, a "mock initiation?"[8] One would think that Isaac's blessing would be transformative for Jacob, carrying him into a realm of spirituality and toward a mature understanding of his mission as the scion of a lineage, a heritage beginning with his grandfather, Abraham. But the trajectory of Jacob's journey after his father's blessing reveals to us that he is not yet ready to truly be a patriarch. God has, in Pitzele's description, "not [yet] brushed him with His power. Jacob's imagination has not yet been fired by vision or dream.... His real potency sleeps and his powers have been put to the ends not of conception but of deception."[9] Jacob will have a long way to go before he finds himself, before he is able to relinquish a false birthright and blessing, before he can return it to Esau and face his brother in sincerity. Only when he can drink in the nectar of Esau's loving and forgiving embrace can he discover his own

7. *The Little Prince.*
8. Pitzele, *Our Father's Wells*, 174.
9. Pitzele, *Our Father's Wells*, 174.

true blessing within himself. Only *then* can Jacob become the *pater familias*, the father of the Israelite family—once he himself has authentically wrestled and become Israel, once he has come to know his purpose in life.

Does Jacob's journey sound familiar to you? The search for self? The stumbling and seeking, and following paths that lead us nowhere? Even the duplicity that we sometimes exercise in thinking we have reached our own self-identity? For most of us there are myriad twists and turns we take in our lives until we finally discover our own *genuine* truth. Jacob's story is our own story clad in different garments—and it resonates for many of us.

And what about Esau—the older son-come-lately who has followed his father's instructions, hunted for game, and now brings Isaac the savory stew Isaac had requested. Expecting his father's sacred blessing, he soon discovers his younger brother's deception:

> And he [Esau] said to his father, "Let my father sit up and eat his son's game so that you may give me your innermost blessing." His father Isaac said to him, "Who are you?" And he said, "I am your son, Esau, your first born!" Isaac was seized with very violent trembling. "Who was it then," he demanded, "that hunted game and brought it to me? Moreover, I ate of it before you came, and I blessed him. Now he must remain blessed!" When Esau heard his father's words, he burst into wild and bitter sobbing, and said to his father, "Bless me too, father!" But he answered, "your brother came with guile and took away your blessing." . . . [Esau said:] "Have you not reserved a blessing for me?" Isaac answered, saying to Esau, "But I have made him master over you: I have given him all his brothers for servants, and sustained him with grain and wine. What, then, can I still do for you my son?" And Esau said to his father, "Have you but one blessing, father? Bless me too, father!" And Esau wept aloud and his father Isaac answered, saying to him:
>
> "See, your abode shall enjoy the fat of the earth
> and the dew of heaven above.
> Yet by your sword you shall live,
> and you shall serve your brother;
> but when you grow restive,
> you shall break his yoke from your neck."
>
> —Genesis 27:31–40

How poignant and sad are these moments between Esau and Isaac. Finally we see how much Esau really *does* care about his father's blessing. Though he laments the loss of his birthright, it is really Isaac's paternal soul blessing that Esau mourns. He craves that blessing because it is a sign of Isaac's love for him, a sign of the father-son bond between them—its loss to Jacob is a terrible blow to Esau and the blessing that Isaac *does* give to him is double-edged, literally (*"yet by the sword you shall live"*). While enjoying prosperity (the *"fat of the land"*), Esau's life will not be tranquil.

What a tragedy—a father who loves *both* his sons—who has given his "innermost" blessing to a son whom he prays will grow into a man of faith, despite the fact that at this moment in his life, he is ambitious, deceptive, and faith*less*. The tragedy is that Isaac loves Esau too, perhaps more—and yet he has deprived Esau of his *innermost* blessing, and has given it to his less deserving son, Jacob, because of a hope, an instinct, perhaps a dream of a future in touch with God, in touch with a better future. If you are a parent, have you perhaps offered more help to a child who you thought needed it more, because that child seemed more "lost?" Perhaps Isaac, though preferring Esau, felt that Jacob needed the blessing more.

Is this not a dilemma that many parents face in their *innermost* being—when they choose one child over another? Perhaps unconsciously, parents sometimes act in ways that affect their children for the rest of their lives, unintentionally inflicting wounds that might never heal, inadvertently causing deep-set psychological injuries that ultimately lead to profound and painful conflicts between siblings into the next generation and even into the next and the next and the next . . . .

Caught up in his grieving for the original blessing, Esau *"harbors a grudge against Jacob . . . and says to himself, 'Let the mourning period of my father come, and I will kill my brother Jacob'"* (27:41).

Text to Life

> This story was told to me by George, the younger brother of Robert, about a decades-long estrangement between them and an ultimate reconciliation, after years of torment and profound pain.
>
> Some twenty-seven years ago, Robert and his wife Judy asked George and his new wife Michelle to babysit for their two young children while Robert and Judy went away for a long weekend to celebrate their anniversary. George and Michelle readily agreed, since they adored their niece and nephew, Lisa and Brian. George and Michelle moved into Robert and Judy's home for the weekend.
>
> All went well the first day and night and the second evening was a time full of fun as aunt and uncle played with the kids.

Some time in the early morning hours, George and Michelle awoke to thick smoke rushing into the bedroom and realized that there was a major fire on the second floor of the house. They immediately ran to Lisa's and Brian's rooms to rescue them, but when they tried to open the doors, an explosion of flames came at them from each door and they were unable to enter the rooms. It was hopeless.

Soon the fire fighters arrived and tried to enter the children's rooms from the roof. It was futile—Lisa and Brian died in the fire, and Michelle and George were in complete trauma as they contemplated letting Robert and Judy know the devastating news. Grieving and almost unable to speak, George called his brother.

Once the ashes settled and the funerals were over, Robert and Judy's emotions took a terrible direction. Turning their overwhelming grief against George and Michelle, they blamed them for their children's deaths, concluding that they didn't try hard enough to save the kids. "We will never forgive you!" Judy and Robert proclaimed. "You are no longer family to us. We never want to see you again."

And so the long estrangement began. Over time, Michelle and George had children, and even Judy and Robert had another child, a son, Raphael. But no news, no family celebrations, no connections were shared between the brothers. Neither brother ever spoke of the other. Yet beyond the grieving, a corrosive anger remained within Robert's heart and a profound yearning and love for his brother remained within George's.

The years went by. Robert's health began to suffer—hypertension, heart disease, ulcers. His doctor kept telling him that he needed to let go of his rage—it was killing him. And George suffered from periods of deep depression, a sense of emptiness, a deep sadness as he craved his brother's love and acceptance that there was nothing he could have done to prevent the outcome of that terrible fiery day so many years ago.

There is a saying that "coincidences are God's way of being anonymous." In Robert and George's case, divine anonymity seems to have brought a kind of miracle. George's son, Michael, and Robert's son, Raphael, born several years after the fire, met "coincidentally" on a Birthright Trip[10] to Israel. Seeing that they had the same unusual surname, they began to share their

---

10. The Taglit-Birthright trips to Israel offers free ten-day trips to Israel in an effort to strengthen young diaspora Jews' connection to the State of Israel.

family history and somehow discovered that they were first cousins. Bits and pieces of what each knew about the fraternal estrangement tumbled forth. The cousins resolved to bring their fathers together—to try to heal the rift and to try to bring forgiveness and love back to the family.

A long process ensued—stubborn refusals to meet, tears, shouting—but finally, after so very long, the brothers agreed to meet in the presence of their sons and their wives (Judy had long ago let go of her anger toward George and Michelle), and a rabbi they all trusted. Once again, "coincidence" played a part: the brothers lived in adjoining towns and were acquainted with one rabbi they each admired, respected, and trusted. Ultimately, Robert acknowledged that his rage and anger was destroying him, that he yearned for George's love and that in his heart of hearts he knew that George and Michelle could not have saved the children. And George admitted that he had lived for these decades with a deep sense of guilt even though he knew in his rational mind that he could have done no more than what he had attempted. He, too, said that he yearned for Robert's love. The brothers embraced—and a profound healing began that day. A family was restored and peace returned after years of painful struggle.

Exploring the Text Within

Find a quiet and comfortable place to sit in contemplative silence with the above teachings and with the following questions about you and your life's experience. You may choose to focus on one question or sit with several. Ask yourself: what do the biblical text and these teachings mean to me in my life?

> So Jacob drew close to his father Isaac, who felt him and wondered, "The voice is the voice of Jacob, yet the hands are the hands of Esau."
>
> (Genesis 27:22)

Have I ever spoken in a voice that was not my own?

Have I, even metaphorically, pretended to be someone I am not in order to attain something I yearned for?

[Esau said:] *"Have you not reserved a blessing for me?"*

(Genesis 27:36)

Have I ever longed for the love and blessing of someone I loved deeply but the blessing came too little, too late?

How did I fill that empty place in my heart?

Let the mourning period of my father come, and I will kill my brother Jacob.

(Genesis 27:41)

Have I ever been so angry and hurt that I have vowed revenge?

How has that anger affected me?

Do I still hold that anger or have I really learned to let it go?

Chapter 12

Vayeitzei I

Awakening

*"Surely God is in this place,
and I, i did not know it!"*[1]

—Genesis 28:10–18

Finding Our "Place"—Makom

The family intrigue unfolds; Jacob has taken Esau's birthright from him for a bowl of red lentil soup, and he has received Isaac's innermost birthright blessing. As described in the preceding chapter, Esau is profoundly hurt by Jacob, is angry and seeks revenge, vowing to kill his younger twin.

Hearing from his mother Rebecca of Esau's threat, Jacob now fearing for his life, flees. A refugee from his brother's jealousy, pain, and wrath, Jacob is an exile from his father's house. He is homeless. He is a man with no place.

> *Jacob left Beer Sheba, and set out for Haran. He came upon a certain place and stopped there for the night, for the sun had set. Taking one of the stones of that place, he put it under his head and lay down in that place.*
>
> *He had a dream; a stairway was set on the ground and its top reached to the sky, and angels of God were going up and down on it. And the* LORD *was standing beside him and He said, "I am the* LORD, *God of your father Abraham and the God of Isaac: the ground on which you are lying I will assign to you and your offspring. Your descendants shall be as the dust of the earth; you shall spread out to the west and to the east, to the north and*

---

1. This translation is taken from Rabbi Lawrence Kushner's book of the same name.

> *to the south. All the families of the earth shall bless themselves by you and your descendants. Remember, I am with you: I will protect you wherever you go and will bring you back to this land. I will not leave you until I have done what I have promised you."*
> *Jacob woke from his sleep and said: "Surely, God is in this place and I, i did not know it!" Shaken, he said, "How awesome is this place! This is none other than the abode of God, and this is the gateway to heaven."*
>
> *Early in the morning, Jacob took the stone that he had put under his head and set it up as a pillar under his head and set it up as a pillar and poured oil on the top of it. He named that place Bethel.*
>
> —Genesis 28:10–19

The word "place" is repeated six times in this very short vignette, which spans only ten verses of the biblical text. It is clearly very important—for Torah repeats specific words only when it wants to draw our attention to them. The Hebrew word for "place" is *makom*, a word rich with meaning. Its plain meaning simply denotes a location—but there is much more to this word. *Makom* also means God! In Jewish tradition, when someone has died, the mourner is comforted with the words, "*Ha-Makom y'nachem . . .*" "May God [or literally, "the Place"] comfort you along with all those who mourn . . . ," indicating that God is the "place" of the *whole* world! So this comforting phrase thus means—God is everywhere, encompassing the whole universe, so may you be comforted everywhere you go, in all places.

Similarly, when different categories of commandments, *mitzvoth*, are divided in Judaism, they are called *mitzvoth beyn adam l'chaveróh*—commandments between one human being and another and *mitzvoth beyn adam la-Makom*—commandments between a human being and God (the "Place"). So, when we observe a commandment given by God—we are engaging in a kind of eco-adherence: the whole word is affected by our deeds, for the "place" is truly *all* places and what we do in one micro-place does indeed affect the macrocosm: we are not as insignificant as we think we are—every small deed is important in the cosmic scheme of things.

Moreover, if we study with these verses deeply, as sages of the Bible have for millennia, we might transform them into something even more profound and mystical by substituting the word "God" for "place" in some of the verses and reading this section in the following way:

- He came upon a certain GOD (*makom*/place) (28:11)
- Taking one of the stones of that GOD (*makom*/place) (28:11)

- he put it (GOD'S STONE) under his head and lay down (WITH GOD) (28:11)

- "How awesome is this GOD! (28:17)

Something amazing is happening to Jacob as he sleeps and as he awakens from his dream—and until the moment of his awakening, he is not even aware of it!

Becoming aware of God's Presence when perhaps we have never experienced this sensation before changes us in some essential way. Rabbi Simcha Zevit writes that

> *Makom* [is] a place of touching our innermost selves with all our faults and blemishes as well as our potential for greatness and finding our connection to something so much greater than ourselves, a place where we touch eternity in the present moment and feel our rightful place in the totality of God's plan.[2]

Perhaps this is what has happened to Jacob—and perhaps it can happen to each of us at sublime and extremely rare moments in our own lives.

God came to Jacob as he dreamed. For some of us, God comes in ordinary moments when we look into the face of another person, when we witness a sublime moment in nature, even when nothing special is happening. How or why this happens is a mystery (or a Mystery?). My friend and colleague, Rabbi Benjamin Shalva writes: "I suspect that God's voice works upon us the way that love works upon us. God's voice bypasses our brains and works directly through our cells. It vibrates our very atoms. If we're still and silent, listening closely . . . we might hear something. With the word, God will move us where we need to go."[3]

Let's explore further.

Angels

> *He had a dream; a stairway was set on the ground and its top reached to the sky, and angels of God were going up and down on it.*
>
> —Genesis 28:12

How odd! The angels are going *up* and down! If we imagine celestial beings at all, shouldn't it be the other way around? Shouldn't the angels *first*

---

2. Rabbi Simcha Zevit, unpublished commentary on *Parashat Vayetzeh*.
3. Shalva, *Spiritual Cross Training*, 41.

be coming down the stairway, and *then* be going up? Why is the order reversed? Why do the angels start on earth and only then ascend to heaven? Interpretations abound. Here are just a few:

(1) In one of the commentaries in the ancient collection of Leviticus Rabbah, the angels are said to have symbolized the rulers of many nations surrounding Jacob's people, who were destined, in the course of future history, to ascend to power and vanquish Israel and rule her for a period of time and ultimately descend from power. The message was that in the end of all these trials and tribulations, Israel would never be destroyed. This *midrash* is a way of giving hope to the Jews of antiquity who repeatedly found themselves as a subjugated people under the might of foreign rulers:

> Said Rabbi Samuel bar Nachman: Is it possible that these were the ministering angels [whose job it is to serve before God in heaven]?
>
> Were they not instead the guardian angels of the nations of the world [that would rule Israel in the future?]. He [God] showed him [Jacob] Babylon's angel climbing up seventy rungs and going down again.
>
> Then he showed him Media's angel going up and down fifty-two and then Greece's going up and down one hundred and eighty. Then Rome's went up and up and he [Jacob] did not know how many [rungs it would ascend].[4] Jacob took fright at this and said, "Oh LORD, do you mean that this one has no descent?" God said to him: "Even if you see him reach the very heavens, I will still cause him to go down, as it is written, 'Though you soar aloft like an eagle, though your nest is set among the stars, from there will I bring you down, says the LORD.'" [Obadiah 1:4].[5]

(2) In the first century C.E., Philo, a Jewish philosopher from Alexandria, Egypt, suggested that the "stairway" or ladder symbolized Jacob's or his descendants' futures: "The affairs of men are by their very nature comparable to a ladder because of their irregular course. For a single day . . . can carry [a] person set on high downward and lift someone else upward, for it is in the nature of none of us to remain in the same circumstances, but rather to undergo all manner of changes. . . . So the path of human affairs goes up and down, subjected to unstable and shifting happenstance."[6]

---

4. This *midrash*, written after the Roman Empire's conquest of the Land of Israel, the destruction of the Second Temple in 70 C.E., and the expulsion of the Jewish people, which brought with it the beginning of the long diaspora of the Jews from the Land of Israel, reflects the Jews' fears that Roman rule would never end.

5. Leviticus Rabbah 29:2.

6. Philo, *On Dreams*, 1:150. 153–56 quoted in Kugel, *The Bible as It Was*, 211–12.

How true this is for all of us—the circumstances of our lives change from day to day. The believers among us sense that as changes occur in our lives, we are visited by "angels"—not celestial, cherubic, winged creatures, but messengers from the Divine who come to us as insights ("in-sights") that assist in navigating the vagaries of life. Thus, the syntax is important in the sentence about angels ascending and descending the ladder next to which Jacob falls asleep—*these* angels *are right here with us on earth* to offer us deeper understandings, and clearer perceptions about our lives. As we ourselves experience the "ups and downs" of life, the angels are there to guide us and to help us live our lives in the best possible way.

In his interpretation of the angels ascending to heaven and then coming back down to earth to help us lead our ordinary lives, Philo is addressing our most prosaic existence—the angels are instruments to guide us in the most mundane parts of living.

(3) Rabbi Samson Raphael Hirsch, a nineteenth-century German commentator, sees the angels' ascent and descent from a much loftier perspective. He understands the angels' ascent to heaven as a kind of exploratory mission: they are hoping to receive God's guidance as what kind of man Jacob should become (perhaps fulfilling his father Isaac's hopes and prayers) when he awakens from his dream. Rabbi Hirsch writes: "the fate of men is not made on earth by the material world . . . these messengers of God [the angels] go up the ladder to get a picture of ideal humanity, how human beings really should be, and then come down and compare what they find here below."[7]

Rabbi Hirsch quotes the Babylonian Talmud[8] that "they [the angels] ascended and saw a picture depicted of him [Jacob] above, and came down and considered the picture he actually made here below." What the angels saw was that above in the heavens, Jacob was glorifying God and that below on earth, he was simply sleeping, with his head using the stone of the "place" as a pillow. The *midrash* goes on to say that Jacob's mind "should have been awakened" to "thoughts of his glorious mission" which, was, of course, to glorify God.[9] It is this exact moment that Jacob awakens from his dream and speaks the key words: *"Surely God is in this place, and I, i did not know it!"* (28:10–18).

It is almost as if Jacob's elderly father Isaac's hopes, prayers, and vision for his son are coming to fruition at this very moment, when the angels (seeing in the heavens a vision of Jacob glorifying God), descend

---

7. Hirsch in *The Pentateuch: Translation and Commentary,* 459.
8. Babylonian Talmud, *Chullin,* 91b.
9. Hirsch in *The Pentateuch: Translation and Commentary,* 459.

from the heavenly stairway, and wake Jacob up—both physically and spiritually—and Jacob becomes a new man, filled with an awareness of God's Presence, and an understanding of his own lack of awareness of God until this very moment. It is as if the more profound blindness has been revealed here—the old man Isaac, though physically blind, *knew* which son he was blessing when he offered his innermost blessing—it was no mistake; he gave the blessing to his spiritually blind son, Jacob. And only a short while, as Jacob sleeps, alone in that "Place," in that *God-Place (Makom)*, Jacob awakes, now finally able to *see*—the pall of blindness has been lifted and he is able to say, "Surely God is in this place, and I, i did not know it!" Now, Jacob is able to glorify God and embody the angels' vision. Now, he is able to move forward on his life's mission.

Clarity is coming to Jacob—the kind of clarity that comes to many of us, if we are lucky, perhaps once in a lifetime, when the veil of obscurity, confusion, and lack of awareness lifts for us and we *know* who we are, where we stand, and in what direction we must travel. This clarity comes not from a purely intellectual place, but from a Place/*Makom*/God deep, deep inside us. I repeat Rabbi Benjamin Shalva's words: "God's voice bypasses our brains and works directly through our cells. It vibrates our very atoms. If we're still and silent, listening closely . . . we might hear something. With the word, God will move us where we need to go."[10]

How rich is the angel imagery of this seemingly simple story! From the political perspective of an ancient rabbinic *midrash* (Leviticus Rabbah) to a first-century Hellenistic-Jewish theologian's commentary on the "ups and downs" of daily life (Philo) to a nineteenth-century German rabbi's evocation of the celestial angels' vision of Jacob's adoration of the Divine Presence, we have already traveled a long way in understanding that many angels dance on the head of our spiritual pins! And yet there is more.

In the early twentieth century, Rabbi Zalman Sorotzkin, who survived the Holocaust and died in 1966 in Israel, wrote that the angels' ascent into heaven (before they returned to earth) was a way of first taking human beings' prayers to God and *then* returning to earth to take up new prayers to the Holy One. Indeed, according to Rabbi Sorotzkin, the angels were messengers—but they were mortals' servants first and then perhaps they served God second. Human yearnings were so important to God, Sorotzkin asserted, that the Holy One, provided a "messenger service" to bring our thoughts and the longings of our hearts upwards into the celestial realms![11]

---

10. Shalva, *Spiritual Cross Training*, 41.

11. Rabbi Zalman Sorotzkin, discussed by Rabbi Morrison Bial in an excerpt from a Torah commentary (*d'var Torah*) on *Vayeitzei* in Person, ed., *Voices of Torah*, 79.

For the believers amongst us, it is comforting to think that perhaps such a delivery service exists! For those of us who do not believe or envision in such a way, perhaps the notion that there *might* be a listening deity may be enough. And for those of us who cannot accommodate Rabbi Sorotzkin's view—I would offer his idea as a metaphorical advocacy of simple *kindness*. The angels, whether they exist or not, might be imagined as an energy flow of lovingkindness—reaching out to us in love when we need that energy flow, seeking to know and understand what it is that we need and desire. I imagine that this energy flow might come in the form of a real-life human being, a gentle person, who simply says to us when we are most vulnerable, "I care about you. What do you need? How can I help?"

(4) And this leads me to my own sense of what an "angel" might be. For me, angels can be gentle and angels can be challenging. There are angels we dance with and angels we wrestle with. These angels can be the people who are most loving and caring to us—the ones who sit with us by hospital beds when we are ill and weak, or hold our hands, or stroke our heads when we are most in need of comfort and solace. They are the angels who touch our hearts and our souls and who remind us how precious we are, how loved, how cherished. Sometimes such angels can save a person's life. I wonder if there has been an angel in your life that made all the difference for you at any point in your life.

There are also angels in our lives who present us with life's greatest challenges. They are the thorns in our sides: the child who is rebellious, who cannot help her or his rebellion, but who screams out in pain "I hate you," when we try to offer discipline, who defies all order in a household, who is caught up in behaviors they don't want but cannot stop.

There is the terrible angel of an abusive spouse or life-partner, who, caught up in their own pain, lashes out and hurts others.

There is the awful angel of an addicted family member, who is enmeshed in actions they cannot control.

There is the tortured angel of a mentally ill relative or dear friend, one with an unquiet mind, beset by demons which dominate their world.[12]

There are the "angels" who are caught up in conflicts that seem completely unsolvable, trapped in anger and pain stemming from family dysfunction going back a long, long time—cycles of quarrels and words hurled in rage, arrows of venom shooting between people who love each other, but don't know how to break the cycle of conflict and enmity.

---

12. The words "unquiet mind" comes from the title of a brilliant book by Dr. Kay Redfield Jamison, a prominent psychiatrist who writes about bipolar disorder.

These angels teach us too—about learning to be patient, about trying to forgive, about trying to set aside past bitterness and finding peace and reconciliation. We wrestle mightily with these angels, sometimes for decades—and sometimes we wrestle them to the ground and are able find peace. Sometimes we are unable to find that more peaceful place of resolution and reconciliation. Then we must learn to let them go, to say goodbye to these angels and send them on their way, understanding that holding on to destructive angels does not feed the healthy places we need to go in our lives.

(5) Angels may also reflect different parts of our personality—the arrogant and the humble—and these aspects of our personality often determine how we get along in life, how we relate to other people, and how the course of our lives flows. Let's return to Jacob:

When Jacob lays down to the sleep in the *Makom* ("place") he has found for the night, and has his dream of the ladder reaching up to heaven, he falls into a deep sleep. When he awakens, as we know, he says: "Surely God is in this place, and I, i did not know it!" And as we have said, this is Jacob's crucial discovery—there is holiness in this place, this ordinary place with stones on the ground. How did Jacob come to this realization? Was it a profound dream or did a deeper transformation take place within Jacob?

As Rabbi's Lawrence Kushner and Kerry Olitzky write here, "we come to the edges of the Hebrew language itself."[13] In the Hebrew, Jacob says, "*Achen, yesh Adonai ba-makom ha-zeh v'anochi lo yadati*" (ואנכי לא ידעתי). The Hebrew word *anochi* means "I." It is a grand word. It is the word that God uses when He introduces Himself in the Ten Commandments:

Anochi Adonai Eloheicha . . . אנכי יהוה אלהיך, "I am Adonai your God, who brought you out of the land of Egypt, the house of bondage" (Exodus 20:2).

A second Hebrew word to pay attention to in this sentence is *yadati* as in *"lo yadati"*—"I did not know." Here, too, we have the first person singular pronoun, "I." So this sentence, *yesh Adonai ba-makom ha-zeh v'anochi lo yadati* literally means, *"God is in this place and I, i did not know."* Note the redundancy: "I, i, did not know." So what does this redundancy signify?

A nineteenth-century Hassidic rabbi named Shlomo of Radomsk suggests that what has happened to Jacob in his sleep is an obliteration of the ego, a kind of contraction of those parts of Jacob that made him previously unable to recognize the Presence of God (indeed the Presence of God in other people, like his brother Esau, his father Isaac, and others), and that when he awoke, he was a much more humble man, now able to "leave space" within his heart, mind, and soul for others. Here are Rabbi Shlomo's words:

---

13. Kushner and Olitzky, *Sparks Beneath the Surface*, 34.

If the presence of the Holy One indeed dwells here, if I have invoked the holiness in this place, it must be because *my I, i did not know*. I obliterated everything that was in me; my sense of self-awareness; any consciousness of ego; any trace of self-intention.[14]

Has this ever happened to you? Have you ever been in a state of mind, heart, or soul when you have been so self-centered that you were unable to make space in your mind or heart for other people or God? This is what Rabbi Shlomo is saying about Jacob. The rabbi is suggesting that somehow, in that dark, lonely night as Jacob was fleeing from Esau, as he lay down to sleep with a stone as his pillow, he came to realize (within his dream), that God is everywhere and that God also resides within other human beings. This transformed his life for the future. I know from my own personal experience that when we make room for others—for their feelings, their hopes, their dreams, their perspectives, our own lives are immeasurably deepened and enriched—and the texture of our relationships is finer, stronger, and more splendid.

Text to Life

> Shirley was my high school English teacher. I arrived to her class a lonely teenager with a dark view of life. I believed that I was "dust and ashes," but Shirley saw my divine spark—the light behind the outer darkness. She discerned my gift for words, a talent for poetry and drama, and she lifted me up, inviting me to join in—in the poetry and drama clubs, the school play, in long conversations about life and love. Shirley made me feel as if I mattered in the world—as if "the world were indeed created just for me." For all the tumultuous years of high school had it not been for my "angel" Shirley, I am not sure I would have made it through. My angel guided me. She taught me about love, about compassion, about humor, and about self-esteem. I am eternally grateful for that guidance, and I have tried to follow Shirley's way in relating to other people of all ages—with kindness and respect.
>
> LGB

---

14. Kushner and Olitzky, *Sparks Beneath the Surface*, 34. Italics added.

Exploring the Text Within

Find a quiet and comfortable place to sit in contemplative silence with the above teachings and with the following questions about you and your life's experience. You may choose to focus on one question or sit with several. Ask yourself: what do the biblical text and these teachings mean to me in my life?

> Makom [is] a place of touching our innermost selves with all our faults and blemishes as well as our potential for greatness and finding our connection to something so much greater than ourselves, a place where we touch eternity in the present moment and feel our rightful place in the totality of God's plan.
>
> —Rabbi Simcha Zevit

What is my most sacred and safest *Makom*?

> *Surely, God is in this place, and I, i did not know it!*

Clarity comes to Jacob—the kind of clarity that comes to many of us, if we are lucky, perhaps once in a lifetime, when the veil of obscurity, confusion, lack of awareness lifts for us and we *know* who we are, where we stand and in what direction we must travel."

> *... a stairway was set on the ground and its top reached to the sky; and angels of God were going up and down on it.*
> (Genesis 28:12)

Who are the "angels" in my life?

With which ones do I dance?

With which ones do I struggle?

> *I obliterated everything that was in me; my sense of self-awareness; any consciousness of ego; any trace of self-intention....*
>
> —Rabbi Shlomo of Randomsk

> Has there been a time in my life when I have been so self-centered that I could not find space for other people or God?
>
> Has there been a time when I simply had to get out of my own way in order to come back into relationship with God or other human beings?

Chapter 13

Vayeitzei II

Two Sisters

"Now Laban had two daughters: the name of the older one was Leah, and the name of the younger was Rachel. Leah had weak eyes; Rachel was shapely and beautiful. Jacob loved Rachel...."

—Genesis 29:16–18

"The saddest thing is to be a minute to someone, when you've made them your eternity."

—Sanober Khan[1]

Our story continues with the connective tissue of Jacob's lineage. Here we are introduced to two sisters—Rachel and Leah—who will both become Jacob's wives. Along with two maidservants, Bilhah and Zilpah, they will become the mothers of Jacob's twelves sons, who in later Jewish tradition, comprise the "twelve tribes of Israel."

Here we pause to reflect on Jacob's sojourn with Laban and his two daughters, his marriage, first to the elder daughter, Leah, and then to the beloved of Jacob's heart, Rachel. When Jacob arrived in Haran, the land where his uncle Laban lived, he came to water his flocks at the local well. Inquiring from the people gathered there if they knew "Laban, the son of Nahor," they answered, *"yes we do, . . . and there is his daughter Rachel, coming with the flock"* (29:4–6).

---

1. Twentieth-century Indian poet.

Jacob was powerfully attracted to Rachel when he first saw her. Approaching Rachel and rolling the stone away to open the well, for the flocks to be watered, *"Jacob [then] kissed Rachel and broke into tears"* (29:11)

What an unusually emotional reaction to a cousin he has met for the first time! The ancient sages, with their fertile imagination, want to know whether Jacob has been smitten with "love at first sight," whether, in Jerry Rabow's words, his kiss was "just a kiss or was this a *kiss*?"[2] It would seem to me, as events unfold, that Jacob is indeed in love with Rachel from the moment he meets her, so in love, in fact, that he is willing to work for her father Laban for seven years to gain her hand in marriage, as Laban demands of him.[3]

Soon we learn more about Rachel's family. Laban, Rachel's father, comes to welcome Jacob, embracing and kissing him and saying to him, *"You are truly my bone and flesh"* (Gen 29:14). Then, Jacob is introduced to Rachel's sister, Leah: *"Now Laban had two daughters; the name of the older one was Leah and the name of the young was Rachel. Leah had weak*[4] *eyes; Rachel was shapely and beautiful. Jacob loved Rachel"* (29:16–18).

Rabbis over the ages have had a lot to say about Leah's eyes. Some have translated the Hebrew words עינים רכות / *eynayim rakot* as weak, dim, or lifeless eyes, as if to suggest that because of her eyes, Leah appeared simple-minded, dull, and unattractive, perhaps justifying Jacob's lack of attraction to her. Rabbi Chayim ben Attar, an eighteenth-century Moroccan rabbi, reflecting many other earlier rabbis' views, has written: "Leah was not only not as beautiful as her sister Rachel, but she suffered from a blemish, i.e., her eyes were not attractive."[5] Others, like Rabbi Samson Raphael Hirsch in the nineteenth century, have interpreted *eynayim rakot* as "soft and tender" eyes,[6] suggesting that Leah was indeed a kind, loving, lovely, and tender woman, worthy of Jacob's love. *Targum Onkelos,* a first/second century C.E. Aramaic translation and commentary on the Torah, notes that Leah's eyes were "lovely."[7] *Midrash Rabbah* (according to Rabbi Yohanan) suggests that Leah's eyes are "weak" because "this was the arrangement; the elder daughter [Leah] is for the elder son [Esau], and the younger daughter [Rachel] is

---

2. For a detailed discussion of Jacob's kiss and feelings toward Rachel at their moment of meeting, see Rabow, *The Lost Matriarch,* 17–20.

3. In general, romantic love is not something we see in the Bible, yet clearly it is present in the story of Jacob and Rachel. See Rabow, *The Lost Matriarch,* 13, for a discussion of this topic. Rabow cites several sources about the history of romantic love in footnotes 1 and 5 for chapter 1 on p. 204.

4. See Rabow's discussion in *The Lost Matriarch,* 31–34.

5. Chayim ben Attar, *Or Hachayim—Vayetze,* 29:16, 248.

6. Samson Raphael Hirsch, in *The Pentateuch,* vol. 1, 470.

7. See citation in Rabow, *The Lost Matriarch,* 207, footnote 32.

for the younger son [Jacob], while she used to weep and pray, 'May it be Thy will that I do not fall to the lot of that wicked man.'"[8]

When Jacob arrived at Laban's homestead, and it became apparent that a marriage was in the offing, perhaps Leah's "weak eyes" brightened with the hope that it would be she, as the elder, who would marry Jacob and she would avoid her terrible fate, of being compelled to marry Esau. Indeed, Leah's prayer was fulfilled, as things turned out, for, as Rav Huna, an ancient sage, wrote, "Great is prayer, that it annulled the decree [that she would marry Esau] and she even took precedence over her sister."[9]

Why would the quality of Leah's eyes matter? Perhaps they marked the sharp contrast between her and the *beautiful* Rachel. There is an echo here back to the story of Jacob and his elderly and blind father Isaac. Isaac's eyes are "dim" too—and he is taken advantage of by Jacob. In our story, we shall see that Jacob is the one who will be both an exploiter and the one who is taken advantage of. Continue reading and you will see how the plot thickens as the story unfolds!

Laban, who may not be as prosperous as he pretends to be,[10] demands that Jacob work for him while he sojourns with him. When Laban discovers that Jacob wants to marry Rachel, he requires seven years of labor before the younger man will be permitted to marry Rachel.

Already, we have a problem. As we have seen in the story of Jacob and Esau, the law and custom of primogeniture (in which the eldest child inherits first and also marries first), it is Leah, the older sister, who should marry first. Jacob's love for, and desire to marry Rachel is highly problematic, violating the customs and culture of his day—he wants to marry Laban's *younger* daughter, while ignoring the elder. How ironic that Jacob is playing out again the same drama that he orchestrated in his own household with his father Isaac by stealing the birthright and blessing of his older brother Esau! He seems to have learned nothing from his actions. Here he goes again, wanting what he wants regardless of the social rules of his time and place. Laban sets strict terms for Jacob, requiring that Jacob work for seven years before he will be allowed to marry Rachel. Jacob agreed—"*So Jacob served seven years for Rachel and they seemed to him, but a few days because of his love for her*" (29:20).

Finally, with the wedding night approaching, Jacob is filled with eager anticipation. Laban (never intending to marry off Rachel the younger first)

8. Midrash Rabbah Bereishit, 70:16.
9. Midrash Rabbah Bereishit, 70:16.
10. See Rabow, *The Lost Matriarch*, 26 where he comments that "midrash portrays a desperate Laban who has lost most of his wealth to drought and who is now consumed with how he can profit from Jacob's arrival."

makes plans to trick Jacob into marrying Leah, his elder daughter. Here, as in a contemporary soap opera, the machinations reach their height:

After the wedding feast, preceding the night of consummation of the marriage, unbeknownst to Jacob,

> *Laban took his daughter and brought her to him* [Jacob]. . . . [It is dark and Jacob cannot see the face of his bride.] *When morning came, there was Leah! So he* [Jacob] *said to Laban, "What is this you have done to me? I was in your service for Rachel! Why did you deceive me?"* [Laban answers:] *"It is not the practice in our place to marry off the younger sister before the older. Wait until the bridal week of this one is over and we will give you that one too, provided you serve me another seven years."*
>
> —Genesis 29:23, 26–27

(Notice how Laban refers to his daughters as "this one" and "that one." He doesn't even use their names! They are merely objects to him—ways to enrich himself via Jacob's labor. So Jacob serves Laban for an additional seven years to earn his marriage to his beloved Rachel.

How could this ruse have happened? How could Jacob have been so brazenly duped?

A fanciful midrash explains that Jacob could not see his bride because "In the evening, having led the bride into the nuptial chamber, the ushers put out the lamps." When Jacob asks why they were extinguishing the lamps, the ushers responded, "What do you think—that we are as shameless as you?"[11] (In biblical time, marriages were not consummated in a lit space.)[12]

Midrash also tells us that though Rachel loved Jacob very much, she could not in good conscience cause her sister Leah to suffer, and so she helped Leah to fool Jacob into believing that he was making love to her on his wedding night: ". . . when the wedding night came, Rachel said to herself: 'Now my sister will be humiliated [if I, Rachel, am married first], so she turned over her tokens [which identified the wearer as Rachel] to her sister, Leah.'"[13]

Another midrash tells this story in more elaborate detail: "And not only so, but I crawled under the bed on which he was lying with my sister [Leah], while she remained silent, and I made all the replies so that he would not discern the voice of my sister. I paid my sister only kindness, and

---

11. Bialik and Ravnitzky, *The Book of Legends (Sefer Ha-Aggadah)*, 47. No. 72.
12. Bialik and Ravnitzky, *The Book of Legends (Sefer Ha-Aggadah)*, note no. 6.
13. Bialik and Ravnitzky, *The Book of Legends (Sefer Ha-Aggadah)*, no. 71.

I was not jealous of her and I did not allow her to be shamed."[14] Rachel's midrashic loyalty to her sister Leah is beautiful, but not all loyalties should be binding when they conflict with one's own well-being.

Thus Rachel acted in the most loving way toward Leah, protecting her dignity and sacrificing her own happiness temporarily as she gives up her own chance to marry Jacob first.

When confronted by Jacob about the deception, the midrash offers Rachel a response in which she teaches her future husband a deep moral lesson about the consequences of one's actions, reminding him that he himself was a trickster, in stealing his older brother Esau's birthright and in deceiving his own old and blind father Isaac into giving Jacob his innermost birthright blessing, instead of to Esau (to whom, according to custom, it rightfully belonged). Rachel is reminding Jacob that he is getting his "just desserts" for his own deception.[15]

Thus, Jacob and Leah's marriage begins—a bitter union of a loving wife and a resentful, unloving husband. In the words of Indian poet Sanober Khan, Leah had made Jacob her *eternity*. Jacob, on the other hand, thought about Leah as a *minute*.

In vain, Leah craves Jacob's affection, hoping that if she does her conjugal duty, and gives birth to sons, her husband will come to appreciate and love her. Indeed, Torah tells us that God gives Leah special fertility, as a consolation gift and a pathway to Jacob's love: *"The LORD saw that Leah was unloved and he opened her womb . . ."* (29:31).[16]

As each son is born, Leah gives him a name that poignantly expresses her deep yearning for Jacob's love:

Leah and Jacob's first-born is Reuben—ראובן, which in Hebrew means, "Look! A son!"[17] Imagine Leah holding up her baby boy and saying to Jacob, "Look! I have borne you a son! Now will you love me?" A second interpretation of the baby's name is *"ra'ah . . . b'onyi*—"the LORD has seen my affliction," with Leah's thought being, *"Now my husband will love me* (ye'ehavni)."[18] "It appears that there is no change in Jacob's feelings.

---

14. Midrash Rabbah, Lamentations, Prologue 24, translated by Jerry Rabow, *The Lost Matriarch*, 55.

15. Bialik and Ravnitzky, *The Book of Legends (Sefer Ha-Aggadah)*, 47, no. 71.

16. Note that the Hebrew word that is translated into English as "unloved" by the JPS TaNaKH is actually שנואה, which means "hated." On this verse, *Midrash Rabbah Bereishit* 71:1 quotes Psalm 69:34: "For the LORD listens to the needy."

17 Genesis 29:32 On Reuben and Simeon's names, see *Midrash Rabbah Bereishit*, 72:3.

18. Rabbi Shai Held, in *The Heart of Torah*, vol. 1: *Essays on the Weekly Torah Portion: Genesis and Exodus*, 61.

A second son is born to Leah—Simeon—שמעון—coming from the Hebrew word, לשמע, "to hear."[19] Is Leah perhaps beseeching Jacob, "Can you hear me? Can you listen to the stirrings of my heart for you?"

Then Leah bears a third son—Levi—לוי—which means "joined to/attached/bound to."[20] Is Leah pleading with Jacob: "Please, dear one, bind yourself to me as my husband!" Rabbi Shai Held observes that Leah's hopes are diminishing: "Notice that when her first son was born, she had the temerity to hope that his arrival would elicit Jacob's 'love'; by the time the third is born, it seems she would settle for her husband's 'attachment.'"[21] There is still no change in Jacob. He is far from connected to Leah; and may be even more alienated, now that at least three years have gone by since the wedding, three years in which he has used Leah as a sexual object, siring sons without growing an emotional attachment to his wife. Rabbi Held comments poignantly, "By this point the reader is ready to cry for her."[22]

Then comes Leah's fourth son—Judah—יהודה—meaning "to praise or be thankful."[23] We might wonder if Leah is asking Jacob if he is thankful to her for bearing him four healthy sons!

It is interesting to note that all Jews are called *Yehudim*, not because we come from the Land of Judea alone, but because we are descendants of Judah, and should cultivate an "attitude of gratitude"—thanksgiving and appreciation for all God's blessings.

Note that when Leah speaks of the birth of her fourth son, Judah, she says, "הפעם—*this time—'I will praise the* LORD'" (29:36). There seems to be a shift in Leah's attitude from yearning to acceptance and, finally, even to gratitude. I myself am grateful to Rabbis Shai Held and Jill Hammer for helping me to understand Leah's gradual shift here. She moves her emotions away from Jacob and now, with the birth of Judah, comes to offers thankfulness for Judah and her previous sons. Now, she can live a more contented life. In Rabbi Held's words, "she sees that this constant yearning [for Jacob's love] will only generate more fantasy and illusion. . . . A new acceptance develops for Leah and, rather than sinking in the sorrow of what she does not have, she becomes able to embrace the beauty and fullness of what she does"[24]—being a mother to four beautiful sons.

Rabbi Jill Hammer points out that in Kabbalah (Jewish mysticism):

19. Genesis 29:33.
20. Genesis 29:34.
21. Rabbi Shai Held, in *The Heart of Torah*, vol. 1, 61.
22. Rabbi Shai Held, in *The Heart of Torah*, vol. 1, 61.
23. Genesis 29:35.
24. Held, *The Heart of Torah*, vol. 1, 62.

Leah represents the "upper mother," Binah, the divine womb from which life and understanding flow. She represents *malkhut shebegevurah*, majesty within strength, because in spite of the painful reality of living with a jealous sister and a man who does not love her, Leah finds the dignity of praise and gratitude. We are most like Leah when we are able to live not only for those we want to love us, but for ourselves and for God.[25]

Then she stops bearing children (30:35), realizing that she is now in competition with Rachel, Leah offers her concubine, Zilpah, to Jacob. Zilpah bears a son whom Leah names Gad—גד, which means "happy," "lucky" [or] "fortunate." It almost feels as if Leah is still in the process of trying to will herself into the emotional state of gratitude.

This is reaffirmed when Zilpah bears a final son for Leah named Asher—אשר, which means "beloved," "fortunate," or "happy." A part of Leah still longs to be Jacob's beloved and to be fortunate enough to find happiness with him!

Leah has done everything right. Jerry Rabow writes:

> [Leah's] ultimate victory can be found in the model that she offers us of moral heroism in the face of adversity. Her most important lesson to us is that even harsh unfair challenges need not automatically call forth equally harsh and unfair responses.[26]

Rather than become entirely embittered and vindictive toward Jacob and Rachel, Leah lives a good (if emotionally unfulfilled) life. She has been a faithful and fertile wife to Jacob, and has lived a loyal and moral life, parenting her children while in a loveless marriage, with little to no support from her husband, and she has raised her children to take on the responsibilities of manhood. Leah is indeed an *eshet chayil*, a woman of valor, a strong woman who finds a way to live while, despite great obstacles, making of her life a positive work-in-progress. And life goes on.

Text to Life

> George, a pastor in a nearby church, told me about his experience with two sets of friends, which reminded him of the plight of the unloved Leah: "We were friends with a fellow pastor and his wife. My wife and I knew them quite well and we considered them

---

25. Hammer, *Omer Calendar for Biblical Women*, 24.
26. Rabow, *The Lost Matriarch*, 188.

friends. We knew their children and we shared a number of times together as couples and with our families. After years of marriage, the husband suddenly announced to his wife that he wanted a divorce. He claimed that he was very dissatisfied with their married life and wanted to be freed from their marriage relationship. Asked if there were another who had caught his affection, he denied it to be so. She was devastated and blind-sided by this, as she had spent her adult life with him, together raising a family and being significantly involved in his ministry."

Eventually they were divorced, much to the wife's distress and feelings of emptiness and abandonment. She felt especially hurt by his claim that he had never really loved her. It was hard for her to believe and it certainly had never been apparent to those who knew them both. Eventually it became clear that there was another to whom he had been drawn and was romantically involved. They were married and the first wife was left to reorder her present and future life without him. There were difficult times for her, but she had strong support systems that helped her through. She developed a career of her own, which she had not done prior to the divorce, and she managed well for herself without him. She never remarried but seems to be doing well. There has never been any real mending in the broken relationship in years since the divorce. The quote seems especially applicable in this case—he was her "eternity" and she was his "minute".

Sadly, there was a second friend and colleague who went through a similar scenario. We knew them and their family for several years and had friendly interactions with them as we were able when they were close by. Some years later, having moved family and ministry to a place more distant, we considered them friends, but we still had limited times to be able to be with them. The husband (a pastor also) declared that he needed to be free of his marriage obligation. It was not her choice and she too found the divorce very difficult. He too was then married to another woman, with whom it seemed clear that he had been involved with for some time prior to the divorce. His first wife needed significant counseling to help her deal with the change that had come in her life. Their children were older and on their own before the divorce, but they continued to provide good support for her as they were able. In this case, the husband and new wife did have a continued relationship with his family and eventually there was some mending and healing from the deep pain to a more cordial relationship in the extended family.

In both cases the divorced wives had invested their lives with their husbands in what they hoped would be happy and life-long commitments that they had covenanted together, but which were torn apart by the withdrawal of their partner. Feelings of abandonment, uncertainty about the future, bitter disappointment, and rejection must have truly been part of their inner experience. Neither of the women has remarried.

My wife and I too were impacted emotionally by these events and have had very little contact with the former husbands, which is reflective of our own difficulty in resolving feelings about the events that took place years ago. In each case, the first wives, who highly valued their relationships, were not valued as highly by their spouses, who found something in another. It seems tragic that one can live for a lifetime and love someone as if that person is their "eternity" and the other person thinks of them only as their "minute."

Exploring the Text Within

Find a quiet and comfortable place to sit in contemplative silence with the above teachings and with the following questions about you and your life's experience. You may choose to focus on one question or sit with several. Ask yourself: what do the biblical text and these teachings mean to me in my life?

> the saddest thing is to be
>
> a minute to someone,
>
> when you've made them your eternity.
>
> —Sanober Khan[27]

> Who have been the "eternities" in my life?
>
> A parent? A sibling? A lover?
>
> Was there ever a time in my life when I felt that any of these people considered me as if I were a "minute"?

---

27. A twentieth-century Indian poet.

Leah had weak eyes.

(Genesis 29:17)

> Leah's eyes caused her to be unloved.
>
> Have I ever felt that I have been unloved or ignored because of my physical appearance or other qualities beyond my control?
>
> Despite emotional obstacles in my life, how am I doing in creating a good life for myself?

She [Leah] conceived again and bore a son, and declared, "This time, I will praise the LORD."

(Genesis 29:35)

> Has there ever been a time when my own emotions have shifted from yearning towards gratitude, from sadness because of what I *don't* have to appreciation for what I *do* have?
>
> How has that shift in emotions and attitude affected my life?

Chapter 14

Vayishlach I

God Wrestling and Reunion

> "Jacob was left alone. And a man wrestled with him until the break of dawn."
>
> —Genesis 32:23–33 (Vayishlach 1)

As Leah raises her children, Jacob continues his time of service to his uncle Laban, to complete his "payment" for being given his beloved Rachel. Finally, after seven more years of labor, Jacob is free to marry Rachel and move on, to return to the land of his father Isaac. Through a ceremonial act of release, Laban and Jacob agree that Jacob may leave with his family. As any father might, Laban warns Jacob to treat his daughters well— *"May the* LORD *watch between you and me, when we are out of sight of each other. If you ill-treat my daughters—though no one else be about, remember, God Himself will be witness between you and me"* (31:49–50). So, *"early in the morning, Laban kissed his daughters and bade them goodbye . . ."* (32:1). Jacob and his caravan, wives, children, servants, and livestock begin the long journey southward.

Twenty years have passed since Jacob has seen his brother Esau, two decades since he stole his brother's birthright and cheated Esau out of their father's innermost birthright blessing. As we shall see in observing Jacob's evolution, Jacob has matured and has come to some understanding of the self-centeredness of his youthful actions. Far less egotistical and arrogant now, he understands how much distress he brought to Esau. Jacob is now remorseful and emotionally ready to seek forgiveness from Esau for his youthful behavior. As he and his family, servants, and livestock leave Laban's territory, Jacob encounters angels of God who guide him to a place that he recognizes as *"God's camp"* (32:2). Jacob's experience of God's Presence has grown immeasurably since his youth; he believes in angels—whether they come in the guise of humans or instincts or strong intuitions—and believes that these angels can guide him to the place where he must be. Jacob now has a moral compass.

As a young man, Jacob showed no sense of a moral conscience. But after he fled his home to escape Esau's wrath, he experienced a profound spiritual moment when he dreamed of a ladder ascending to heaven and angels of God were ascending and descending on it. Waking from his dream, Jacob suddenly realized that *"Surely God is in this place, and I, i did not know it"* (Gen 28:16). From his "ego place" (his "I"), Jacob could not perceive the spiritual dimension of life. But he began to understand that beyond the material, there is such a dimension—and that this realm is God. As he matured during his sojourn with Laban, marriage, and fatherhood, this sense of God in his life increased. Jacob now feels guided by God's angels or by the Holy One Him/Herself.

Jacob is also gradually realizing that God is not bounded by land borders. His moral compass is God—activated everywhere and at all times. Jacob now moves in the direction that this divine compass is leading him.

As Jacob and his entourage set out on their journey from Laban's land, God promises Jacob protection and instructs him to return to his ancestral home in Canaan. Jacob sets out with confidence in God's grace and at the same time, with more than a little trepidation at seeing Esau again. Nearing Canaan, Jacob takes precautions, lest his older brother still seek revenge.

First, in advance of their encounter, he sends his servants to Esau with a message of peace. He learns that Esau *"himself is coming to meet you and there are four hundred men with him"* (32:7). Even more frightened now, Jacob divides his entourage and property into two camps, thinking *"If Esau comes to the one camp and attacks it, the other camp may yet escape"* (32:9). Jacob then lies down to a troubled sleep.

The next morning, Jacob tries a different tactic, and selects the best of his livestock, instructing his servants to take them to Esau, reasoning that if he placates his older brother with all this bounty, *"perhaps he will show me favor"* (32:21). Jacob takes his wives and children to safety across the stream of Jabbok (32:23), but then crosses back to the other side, perhaps sensing that he needs to be alone.

The river Jabbok—say the name out loud, with the "J" pronounced as in Hebrew like a "Y." Yabbok. This is an inversion of Jacob's name, "Ya'akov." It is as if Ya'akov is turned inside out, his heart exposed, vulnerable, his faith unfolding. He is becoming spiritually and emotionally open, available for the struggle to come, even if it hurts. *"Jacob was left alone"* (32:25)

Henri Nouwen once wrote that "solitude begins with a time and a place for God, and God alone."[1] Hermann Hesse wrote that "We must become so alone, so utterly alone, that we withdraw into our innermost self. It is a way of bitter suffering. But then our solitude is overcome, we are no longer alone, for we find that our innermost self is with the spirit, that it is God, the indivisible."[2]

One of the important teachings of the Hassidic mystics was *hitbodedut*—a going out for a time of aloneness, during which one opens oneself up to a conversation with God. In this process, one becomes receptive to whatever lessons that emerge from the conversation and in very intimate vulnerability, one asks deep and honest questions.

Jacob/Ya'akov's aloneness at the bank of the Jabbok river is a *sacred solitude*, an isolation that enables him to feel deeply the repercussions of his youthful deeds, opening possibilities for regret and repentance. It is just at this moment that he falls asleep and dreams a dream that will, once again, like his dream of the ladder, lead him toward further transformation.

> *And a man wrestled with him until the break of dawn. When he saw that he had not prevailed against him, he wrenched Jacob's hip at its socket, so that the socket of his hip was strained as he wrestled with him.*
> *Then he said, "Let me go, for dawn is breaking."*
> *But he answered, "I will not let you go, unless you bless me."*
> *Said the other, "What is your name?"*
> *He replied, "Jacob."*
> *Said he, "Your name shall no longer be Jacob, but Israel,[3] for you have striven with beings divine and human and have prevailed."*
> *Jacob asked, "Pray, tell me your name."*
> *But he said, "You must not ask my name!" And he took leave of him there.*
> *So Jacob named the place Peniel,[4] meaning, "I have seen a divine being face to face, yet my life has been preserved."*
> —Genesis 32:25–31

Who *is* this "man" who wrestled with Jacob? Perhaps he is Jacob's brother Esau, as Rabbi Samuel ben Meir (RaSHBaM) suggested in the twelfth century. Perhaps he is the Esau, the brother from whom Jacob can

---

1. Nouwen, *Making All Things New and Other Classics*.
2. Herman Hesse. https://citatis.com/a21808/16759a/.
3. The name Israel derives from the Hebrew *saritha*, which means "strived" or "struggled."
4. The name Peniel derives from the Hebrew *panim* (face) and *Eyl* (God).

no longer flee, and perhaps the wound to Jacob's hip is inflicted because, despite all that had occurred in his life, despite his maturation, despite his feelings of remorse, Jacob is still trying to flee. So many of us try to flee our remorse and our responsibility to make *teshuva* (repent), even though we know it is the right thing to do. Often it is because of our own woundedness that we finally come to a place of readiness to seek forgiveness—in our own hurt, we become more empathetic to others' hurts.

Contemporary Rabbi Rami Shapiro[5] suggests a Jungian approach in which Jacob's wrestling with the "man" becomes a ritual of initiation into manhood. Carl Jung[6] suggested four elements in the mythology of initiation: 1. "an encounter with a superior being;" 2. "a wounding of the protagonist;" 3. "perseverance of the protagonist despite the wound;" 4. "divine revelation." This seems to be the pattern of Jacob's wrestling dream. Rabbi Shapiro suggests that "the wounding of Jacob is his grounding—. . . some old traditions say that no man is adult until he has become opened to the soul and spirit world, and that such an opening is done by a wound in the right place in the right company."

Rabbi Shapiro further suggests that when Jacob receives the blessing of a new name from the "man," it is the transformative blessing of his life: "This is the third blessing Jacob has received. The *first*, he tricked out of his father Isaac. The *second*, he coerced out of his mother's brother Laban. *The last he earned by his own sweat and pain. This is the blessing that counts.* This is the blessing that will make him new. This is the blessing that he needs in order to face his brother."[7]

And now we are led to another answer to the question, who *is* this man who wrestled with Jacob (Ya'akov) on the banks of the Yahbok river? It is probably Jacob himself! It is the Jacob (Ya'akov) who is turned inside out (Yabbok); it is the Jacob who is wounded and finally, becomes fully adult. It is the Jacob who has been alone in sacred solitude and has been able, finally, to feel and *understand* the awful repercussions of his earlier deeds. It is the Jacob who has come to know himself. *This* Jacob is ready to meet his brother, to face whatever is in store for him with the reunion, to return the original blessings, and the birthright to Esau (for they were never Jacob's) and to leave the encounter more wholly a man.

Rabbi Samson Raphael Hirsch comments on the similarity between the word "struggled" *yeh-avek*/יאבק, which means "wrestled" here, and

---

5. These comments are derived from Rabbi Rami Shapiro's book, *Embracing Esau*.

6. Carl Gustav Jung (1875–1961) was a psychiatrist and psychoanalyst whose work influenced not only psychiatry but also many other realms of thought, such as literature, philosophy, religious studies, and more.

7. Shapiro, *Embracing Esau*, 74.

the verb *chibek*/חבק, which means "embraced": "Related to it ['struggled'] is חבק, the effort to draw somebody close to oneself, to embrace."[8] Could Jacob be learning to embrace *himself*, and in so doing gain the integrity and wholeness to encounter Esau?

God (through an angel) has given Jacob a new name—*Yisra'el*, Israel—the one who has struggled, wrestled, with God and humans and has survived:

> "Your name shall no longer be Jacob, but Israel, for you have striven with beings divine and human and have prevailed."
> —Genesis 32:29

Jacob has wrestled all his life, from the moment of his birth, when he emerged from his mother Rebecca's womb, holding onto his brother Esau's heel. Indeed, Jacob's very name in Hebrew reflects his struggle, for *Ya'akov* is derived from the Hebrew word *ekev*/עקב—"heel." And Jacob is a "heel" in every sense: he steals his brother's birthright and blessing; he is a scoundrel in his youth. Now, after his mighty tussle with the mysterious "man" (angel) he emerges, wounded, yet still more whole, now *Yisra'el* (Israel), to meet his brother Esau again.

Jacob names the place "Peniel," because *"I have seen a divine being face to face, yet my life has been preserved"* (32:31). Just as earlier in his journey he had become conscious of the Presence of the Holy One when he dreamed of the angels on the stairway to heaven, now Jacob palpably feels God around him and *with* him as he advances toward Esau. This heightened God-awareness will enable Jacob to truly repent, to open his heart to Esau and without hesitation return the birthright and the blessing to its rightful owner. Imbued now with faith and spirit, Jacob is transformed from the "heel" of his youth to the "God-wrestler" and believer of his mature years.

Soon, *"looking up, Jacob saw Esau coming, accompanied by four hundred men"* (33:1). Hopeful, but still afraid, Jacob takes one last precaution in case Esau's anger flares against him, placing his most beloved wife and child at the rear of his entourage and his least beloved wives and children in the front, not very noble, but certainly pragmatic.

> He himself went on ahead and bowed low to the ground seven times until he was near his brother. Esau ran to greet him. He embraced him and falling on his neck, he kissed him; and they wept.
>
> —Genesis 33:3–4

---

8. Hirsch in *The Pentateuch: Translation and Commentary*, 504.

Ancient and medieval rabbis wondered if Esau's greeting to Jacob was genuine joy or something else. Was Esau's "kiss" really a kiss or a "bite"? Was Esau's ambivalence about his brother still there? In the Torah scroll, the words, "and kissed him" are adorned with dots. What does this mean?

Mois A. Navon teaches that "Rashi brings the Sifri (Behaalotkha 69),[9] which entertains two interpretations of the meaning of the "kiss"—one maintaining that the kiss was whole-hearted, the other that it was not. The one view holds that the dots come to diminish the word, and thus indicate that the kiss was not sincere. On the other hand, the dots may have been meant to teach that there is something novel here, that at this particular moment Esau was aroused with brotherly compassion and his kiss was sincere."[10]

The Midrash (Genesis Rabbah 78:9) says R. Shimon b. Elazar teaches that where the number of dots and letters are equivalent, the dots come to add to the text, and from this we learn that Esau had pity and kissed Jacob with all his heart. R. Yannai demurs, for if the word keeps its simple meaning of "kiss" (sincere or not), the dots then are effectively meaningless. He thus proposes that Esau wished to "bite" Jacob—the word "kiss" [*vayishakeihu*] and the word "bite" [*vayishakheihu*] differing in only one letter."

When the two brothers embrace, Jacob says to Esau: *"to see your face is like seeing the face of God, and you have received me favorably"* (33:10). At this crucial moment, Jacob tries to return the birthright (Isaac's innermost blessing) that he had stolen from Esau back to his older brother: *"Please accept my blessing which has been brought to [for?] you, for God has favored me and I have plenty"* (33:10). *"And when he [Jacob] urged him [Esau], he [Esau] accepted"* (33:11).

It would seem that peace has finally come between the brothers, and yet when Esau suggests that he and Jacob travel together, with Esau proceeding at Jacob's pace, Jacob makes excuses and ultimately travels in a different direction—peace, yes, but not togetherness:

> And [Esau] said, "Let us start our journey and I will proceed at your pace." But he [Jacob] said to him, "My lord knows that the children are frail and that the flocks and herds, which are nursing, are a care to me; if they are driven hard a single day, all the flocks will die. Let my lord go ahead of his servant, while I travel slowly, at the pace of the cattle before me and at the pace of the children, until I come to my lord in Seir. . . . So Esau started back that day on his way to Seir. But Jacob journeyed on to Succoth, and built a house for himself and made stalls for his cattle.
>
> —Genesis 33:12–15

9. Navon, "The Kiss of Esau."
10. Navon, "The Kiss of Esau."

Seir is a mountainous region between the Dead Sea and the Gulf of Aqaba. Succoth is in Transjordan, far east of Seir and slightly north of the river Jabbok.

A bite and a kiss—perhaps this is a metaphor for the often-complex relationships between siblings: love and resentments, gnarled conflicts that often arise over trivial matters that become magnified and reflect deeper feelings—feelings that twist and bend and become so entangled that there seems no way out. Even in reconciliation not all gets settled, not all is resolved. Perhaps this is why Jacob can not imagine living too close to his brother Esau—for proximity might cause conflict to flare up again. Perhaps love at a distance was preferable than living together. As Rabbi Jeffrey Salkin suggests, "we too, hopefully, achieve a rapprochement with our brothers—yet that moment of understanding and healing will not necessarily last forever. Reconciliation between brothers does not always mean closeness, at least in a world that is not yet Eden."[11]

Text to Life

> In my introduction, I wrote of my few days alone in the desert. This was the first time I had ever really spent any time truly alone and the experience was both daunting and liberating. As I wrote there, I discovered many things—I discovered the Hebrew Bible and its wonders—but my time in the wilderness revealed more: that I actually could *be* alone and that I didn't feel lonely; that I could have deep conversations with myself and realize truths about myself and includes behavior, that amid the silence and lack of distraction I could discern what I really wanted (and didn't want) in my life, who were my real friends and who were hangers-on.
>
> I discovered that aloneness could be a gift rather than a curse, a quiet time to figure life out, without the distractions and the din of other people and others' needs surrounding me. The time alone was profoundly illuminating for me, and it helped me set my course for years to come.
>
> LGB

---

11. Salkin, *The Modern Men's Torah Commentary*, 55.

Exploring the Text Within

Find a quiet and comfortable place to sit in contemplative silence with the above teachings and with the following questions about you and your life's experience. You may choose to focus on one question or sit with several. Ask yourself: what do the biblical text and these teachings mean to me in my life?

Jacob was left alone.
(Genesis 32:25)

Solitude begins with a time and a place for God and God alone.
—Henri Nouwen

> Has there ever been a time in my life when I felt alone but not lonely and did some of my best thinking/feeling?

And a man wrestled with him until the break of dawn.

(Genesis 32:25)

Your name shall no longer be Jacob, but Israel, for you have striven with beings divine and human and have prevailed.
(Genesis 32:29)

(Israel = Godwrestler; one who strives or struggles with God)

> Has there ever been a time in my life when I felt myself in a mighty struggle or wrestle with God?
>
> How did I emerge from the wrestle?
>
> With what insights did I emerge?

Esau ran to greet him. He embraced him, and falling on his neck, he kissed him [Jacob] and they wept.
(Genesis 33:4)

[Jacob said to Esau]: "... for to see your face is like seeing the face of God."
(Genesis 33:10)

> Have I ever had a reunion with someone I love and with whom I have had a deep conflict?
>
> Did I experience complete reconciliation or was there still ambivalence?

We are each created in the image of the Divine, and if we allow ourselves, we can see godliness in each human being, even in those with whom we have experienced troubles.

Chapter 15

Vayishlach II

Rape and Revenge

"Now Dinah, the daughter whom Leah had born to Jacob, went out to visit the daughters of the land..."

—Genesis 34:1–31

Just after Jacob and Esau's reconciliation, Jacob's daughter Dinah,[1] perhaps being curious to explore outside the confines of her tribe, *"went out to visit the daughters of the land"* (34:1). Dinah is the daughter of Leah, Jacob's unloved wife, and is initially noted as *Leah's* daughter. Only later in the story is she identified as Jacob's daughter.

What happens after Dinah *"goes out"* is disturbing and complex:

"Shechem, son of Hamor the Hivite, chief of the country, saw her and took her and lay with her by force" (34:2). Then, the text tells us that Shechem's *"soul cleaved to Dinah and [he was] in love with the maiden"* (34:3)—What an odd and deviant order! First, it seems, Shechem rapes Dinah and only after the rape does he come to love her! We know, of course that rape is an act of obscene violence and a perverse exercise of power of one person over another. It is *never* an act of love. Yet immediately after Shechem's rape of Dinah, he falls in love with her! Is this the text's way of suggesting Shechem's remorse? We can only imagine the answer.

What comes next is a classic tale of male action with complete disregard for Dinah the victim. First, Hamor, the rapist's father, comes to Dinah's father Jacob and asks that the maiden be permitted to marry his son. Hamor proposes that Jacob and his sons marry into his tribe and gain much wealth from the arrangement (34:8–12). Dinah is not consulted.

---

1. Dinah's birth is mentioned in Genesis 30:21.

Jacob's sons, Simeon and Levi, are *"distressed and very angry"* (34:7), and respond on behalf of their father *"speaking with guile"* (8:13), and *they* agree to Hamor's proposal. The brothers insist, however, that since Hamor's men are uncircumcised, they must all circumcise themselves before the marriage and intermarriages take place (34:14–17). Hamor and Shechem agree to this condition and they immediately go back to their own city and circumcise themselves and all the men among them (34:18–24).

Taking advantage of Hamor and his menfolk's post-operative recuperation,

> Simeon and Levi . . . came upon the city unmolested, and slew all the males. They put Hamor and his son Shechem to the sword, took Dinah out of Shechem's house, and went away. The other sons of Jacob came upon the slain and plundered the town, because their sister had been defiled. They seized their flocks and herds and asses, all that was inside the town and outside; all their wealth, all their children, and their wives, all that was in the houses, they took as captives and booty.
>
> —Genesis 34:25–29

During all this time, it seems that Jacob the father is passive, saying nothing about the situation. It is no wonder that at the beginning of this story Dinah is identified as *"Leah's daughter"*! But then, in the manner of a patriarchal society, when Dinah is raped, she suddenly becomes identified as "daughter of Jacob" as if she were nothing more than chattel. Nonetheless, throughout the whole incident until almost its end, Jacob is silent. *After* the attack on Hamor and Shechem and the town, Jacob pathetically laments, *"You have brought trouble on me, making me odious among the inhabitants of the land, the Canaanites and the Perizzites; my men are few in number, so that if they unite against me and attach me, I and my house will be destroyed"* (34:30). Simeon and Levi self-righteously respond to their father: *"Should our sister be treated like a whore?"* (34:31). Suddenly, righteous brotherly indignation is the cause for the attack and wanton violence is justified in the name of their sister's honor. Jacob, the *pater familias*, comes off as a coward, concerned for his own welfare and not at all worried about poor Dinah's well-being!

This is the whole story of Dinah. The text tells us *nothing at all* about what Dinah feels, what she thinks, how she might have responded to Shechem's "love," or what she might have said to Jacob in the wake of the attack. *No one asks her. No one pays attention to her. No one seems to consider her feelings at all. Dinah is invisible.* She is, as Emily Taitz and Sondra Henry have said, "written out of history."[2]

What is most upsetting is that Dinah *as a woman, as a person* is erased from the text. She is utterly objectified. Though the entire story of the attack on Shechem, Hamor, and their city is supposedly *because* of Dinah, she never appears again in the story as a real person. Rabbi Laura Geller writes, "What happens to Dinah in the aftermath of her ordeal? We do not know. We never hear from her, just as we never hear from the women and girls in our generation who are victims of violence and whose voices are not heard.... The feminist educator Nelle Morton urged women to 'hear each other into speech.' Dinah's story challenges us to go even further and be also the voices for all of our sisters."[3]

What is even more upsetting is that in later generations, the rabbis blame Dinah for her own misfortune! In the ancient *midrash*, she is called a "gadabout."[4] Another ancient rabbi, Rabbi Berakiah in Rabbi Levi's name, wrote: "*And Dinah, the daughter of Leah went out*—This may be compared to one who is holding a pound of meat in his hand and as soon as he exposed it a bird swooped down and snatched it away. Similarly, *And Dinah, the daughter of Leah went out,* and forthwith, *and Shechem the son of Hamor saw her.*"[5] Yet another rabbi, Rabbi Samuel, explains, "Her arm became exposed."[6]

In another appalling, mysoginistic midrash, Dinah is blamed for becoming "corrupted":

> The man subdues a woman, and the woman does not subdue a man. But, if she walks about a lot and goes out into the marketplace, she finally comes to a state of corruption, to a state of harlotry. And so you find in the case of Jacob's daughter Dinah. All the time that she was sitting at home, she was not corrupted by transgression; but as soon as she went out into the marketplace, she caused herself to come to the point of corruption.[7]

How awful is this classic case of blaming the victim for a crime of violence against her. The message is that Dinah should *not* have been curious, should *not* have wanted to visit other women, should *not* have wanted to go outside the confines of her tribe. I am reminded of a court case in which

---

2. Taitz and Henry, *Written Out of History: Our Jewish Foremothers.*
3. In Eskenazi and Weiss, eds., *The Torah: A Women's Commentary*, 205.
4. Genesis Rabbah 80:5.
5. Genesis Rabbah 80:5.
6. Genesis Rabbah 80:5.
7. Midrash Tanhuma 8:12.

the victim of a rape is berated for having worn provocative clothing, or having ventured out of her own neighborhood, the suggestion being that *she* was responsible for provoking the hapless rapist! Such disdain of Dinah speaks to a profound contempt of women in general—a symptom of a larger phenomenon that in future centuries would lead to horrific sexual abuse and in our day, sexual slavery and sex trafficking.[8] It is a symptom of a malady that pervades our planet, from so-called "enlightened" societies to the seemingly most "primitive" ones.

And what of Simeon and Levi's horrendous actions against Shechem, Hamor, and the mass circumcision of their menfolk? Pretending to agree to the marriage of their daughters once the circumcisions had taken place, Simeon and Levi take advantage of the weakened state of the recovering Shechemites and slaughtered them all, taking the women and children as prisoners and their possessions as booty. While these two brothers take the lead in plundering the city, their brothers also take part in the mayhem. This reflects the custom of avenging the honor of the tribe for a "dishonor" it perceives has been done to it—the rape of Dinah dishonors her father Jacob, and Simeon and Levi are avenging this affront to their father's status as head of the tribe. Once again, Dinah herself is just the rationale for events and has no say whatsoever in the matter.

Not so much has changed in the millennia since the days of the Bible. Even today there are honor killings in the Middle East and elsewhere—either horrendous killings of the woman who has been raped for *her* dishonor to her family (!)—or murders of the rapist for having brought shame on the *family* of the victim, with little regard for the victim herself. But is the biblical honor killing *justified*? Are Simeon and Levi *right* in their murder and pillaging of the town?

The great twentieth-century biblical scholar Nehama Leibowitz writes, "If the deed was justified why did Jacob angrily reprimand them [his sons Simeon and Levi].... To be sure, Jacob advances a purely utilitarian argument in his words of reproof to the two brothers:

> *You have troubled me to make me odious unto the inhabitants of the land ... and I, being few in number, they will gather themselves together against me and smite me; and I shall be destroyed, I am and my house.*
>
> —Genesis 34:30

---

8. This travesty is even present in the State of Israel. See Rabbi Laura Geller's comments in Eskenazi and Weiss, eds., *The Torah: A Women's Commentary*, 205 and the many articles of the Israel Ministry of Justice, Office of the National Anti-Trafficking Coordinator.

Jacob is worried about *his own* welfare and the well-being of his tribe. He appears entirely unconcerned about *Dinah's* anguish! Years later, close to his death, Jacob seems to have thought more about his sons' actions, and about the morality of their deeds, rather than just the immediate repercussions that would affect the tribe:

> *Simeon and Levi are a pair; Their weapons are tools of lawlessness, Let not my person be included in their council; Let not my being be counted in their assembly. For when angry, they slay men, And when pleased, they maim oxen. Cursed be their anger, for it was fierce, and their wrath for it was cruel.*
>
> —Genesis 49:5–7

At his end-of-life reflection, Jacob seems to have come to finally deeply feel the immorality and cruelty that Simeon and Levi's actions brought on Shechem and his people.

Rabbis over the centuries have debated Jacob's feelings about this incident. In the twelfth century, the great theologian Maimonides (RaMBaM) wrote that "Taking revenge is an extremely bad trait. A person should be accustomed to rise above his feelings about all worldly matters; for those who understand [the deeper purpose of the world] consider all these matters as vanity and emptiness, which are not worth seeking revenge for."[9]

Half a millennium later, in his code of Jewish law, Reb Schneur Zalman of Liadi, a Hassidic master, wrote that "one should erase any feelings of revenge from one's heart and never remind oneself of it."[10]

From a contemporary perspective, I respond in disgust to Simeon and Levi's act. First, that they so disregard Dinah's feelings, and next that they so ignore the perhaps honorable overture of Shechem and Hamor in asking for Dinah's hand in marriage. Resorting to a duplicitous agreement and then to wanton violence is a repugnant reaction to the original violation against Dinah. I wonder what might have happened had the *womenfolk* been left to respond to Dinah's rape and Shechem and Hamor's request to allow Shechem to marry her. How might *they* have responded? One suspects that their reaction might certainly have been less violent, and more humane. They certainly would have empathized with Dinah, cared for her, and perhaps examined more closely Shechem's feelings and motives in his newfound "love" for Dinah and his seeking her hand in marriage.

When I think of this incident of dastardly revenge, I am terribly saddened. For its time, and even now in some countries, such acts of

---

9. Mishneh Torah, *De'ot* 7:7.
10. Shulchan Aruch HaRav 156:3 (end).

righteous indignation ending in violence are not uncommon. They lead to tribal blood feuds, even to wars. How tragic it is that we humans have not found better ways to quell our savage instincts and more peaceful ways to settle our differences.

Text to Life

> Michael and Jill had been married for fifteen years. The initial years of their marriage were happy as they pursued their professional lives, bought a home, and settled into ordinary life. They decided that they did not want to have children—that they were enough for each other.
>
> Over time, however, they seemed to grow apart and Jill became restless. She began to study for a graduate degree, spent more time with her women friends, and generally drifted away from Michael. During this time, Jill met a man at the university who lit up her heart.
>
> Jill tried to avoid the enmeshment of an extramarital affair, but as she came to know this new man in her life, she couldn't resist the feelings that were growing inside of her. She and Joshua sat talking for hours and there seemed to be a whole universe of interests that they shared. It seemed that they always had something to talk about. Soon, they were taking long walks, afternoon coffee, early evening drinks. Eventually, Jill fell in love with Joshua, a man who filled many empty places in her heart that, try as she might, Michael no longer seemed to satisfy.
>
> Jill dutifully asked Michael to go to couples counseling with her. Puzzled by the request (since he had no inkling that there was anything "wrong" in their marriage), Michael nevertheless agreed and together they sought out a counselor. Jill put her relationship with Joshua on hold and vowed not to see him during this time, and was determined to make a genuine effort to repair her broken relationship with Michael. For Jill, this time apart from Joshua was agony; for Michael it was an enigma.
>
> For eight months, Michael and Jill saw their couples counselor, only for Jill to feel affirmed in her conviction that their relationship was truly irreparable. Michael, on the other hand, remained puzzled as to why Jill felt so alienated from him. He didn't seem to change or grow through the counseling. Finally, Jill asked for a divorce and in the most gentle way she could, affirmed the love for Michael she had shared in the early years, but explained that she no longer loved him.

> A few months later, Jill and Michael were legally divorced, without acrimony, it seemed, and a year later, Jill married Joshua and began a new life.
>
> Things were different for Michael. After the divorce, he fell into a deep depression and began to blame the professional setbacks he was experiencing and his profound loneliness on Jill and especially on Joshua, whom he came to hate with a venomous passion. He believed that Joshua had "stolen" Jill from him and that Joshua was an evil presence in his life. Over time, Michael's hatred of Joshua grew deeper, to a pathological and lethal point. Against all his normal impulses, Michael bought a gun. Somehow, in a mind now twisted with a sense of loss and betrayal, Michael came to believe that if he just got rid of Joshua, Jill would come back to him and they could be happy again.
>
> One night, drunk and doped up on depression medications, Michael drove to Jill and Joshua's new home, somehow broke in, and confronted Joshua, screaming obscenities at him. Then, in a moment of complete irrationality, Michael shot Joshua dead. Then he begged Jill to take him back.
>
> Revenge—tragedy—and the destruction of three lives.

Exploring the Text Within

Find a quiet and comfortable place to sit in contemplative silence with the above teachings and with the following questions about you and your life's experience. You may choose to focus on one question or sit with several. Ask yourself: what do the biblical text and these teachings mean to me in my life?

> *Now Dinah, the daughter whom Leah had born to Jacob, went out to visit the daughters of the land....*
>
> (Genesis 34:1–3)

> Has there ever been a time in my life when my curiosity, my urge to explore led me to "go out," to travel, to seek out new places, new lands, new experiences?
>
> What did I find when I allowed myself to "go out?"

Now Dinah, the daughter whom Leah had born to Jacob, went out to visit the daughters of the land....
(Genesis 34:1–3)

> Have I ever been hurt by taking a risk to explore?
>
> What happened in the aftermath of the hurt?
>
> How was I treated by those for whom I cared most?

Jacob said to Simeon and Levi, "You have brought trouble on me!"... They answered, "Should our sister be treated like a whore?"
(Genesis 34: 30–31)

> Has there ever been a time when I felt profoundly ignored and unseen, when I felt that my own deepest feelings and thoughts were not considered?

Chapter 16

Vayeshev I

Parental Favoritism

> *"At seventeen years of age, Joseph tended the flocks with his brothers, as a helper to the sons of his father's wives, Bilhah and Zilpah. And Joseph brought bad reports of his brothers to their father. Now Israel [Jacob] loved Joseph best of all his sons...."*
>
> —Genesis 37:1–3

The sibling relationship between Joseph, son of Jacob [Israel][1] and Rachel, and his step-brothers, sons of Jacob and Leah and the sons of Jacob's concubines Bilha and Zilpah, is destined from the outset to be troubled and contentious. Jacob loves Joseph's mother, Rachel, passionately, while merely tolerating his first wife, Leah, Rachel's older sister. He had worked for seven extra years for Rachel, after already working seven years and being tricked into marrying her older sister Leah.[2] Yearning for his love and approval, Leah bears Jacob six sons[3] and a daughter (Dinah), but is never able to gain her husband's affection. No doubt, their father's lack of love (and perhaps even disdain) for their mother provokes Leah's sons to greatly resent Joseph, son of Jacob's most-loved wife Rachel.

---

  1. As noted in chapter 14, Jacob had received the name "Israel" after wrestling with an angel of God (32:25–29) and having survived.
  2. In biblical times, men were permitted to marry more than one wife.
  3. Leah's sons were Reuben, Simeon, Levi, Judah, Issachar, and Zebulun. Rachel gave birth to Joseph and Benjamin and the maidservants, Bilhah and Zilpah, each bore two sons. Bilhah gave birth to Dan and Naftali and Zilpah bore Gad and Asher. These twelve sons of Jacob comprised the twelve tribes of Israel.

Additionally, Jacob's special love for Joseph and his baby brother Benjamin is significantly heightened when Rachel dies while giving birth to Benjamin, leaving him and his older son Joseph bereft and emotionally devastated. Jacob's natural preference for Rachel's two sons is compounded after Rachel's death and his attentions are now even more focused on his motherless boys. Finally, from his early youth, Joseph is a dreamer, and he innocently (perhaps arrogantly?) recounts his dreams to his father and half-brothers, dreams that depict him lording power over the other brothers: metaphors of eleven wheat sheaves that bowed down to his sheaf, and later that the sun, moon, and eleven stars are also bowing in reverence to him. These metaphors do not escape Joseph's brothers. Needless to say, these dreams rankle them and they hate him even more.

In commenting on this family situation, nineteenth-century German rabbi, Samson Rachel Hirsch, wrote that

> [Joseph's] life and aspirations during his formative years developed in the company of the sons of the maidservants whom the text here describes not as his brothers, but as the sons of his father's wives. Thus we see before us a youth who had grown up without a mother and without true siblings. All the others had grown up in the company of siblings and under the protection and guidance of a mother's love. Joseph, by contrast, was all alone. He had lost his mother early in life; Benjamin was still a child and hence no companion for the youth.[4]

Thus, Joseph grows up a lonely, motherless child, burdened by his half-brothers' hatred, which only grows more acute with time as their father makes no secret of his preference for Joseph, *"the child of his old age"* (37:3). Showing him favoritism, Jacob fashions *"an ornamented tunic"* for Joseph (37:3)—the garment made famous in the Tony-Award-winning musical, *Joseph and the Amazing Technicolor Dreamcoat* by Tim Rice and Andrew Lloyd Webber. Now Joseph wears his flashy new coat, a constant irritant to his brothers.

People in "blended" families always face special challenges.[5] Often children in such families grieve the loss of their original families' unity, which is shattered either by the death of a spouse or parent, or by divorce. In the case of death, especially in a happy family, the bereaved spouse and

---

4. Hirsch, *The Pentateuch, Haftaroth and the Five Megilloth*, 162.

5. For more information on blended families, see Friedman, *The Jewish Factor in Remarriage and Stepparenting*, and Friedman, *Remarriage and Stepparenting in the Jewish Community*. There is also a wide literature of non-sectarian books on the subject of blended families. Two representative samples are Carstens, *The Secret to Blended Families* and Marsolini, *Blended Families*.

children grieve deeply. Later, regardless of the amount of time that has elapsed, they face a new reality if there is a remarriage—the entrance of a new "significant other" into the widow/widower's life, and a new stepparent into the children's lives. Life is disrupted.

When a new stepparent comes along with children of her/his own a new family constellation is formed, and the seemingly simple stuff of daily life becomes immeasurably complicated. New questions face the family: Everyone asks: *How will we all live together?* Children ask: *Will our parent favor some children over the others? Will each of us get the nurturing and comfort we need? What will be expected of us? Am I required to love my stepparent? What shall I call my new stepparent? Will there be enough love to go around for all of us?*

In Joseph's case, complexity came in a different form. His father's overt lack of love for his first wife, Leah, and her sons' bitter awareness of their mother's suffering exacerbated an already-tense situation. Once again, many questions arose: *How will Leah's sons relate to their half-brothers? How will they try to regain their father's favor in the face of his obvious preference for Joseph and baby Benjamin?*

No doubt Joseph feels deep grief after the death of his mother Rachel, but our text tells us nothing of his feelings. Does he feel protective of his baby brother Benjamin, overly possessive of his father Jacob, and gratified by Jacob's overt expressions of favoritism towards him? Does Joseph feel that by recounting his dreams of dominance over his half-brothers that he was "one-upping" them? Is he somehow compensating for the loss of his mother? We can only speculate. Nonetheless, we can see clearly that Jacob, Joseph, and his half-brothers show all the signs of an unhappily blended family in which dysfunctional behavior erupts—a father who plays favorites and loves one son over the others; the other sons deeply resenting the "favorite" son; and the "favorite" son (despite his special status) feeling lonely, small, and vulnerable, acutely sensing his half-brothers' resentment.

Perhaps in an attempt to gain power over his half-siblings, Joseph becomes an insufferable tattletale, bringing false "bad reports" about them to his father. Joseph became a bearer of what Jewish tradition calls *lashon hara*—evil speech—speech that damages both the speaker and the object(s) of the speech. Rabbi Shlomo ben Yitzchak (known as *RaSHI*), the great northern European medieval rabbi and Torah commentator, taught that Jacob punished Joseph for his tale bearing:

> [A]ny evil that he [actually] witnessed in his brothers, Leah's sons, he would tell his father. [He related] that they would eat [the flesh] of a limb [taken] from a live animal, that they would

degrade the handmaids' sons, calling them "slaves," and that they were suspected of illicit relations with women. [However, in actual fact, he was mistaken in all of the above], and he was beaten [as respective punishments] for all three cases [for not having investigated the matter thoroughly with the brothers, before he reported them as "faits accomplis" to his father] . . . .[6]

Joseph's tattle telling reminds me of the film *Atonement* set in World War II England. A young girl, Briony, becomes aware of a budding romance between her sister Cecilia and the housekeeper's son, Robbie, and witnesses a series of events that she misunderstands. She then falsely accuses Robbie of having raped a young relative, Lola. Though he is innocent, Robbie is arrested, convicted, and serves four years in prison and is then released into the British army and dies at Dunkirk. Cecilia and Robbie's love affair and their hopeful future is torn apart and their dream of living a happy life together never comes to be, all because of Briony's false accusation. Briony's own life, too, turns out to be a sad and hollow existence. In her old age, she writes a "novel" entitled *Atonement*, confessing the sin of her accusation and revealing its repercussions. Her accusation against Robbie was *lashon hara*, speech in its most evil manifestation.

Judaism teaches that "death and life are in the power of the tongue."[7] In the story of *Atonement*, this proverb becomes a truism. Robbie dies a soldier's death, a great love ends as lovers are separated, sisters are estranged—and a *social* "death" occurs when falsehood is perpetuated through gossip and slander. The family's social community is torn asunder.

In the thirteenth century, the Spanish rabbi Jonah ben Abraham Gerondi wrote,

> Take heed and know that a person who agrees with a slanderous statement when he hears it is as bad as the one who says it, for everyone will say: "That person who listened to what has been said agreed with it, and that shows it must be true." . . . Even if the hearer only turns to listen to the gossip and gives the impression of believing it to be true, he helps spread the evil, brings disgrace on his neighbor, and encourages slanderers to carry their evil reports to all people.[8]

And in our own time, Sissela Bok writes,

---

6. Rashi, commentary on *Vayeshev* ch. 37:4–10 (in Rashi, *Pentateuch with Rashi's Commentary*, 180).

7. Proverbs 18:21.

8. Sha'arei Teshuva, section 3.

As lies spread—by imitation, or in retaliation, or to forestall suspected deception—trust is damaged. Yet trust is a social good to be protected just as much as the air we breathe or the water we drink. When it is damaged, the community as a whole suffers; and when it is destroyed, societies falter and collapse.[9]

In *Atonement*, Briony's accusation against Robbie rips apart the entire family social system; in Joseph's family's social system, his tale-bearing corrodes the larger system of the brothers' tribes. Joseph's lies have corroded the social fabric.

Text to Life

> My friend Jill was caught in a troubled relationship with her long-time partner, Seth. Jill confided in another friend, Naomi, that she had been strongly tempted to begin an affair with another man but had so far resisted. (In fact, Jill had planned to ask Seth to go into couples counseling with her.)
>
> A few weeks later, for unexplained reasons, Naomi not only told Seth about Jill's temptation, but lied and said that Jill had actually begun an affair. The ensuing explosion ended any possibility of working through Jill and Seth's relationship and they separated with bitterness. Naomi's lie had ruptured any possibility of healing.
>
> LGB

Exploring the Text Within

Find a quiet and comfortable place to sit in contemplative silence with the above teachings and with the following questions about you and your life's experience. You may choose to focus on one question or sit with several. Ask yourself: what do the biblical text and these teachings mean to me in my life?

> At seventeen years of age, Joseph tended the flocks with his brothers, as a helper to the sons of his father's wives, Bilhah and Zilpah. And Joseph brought bad reports of his brothers to their father. Now Israel [Jacob] loved Joseph best of all his sons.
>
> —Genesis 37:1–3

9. Bok, *Lying*, 26–27.

As a lad, Joseph was a lonely, motherless child. His father's *extra love* for him made matters worse.

> Can I recall a time when I have felt lonely within my own family?
>
> How did that feeling affect my family relationships?

In his youth, Joseph brought false *"bad reports"* about his half-brothers to his father.

> Can I recall a time when I was a tattletale?
>
> Did my "bad reports" against siblings or friends cause pain or disruption in my family or among my friends?

> Can I recall a time in my family or within my closest circle of friends when gossip or lies tore apart the possibility of loving relationships?

Chapter 17

Vayeshev II

Joseph and the Stranger

"A man found him wandering in the fields.
The man asked him, what are you seeking?"
—Genesis 37:15

Tensions continue to grow between Joseph and his brothers. Jacob's older sons have gone off with their flocks to pasture north of their father's encampment and Joseph is left behind with the maidservants.

Jacob summoned Joseph and said to him:

> "Your brothers are pasturing at Shechem. Come, I will send you to them." He [Joseph] answered, "I am ready [Hineni/הנני]. And he [Jacob] said to him, "Go and see how your brothers are and how the flocks are faring, and bring me back word." So he sent him *from the valley of Hebron.*
>
> —Genesis 37:13

Perhaps in a fatherly attempt to affect a reconciliation between Joseph and his brothers, Jacob decides to bring them together in the fields where the older brothers are pasturing their flocks. Perhaps Jacob hopes that if Joseph and his brothers work together in a shared endeavor, they might find some common ground as brothers. Certainly Joseph, the lonely youth, desired the friendship of his brothers; no doubt his father hoped for this as well.

As previously mentioned, the Hebrew word *hineni* often signifies the beginning of a story of transformation. As with the story of the *Akedah*, the binding of Isaac (see chapter 8 above), when God calls and Abraham responds to the divine call to take his son for sacrifice, here too, Joseph responds to his father's call to embark on an uncertain journey with *hineni*.

Joseph doesn't know exactly where he will meet his brothers, though, given their animosity toward him, he knows that he will not receive a very warm welcome. RaSHI comments on the word *hineni* as "an expression of humility and eagerness [to fulfill] that which is requested of a person."[1] "This Scripture," RaSHI continues, "is telling us that Joseph readied himself to [fulfill] his father's command [to join his brothers] even though he knew that his brothers hated him."[2] From the outset, then, Joseph knows that this journey is fraught with the possibility of danger. Nonetheless, he responds to his father's instruction to meet his brothers with that one faithful, humble, and determined word, *hineni*—"Here I am" or "I am ready."

Sometimes we embark on journeys that we know might be treacherous, but we do so anyway because we know in our hearts that there is a deeper reason for the journey. Though we may be deeply fearful, we nonetheless begin the journey with hope and faith that we will be safe on our way.

Rabbinic commentary is mixed about how Joseph might have felt as he began his trek towards his brothers. Rabbi Samson Raphael Hirsch wrote that Joseph was "at once ready to go," and seems to have felt no trepidation on his journey because "his conscience is quite clear,"[3] since he did not understand that his brothers and his father experienced the dreams he had shared with them as arrogant and grandiose. On the other hand, several other commentators note that Joseph's readiness to meet his brothers was admirable given their hostility toward them, and that Jacob was well aware that he was sending his younger son into a hostile situation: "I knew that your brethren hate you, and yet you answered me: Here I am."[4]

A while after Joseph set out on his journey, he finds himself "wandering in the fields" (37:15) and he becomes lost. Suddenly, out of nowhere, much like a *deus ex machina* in an ancient Greek play, a "man" appears:

> When he reached Shechem, a man came upon him [literally: "found him"]. The man asked him [Joseph], "What are you looking for?" He answered, "I am looking for my brothers. Could you tell me where they are pasturing?" The man said, "They have gone from here, for I heard them say: 'Let us go to Dothan.'" So Joseph followed his brothers and found them at Dothan.

—Genesis 37:14–17

---

1. RaSHI on Gen 22:1, quoted in *Chok L'Yisra'el*, 248.
2. Genesis Rabbah 84:13, quoted in *Chok L'Yisra'el*, 248.
3. Hirsch in *The Pentateuch*, 545.
4. Rabbi Dr. H. Freedman, *Midrash Rabbah: Genesis, Vol. II*, Genesis Rabbah: 84:13, 779. See also, *Or Hachayim: Commentary on the Torah* by Rabbi Chaiyim Ben Attar (translated by Eliyahu Munk), 37:14, 304–5.

What a strange episode! Joseph walks from Hebron to Shechem[5] and then loses his way and a mysterious stranger unexpectedly appears to assist him. Like in the old western movies, the stranger points his finger in a certain direction and says to Joseph, "they went thattaway!" Then the man disappears as quickly as he had appeared! Imagine if that stranger *hadn't* come along! Joseph could have wandered for some time without finding his brothers, and he could have returned home to his father's encampment near Hebron, reporting a failure to fulfill his mission. Had this occurred, his brothers would not have had the opportunity to get Joseph alone, without Jacob nearby to protect him and they would not have had a chance to throw him into a dry well and sell him into slavery to a caravan of Midianite traders. Joseph would never have descended as a slave into Egypt and the whole story of Joseph and our people in Egypt could not have unfolded as the Bible narrates it! This whole chain of events is set in motion because a mysterious person appears at just the right moment in just the right place to guide Joseph.

Who is this mysterious man? Noting that all this is taking place in the valley of Hebron where the patriarch Abraham is buried, RaSHI draws a connection: Hebron is not only Abraham's burial place; it is also the place of the covenant where God promised the patriarch offspring who *"shall be strangers in a land not theirs"* (15:13). Now comes the story of Joseph, soon to be exiled by his brothers to Egypt—a land not his. Thus, the "man" is a symbol of God moving Joseph's destiny along. This anonymous guide, the man who tells Joseph the way to his brothers, is the Prime Mover[6] and, suggests Nechama Leibowitz, the "dialogue is inserted between two worlds, between the quiet and tranquil world of Joseph at home, shielded and spoilt by his father, and the stormy, troubled ruin of a world that was his after he met his brothers."[7]

RaMbaM, a thirteenth-century northern Spanish sage, reaffirms and elaborates on RaSHI's point. He "maintains that Torah inserts the details of Joseph's dialogue with the *man* to stress the workings of Divine Providence. By all accounts, Joseph should have turned back and not found his brothers. . . . Only the predestined decree of the God working behind the scenes led him to his brothers. God's unwitting instrument was the *man*, the chance passerby who constituted . . . a Divine messenger."[8]

---

5. The distance between Hebron and Shechem is approximately 143 kilometers (about eighty-nine miles). This would take a man in biblical times a minimum of four days walk.

6. Leibowitz, *Studies in Bereshit*, 395.

7. Leibowitz, *Studies in Bereshit*, 396.

8. Leibowitz, *Studies in Bereshit*, 396–97.

Sometimes individuals come into our lives for just a moment to serve a specific purpose and then they recede from our sphere of consciousness never to be encountered again. What is their purpose? Why have we encountered them?

Was the stranger's appearance to guide Joseph just a coincidence? Perhaps. But I think that there is more to this moment than mere synchronicity. If the stranger's appearance is no coincidence, but a godly plan, the word for the encounter now makes sense: *"A man found* (וימצאהו) *him wandering in the fields"*—it is almost as if the stranger were *looking* for Joseph, waiting to find him so that he could direct him toward his brothers!

Albert Einstein is believed to have commented once that "coincidences are God's way of remaining anonymous." The ancient rabbis believed that Joseph's being sold into slavery by his brothers was indeed part of a divine plan, to bring him down into Egypt so that ultimately he could save Egypt (and his father and brothers) from starvation. Indeed, as the story of Joseph and his brothers unfolds, even Joseph believes that all that has happened to him was divinely designed (*"it was to save life that God sent me ahead of you"*; Genesis 45:5).

The question that the man asks Joseph, while ostensibly simple, is actually quite profound—*"What are you seeking?"* This is *the* existential question; the man is asking Joseph not only *who* he is looking for, but *what* he is looking for, and in Joseph's simple reply—*"I am looking for my brothers"*—a universe of meaning is conveyed. Joseph is really saying, "I am looking for my brothers' love, I am looking for peace in my deeply fragmented family, I am looking for my purpose in life." Joseph himself may not be entirely sure of what he is seeking, but senses that the journey upon which he is embarking is crucial to his future. Joseph intuits that God is leading him on a journey of discovery—a discovery of self and of future.

When one is asked "what are you seeking?" one is challenged to delve deeply into one's heart and soul for the truest answer—and this is what is being asked of Joseph. The youthful Joseph at this point in his journey is not yet ready to answer the deeper question and perhaps this is the reason that God sends him on the difficult journey ahead, into a dark pit, into slavery, into imprisonment and liberation, from nadir to apex, from the depths of powerlessness to the heights of influence and authority. Joseph's journey, beginning with his encounter with his brothers, is about self-realization, and responding to that deep existential question, "What are you seeking?"

Rabbi Menachem Mendel of Kotzk, the Hassidic master, believed that the "man" Joseph encountered in the field was actually an angel (perhaps the angel Gabriel) sent by God to set Joseph on his way and to give him a central guiding question for his life:

The angel [the unnamed person] taught Joseph here that whenever he finds himself wandering on life's paths, when his soul weeps inside him from despair and doubt, he should remember first to become clear about what he really wants and yearns for. Then he will be able to return to his task; his vision and his path now will be the same.[9]

Rabbis Lawrence Kushner and Kerry Olitzky elaborate on the Kotzker's comment by adding: "When what you seek on the path of life eludes you, and you are confused about what you seek, reach deep inside yourself and God will help you clarify the truth you seek."[10]

Text to Life

> *Rissa, a rabbi and therapist in the eastern United States, writes the following:*
>
> Our ancient rabbis wondered about this man who appeared so suddenly on Joseph's path, a man who walked by—in and out of the narrative—in three sentences. They taught that perhaps the "man" was an angel and that sometimes angels present themselves as human beings to give us direction when we need it. It's 2001. I am in my second year of internship in addictions counseling. My first year of internship had been at the Jewish Family Service. I have taken a group of women to an Alcoholics Anonymous meeting. There is a speaker at the meeting who tells her tale. I do not recognize the speaker or her name. As she begins her story, recognition dawns. She told about coming to the Jewish Family Service needing placement in a Rehabilitation facility. And there, she said, she met an angel, an intern who was so kind to her, who told her over and over not to be ashamed, that she had a disease and could heal from it. That angel, she said, changed my life.
>
>   I had not recognized the speaker, but I did recognize the story. *I* had been that woman's angel. But from my side of the story, I had tried to get a woman into Rehab and couldn't do it. There were no openings. Until that AA meeting, I thought I had failed her.

---

   9. Menachem Mendel of Kotzk, quoted in Kushner and Olitzky, *Sparks Beneath the Surface*, 44. A number of rabbis identify the unnamed man with the angel Gabriel. See, for example, RaSHI's commentary on Genesis 37: 15.

   10. Kushner and Olitzky, *Sparks Beneath the Surface*, 45.

> The rabbis say that angels masquerade as humans. I say we are *all* God's angels. We all constantly step into the function of angels and step out again. We most often do this and have no idea of the lives we have influenced. In Joseph's case, the man walked on. Joseph found his brothers—and his destiny—and the mysterious stranger perhaps never knew how profoundly he had influenced the future of the Jewish People.

Exploring the Text Within

Find a quiet and comfortable place to sit in contemplative silence with the above teachings and with the following questions about you and your life's experience. You may choose to focus on one question or sit with several. Ask yourself: what do the biblical text and these teachings mean to me in my life?

Despite whatever dangers might lie ahead, Joseph responded with *hineni*, readiness to his father Jacob's instructions to find his brothers as they pastured the flocks.

> Can I recall a time when I moved ahead toward a destination, despite my own fears?

A mysterious man appeared to Joseph as he wanders lost in the fields and helps redirect him toward his brothers. *"Coincidences are God's way of remaining anonymous."*

> Can I recall a time when an unexpected stranger appeared and disappeared after making a significant difference in my life?

When what you seek on the path of life eludes you, and you are confused about what you seek, reach deep inside yourself and God will help you clarify the truth you seek.

> Can I recall a time when I knew that I must refocus myself, and reach deep inside to ask myself the question, "What do I seek?" in order to move forward in a healthy way?

Chapter 18

Vayeshev III

Murderous Thoughts

"They saw him [Joseph] from afar, and before he came close to them, they conspired to kill him."

—Genesis 37:18

When Joseph finally finds his brothers, none of them are happy to see him. All their resentments towards him come roaring back. They remember how their father Jacob had sewn a special ornamented tunic for Joseph. How jealous they felt then: *"And when his brothers saw that their father loved him more than any of his brothers, they hated him so that they could not speak a friendly word to him."* They remember Joseph's arrogant recounting of his dream—eleven sheaves of grain (representing the brothers) bowing down to Joseph's upright sheaf—*"and they hated him even more"* (37:3–8). They remember Joseph's second dream in which *"the sun, the moon and eleven stars are bowing down to [him]."* (37:9–11). They truly hate Joseph and when he approaches them, they plot to kill him.

Joseph's eldest brother, Reuben (who intends to return later to rescue Joseph and bring him back to his father Jacob) convinces the other brothers not to actually kill him, but to cast him into a dry well (or "pit"), and leave him to die. The brothers agree.

"The pit was empty. There was no water in it."

—Genesis 37:24

Joseph lies at the bottom of the dry pit. Alone and frightened, he has no idea what will happen next. The ancient rabbis who read the text noticed a redundancy in the verse that made them curious. Why are we told that the "pit was empty and there was no water in it?" Certainly without water, the pit is empty! According to the rabbinic mind, this seemingly repetitive statement must have deeper significance, and indeed it does.

Water is a powerful source (and force) in any culture. In Jewish tradition, the word *mayim* (water) has myriad meanings. *Mayim chayim*—living waters—may represent God and is also one of the names given to the Torah.[1]

The word *mayim*/מים (*mem*/מ—*yud*/י—*mem*/ם) contains within it the name of the Holy One: the *yud* projecting "the timeless pulsating energy of *aleph*/א (the divine force) into time and conditioned physical existence."[2] Water is, of course, *the* life-sustaining liquid. "It flows freely. It is formless, and takes the shape of its container."[3]

A kabbalistic (Jewish mystical) text, *Sefer Ha-Bahir*, teaches that the shape of the letter *mem*/מ in the word is identified with the wetness of the amniotic fluid of the womb, *rechem*, which is associated with the *sefirah* or divine emanation of *chesed*, lovingkindness. Mem is the womb. *Look at the shape of the letter: it has an opening through which it can give birth.* This is the female aspect of the *mem*.

מ

In contrast, the *mem sofit,* the final *mem* is entirely closed.

ם

Sefer Ha-Bahir teaches that this is the *womb of the past and represents the male aspect and symbolizes the sefirah or divine emanation of bina, understanding.* Thus we are taught that the *mem* (מ) is the balancing point of all manifestation—*the womb of the future and the womb of the past. Past and future are linked by the letter yud (י)—the symbol of the Holy One—thus godliness is restored and is always Present in mayim (water)*—מים.[4]

What does all this have to do with Joseph in the empty, waterless pit?

We can sum it up this way:

---

1. See Midrash Rabbah 84:16 Soncino edition, 782.
2. Harelick, *The Inner Meaning of the Hebrew Letters*, 198.
3. Harelick, *The Inner Meaning of the Hebrew Letters*, 198.
4. Harelick, *The Inner Meaning of the Hebrew Letters*, 198.

- On one hand, Joseph is thrown into a godless pit, devoid of living waters.
- On the other hand, Joseph himself becomes the container for *mayim chayim*, living waters. (Hence the redundancy of the text.) *He becomes the vessel for God; he holds within him the bitter waters of the womb of the past and he carries forward into his journey the womb of the future—he holds within his soul both* rechamim, *i.e., both wombs, representing* chesed *(lovingkindness) and* binah *(understanding).* These attributes will emerge in Joseph as he matures and grows.

"The pit was empty. There was no water in it." But Joseph is fertile.

We are discovering that this simple verse is more complicated that it seems on the surface. Let's look at another perspective:

"The pit was empty. There was no water in it."

—Genesis 37:24

The Talmudic-era rabbi Acha interpreted the words, *"the pit was empty,"* as follows: "Jacob's pit was emptied," meaning that Jacob's children "were emptied of their finer feelings" of love and brotherly loyalty to their brother Joseph.[5] How sad it is when siblings are in conflict and embittered toward one another. How tragic when they become so alienated from one another that they even contemplate violence. Jacob himself knew such conflict and bitterness—Esau his brother had vowed to kill him when Jacob had stolen Esau's birthright. The dark specter of violence had plagued his own life until his reconciliation with Esau.

So what was Joseph's fate? Reuben mysteriously disappears from the scene and before he returns, the other brothers have sold Joseph to a caravan of passing Midianite traders. Soaking Joseph's coat of many colors in goat's blood, the brothers bring it to their father Jacob, telling him that Joseph has been devoured by a wild beast. Jacob descends into deep, inconsolable grief.

Now captive, Joseph must grow up all too fast. Arriving in *Egypt—Mitzrayim* in Hebrew—he is now both geographically and physically in a place of tight constriction, as the word *Mitzrayim* connotes—its Hebrew root מצר/*meytzar* means "a strait." In *Mitzrayim*, in the "straits," Joseph undergoes a cascading series of experiences: servitude in Pharaoh's court, temptation, downfall and imprisonment, and finally triumph and elevation to the highest position in the land, just below Pharaoh himself.

5. Midrash Rabbah, 84:16, Soncino edition, 782.

When he first arrives in *Mitzrayim*, Joseph is sold by the Midianite traders to Potiphar, a minister in Pharaoh's court. There, Joseph succeeds masterfully as Potiphar's assistant and is raised to a high status in his household. Soon enough matters turn sour when Potiphar's wife becomes attracted to the "well-built and handsome" Joseph and orders him to have sex with her. At this dramatic moment, Joseph is sorely tempted, but manages to resist the seduction: *"After a time, his master's wife cast her eyes upon Joseph and said, 'Lie with me.' But he refused"* (39:7-8).

RaSHi tells us that at first, when Joseph came into the good graces of Potiphar, Pharaoh's minister, he began "to see himself as a ruler [and] started to eat and drink and curl his hair to groom himself [for a higher exalted position]. The Holy One, Blessed be He, said: Is it right that your father is in mourning and you curl your hair?! I shall now send the bear [in the form of Potiphar's wife] to attack you!"[6]

Though the text simply tells us that Joseph "refused" Mrs. Potiphar's advances, the rare, three-part *shalshelet* cantillation mark that appears only four times in the entire Torah hints at a different story. The *shalshelet* is a three-part quivering, fluctuating sound moving upwards and downwards, seeming to waiver between "yes" and "no." Musically, it can connote emphasis or profound vacillation. Joseph is formidably tempted by Lady Potiphar's[7] enticements, "but he refused" (39:8)—*va'y'ma'eyn*—וַיְמָאֵן. So much drama for such a short Hebrew word! In English, perhaps Joseph's attempt to resist temptation might have sounded something like this: *No, no, no, no, no, no, no, no, no, no—Well, maybe, maybe, maybe, maybe, no, no, no, no, no, no, no, no, NO!* Thus, the *shalshelet* dramatizes Joseph's vacillation, giving extra life to the telling of the story. A community of worshippers listening to this chanted Torah reading in synagogue, and the up-and-down notes of the *shalshelet:* cannot fail to notice the drama of the moment!

The sages of old taught that Joseph was able to resist his mistress' sexual advances because of his deep loyalty to his father, Jacob, and due to his faith in his lineage and to the God of Israel. In the Talmud, we read that one rabbi, Rav Huna, said in the name of Rav Mattona: "'Joseph saw his father's face and his blood was cooled.' Thus it continues. By the hands of the Mighty One of Jacob, from that One, the Shepherd, *Tzur Yisrael* (the Rock of Israel), [Joseph was able to resist]. By the God of your father, who helped you, Joseph!"[8]

6. Rashi in Chok L'Yisrael (Hebrew-English version) "Vayeishev for Friday," 299.

7. Note that Potiphar's wife is nameless here, referred to simply as "the wife of Potiphar." Sadly, this is the condition of the many women in the Hebrew Bible. See, for example, Noah's wife (7:7), Jeftah's daughter, (Judges 11:30-39), etc.

8. *Bereishit Rabbah* 87:7 Soncino ed. 3rd ed., 812.

This interpretation has been supported through the millennia by the thirteenth-century kabbalists of the Zohar and by an eighteenth-century Hassidic rebbe, Reb Levi Yitzchak of Berdichev, who recalls the Zohar's teaching that the three-part *shalshelet* was "strengthened by [Joseph's] recollection of the three patriarchs Abraham, Isaac, and his own father, Jacob, to enable him to withstand the seduction of Potiphar's wife."[9] In the moment of temptation, Jacob chooses to respect his family and his lineage—he does not besmirch his family's honor.

Enraged at the rejection, Mrs. Potiphar accuses Joseph of rape—which lands him in prison. From elevation to downfall. From the heights into another pit.

Languishing in jail, Joseph correctly interprets the dreams of two other inmates—the chief baker and the chief wine server (40:4–23). When the chief wine server is released, he forgets all about Joseph, until a time when Pharaoh has a series of dreams that no one can interpret. Recalling Joseph's ability to interpret dreams, the wine server tells Pharaoh about Joseph and the young man is summoned (41:12–14). Interpreting Pharaoh's dreams—seven fat cows and seven scrawny cows as seven years of plenty and seven years of famine, Joseph counsels storing grain for the lean years. Indeed, everything turns out as Joseph has predicted and in reward for his prescience, Pharaoh appoints Joseph chancellor of *Mitzrayim*, in charge of the stored grain and its distribution. Again, from downfall to triumph. Joseph now becomes the most powerful man in Egypt just beneath Pharaoh. Now Joseph gradually becomes an Egyptian, in dress, in mannerism, in all outward affect. Years go by as Joseph grows and matures.

Text to Life

> Logan is a man in his fifties, a pillar of his community. He teaches classes in his local congregation, often studies in adult education classes himself, reads omnivorously, attends consciousness-oriented seminars, is a generous donor to community charities and is considered to be one of the more sensitive and spiritually attuned men in his community.
>
> In his thirties, Logan worked for an investment firm where he was faced with a formidable temptation—an opportunity to embezzle about $50,000 from his company. Agonizing over the temptation, Logan finally succumbed and stole the money. Amazingly, due to the poorest of bookkeeping practices at the firm,

---

9. Levi Yitzchak of Berdichev, *Kedushat Levi*.

Logan's theft was never discovered. He has lived with the internal consequences of his decision every day since the theft. Unhappy in myriad ways throughout the past quarter of a century, Logan has found that his guilt has plagued him ever since. Unable to return the money because he had spent it, and also fearful of being exposed, Logan lives with his guilt every day.

In the meantime, Logan has lived an exemplary life. Yet "no good deed, no act of kindness or charity seems to be able to atone for my sin. My guilt has seeped into the marrow of my bones," Logan told me. "Whenever I read the story of Joseph's resisting temptation, I remember that Joseph understood the consequences of *not* resisting temptation and he refrained from guilt. Even though I understood what could happen if I were caught embezzling, I could *not* resist the temptation of the money. I was never apprehended, but my punishment has been the guilt I have lived with for decades. Every time I read of Joseph's strength, I envy him."

Cheryl is a retired school teacher. When she was a young woman, she found herself dating two very different men. One, Sam, was a very interesting, somewhat dramatic man who was very much in love with her and promised her a life of fascinating adventure. The other, Joe, was a kind, sweet man, who also loved Cheryl deeply, and offered her a good life, but more ordinary in its goodness. With Sam she imagined a future full of adventure with many ups and downs and fine stories to tell. With Joe she foresaw have a fine, solid life with steady, abiding love. "I was sorely tempted to marry Sam," Cheryl told me. "I could just imagine in my mind's eye all the exciting places we would go and things we would do. Sam was my passion, and Joe was my quiet, steady kind of love. I chose to marry Joe. I resisted the exciting temptation—and have never been sorry. My life has been good. *Very* good." Every time I read of Joseph's resisting the temptation of Potiphar's wife, I think that he was like me with Sam—he knew that it would be a flash in the pan, but not a quiet, steady kind of love, the kind of love I have shared for decades with Joe. *Two roads diverged in a wood and I took the one MORE traveled by and that has made all the difference.*[10]

---

10. With apologies to Robert Frost!

Exploring the Text Within

Find a quiet and comfortable place to sit in contemplative silence with the above teachings and with the following questions about you and your life's experience. You may choose to focus on one question or sit with several. Ask yourself: what do the biblical text and these teachings mean to me in my life?

> *The pit was empty. There was no water in it.*
>
> (Genesis 37:24)

Joseph is growing up and is beginning to face the harsh realities of life. He begins a long journey of trials, tribulations, ascent and descent. Yet his destiny is to become the container for *mayim chayim* (living waters), to embody the closed final *mem* ם, the open *mem* מ, representing the femininity of the open womb, the womb of the future. It is with God's help throughout his journey, represented by the *yud* in the middle of the word *mayim*, that Joseph grows and matures into the *future—carrying the open, fertile womb forward, filling the "empty pit" with hope.*

> Has there ever been a time in my life when I felt poised between what *was* and *what might be*, between past emptiness and future fullness, eager to give birth to my own hopeful new life?

> *The pit was empty There was no water in it.*
>
> (Genesis 37:24)

> *After a time, his master's wife cast her eyes upon Joseph and said, "Lie with me." But he refused.*
>
> (Genesis 39:7–8)

Jacob's pit was emptied, there was no *mayim chayim* (living waters). Jacob's children "were emptied of their finer feelings" of love and brotherly loyalty to their brother Joseph, who is now trapped in a godless place. How sad it is when brothers and sisters are in conflict and embittered toward one another.

> Has there ever been a time in my life when I felt deep conflict with my siblings or other family members or loved ones?

> Have I reached a place of peace and true reconciliation with them or am I, like Joseph, still on my journey?

After a time, his master's wife cast her eyes upon Joseph and said, "Lie with me." But he refused.

(Genesis 39:7–8)

> Has there ever been a time in my life when I have felt sorely tempted by something or someone that I knew was not good for me?
>
> Was I able to resist the temptation?
>
> Resist or not, what were the consequences?

Chapter 19

Mikkets and Vayiggash

The Stuff of Dreams—and Reunion

"Pharaoh dreamed that he was standing by the Nile when out of the Nile, there came up seven cows, handsome and sturdy, and they grazed in the reed grass.
But presently seven other cows came up from the Nile close behind them, ugly and gaunt and stood beside the cows on the bank of the Nile; and the ugly gaunt cows ate up the seven handsome sturdy cows. And Pharaoh awoke."

—Genesis 41:1 (Mikkets)

"Dreams have prophetic qualities: they are 'one-sixtieth of prophecy.'"

"The gift of a dream often comes in disguise. It has to be interpreted: 'A dream that is not interpreted is like a letter that is not read.'"

—Talmud, Berachot 55a[1]

"I am your brother Joseph, he whom you sold into Egypt. Now do not be distressed because you sold be hither; it was to save life that God sent me ahead of you. . . . God sent me ahead of you to ensure your survival on earth and to save your lives in an extraordinary deliverance. So it was not you who sent me here, but God."

—Genesis 46:1–7

---

1. Frankiel and Greenfield, *Entering the Temple of Dreams*, 129.

Dreams can be life changing—for the dreamer, for the one who understands the dream, even for a whole nation. Now, we begin to explore the stuff of dreams—the powerful dreamer, who didn't understand his own dreams, the young man who could interpret them and how that man's understanding changed the fate of his own family and an entire nation.

We pick up our story at the moment where Joseph interprets Pharaoh's two dreams—the first, of seven *"handsome and sturdy cows"* being devoured by seven *"ugly and gaunt"* cows, and the second dream about a single stalk with seven ears of *"solid and healthy"* corn and close behind them a stalk that sprouted *"seven ears, thin and scorched by the east wind"* (41:1-6).

When all of Pharaoh's magicians could not interpret his dreams, his cupbearer, who had been in prison two years earlier with Joseph, remembered Joseph and mentioned him to Pharaoh.

Joseph was summoned to Pharaoh's court and Pharaoh retold his dreams to Joseph, who interpreted them. Joseph concluded that both were really one unified dream (*"Pharaoh's dreams are one and the same"*),[2] explaining that they were related to the famine in all the lands surrounding Egypt, but had not yet spread to Pharaoh's land. Joseph advised Pharaoh to take measures to store the grain for a time when then *"ugly and gaunt"* cows and shriveled corn would take over—symbolically indicating that eventually famine would come to Egypt as well. Joseph was saying, "Be prepared, O Pharaoh, so that Egypt will not starve but survive and thrive!"

> *Accordingly, let Pharaoh find a man of discernment and wisdom, and set him over the land of Egypt. And let Pharaoh take steps to appoint overseers over the land, and organize the land of Egypt in the seven years of plenty. Let all of the food of these good years that are coming be gathered, and let the grain be collected under Pharaoh's authority as food to be stored in the cities. Let that food be a reserve for the land for the seven years of famine which will come upon the land of Egypt, so that the land may not perish in the famine.*

—Genesis 41:33-36

A seemingly small but important point here: the first words of this Torah portion are *Vayehi mikketz sh'natayim yamim*—*"After two years' time"* (41:1). From the time the cupbearer was freed from the dungeon in which he had been imprisoned with Joseph, twenty-four months had gone by. When the cupbearer was liberated, Joseph asked the servant to remember him and mention him to Pharaoh. The cupbearer forgot—until Pharaoh dreamed and

---

2. Genesis 41:25.

could not find an adequate interpreter of his dreams among all the magicians of Egypt. All this time, Joseph languished miserably in prison. Then, finally, when the cupbearer remembered, Joseph was hastily bathed, clothed in fine garb, and brought before Pharaoh. After waiting so long, Joseph understood that this must be Divine Providence. For a long time and to no avail, Joseph had willed his release, but now that Pharaoh had dreamed seemingly inscrutable dreams and Joseph was the only one who could understand them and interpret them correctly, God had intervened!

Joseph had come to a mature awareness that even though the Holy One endows each of us with free will, there is much that is not in our control. He had suffered mightily from the days of his youth until his time in the Egyptian prison. He had been thrown into a dry pit by his brothers and left to die; he had been rescued by Midian traders and then sold into slavery, and then he had been thrown into prison after refusing the advances of Potiphar's wife. There he had wasted away for years until finally, he was summoned by Pharaoh.

Suffering through this long series of tribulations Joseph became a much more humble man, coming to realize that his life had been saved not by his own will, but by God and that ultimately the future was not in his hands. Rabbi Aryeh Ben David writes that "Joseph's suffering has diminished his pride. He now understands that God is the source of the dreams. No longer absorbed with his own powers of dream interpretation, Joseph now regards himself as a medium, a person capable of providing greater insight and understanding."[3] Thus, when he approaches Pharaoh to interpret the king's dreams, Joseph is determined to introduce God to Pharaoh: *"Pharaoh's dreams are one and the same; God has told Pharaoh what He is about to do"* (41:25). Rabbi Ben David continues, "Joseph has finally realized that a dream is God's transmitting of a responsibility; it is less a special privilege than a task with which one has been charged. . . . Joseph, through suffering and tragedy, learns the lesson of humility. Originally blinded by his own exceptional potential, he realizes that these powers are indeed gifts from God and bring with them responsibility."[4]

With great relief, and recognizing Joseph's connection to God, Pharaoh responds to Joseph's advice: *"Could we find another like him, a man in whom is the spirit of God? Since God has made all this known to you, there is none so discerning and wise as you. You shall be in charge of my court and by your command shall my people be directed; only with respect to the throne shall I be superior to you. . . . See, I put you in charge of all the land*

---

3. Ben David, *Around the Shabbat Table*, 72.
4. Ben David, *Around the Shabbat Table*, 73.

of Egypt" (41:38–41). Thus Joseph is elevated from a debased prisoner to the vizier of Egypt, dressed in fine robes and endowed with power second only to Pharaoh himself.

> *The seven years of abundance that the land of Egypt enjoyed came to an end, and the seven years of famine set in, just as Joseph had foretold. There was famine in all lands, but throughout the land of Egypt there was bread. And when all the land of Egypt felt the hunger, the people cried out to Pharaoh for bread; and Pharaoh said to all the Egyptians, "Go to Joseph; whatever he tells you, you shall do."—Accordingly, when the famine became severe in the land of Egypt, Joseph laid open all that was within, and rationed out grain to the Egyptians. The famine, however, spread over the whole world. So all the world came to Joseph in Egypt to procure rations.*
>
> —Genesis 42:53–57

Now that Joseph has risen to great power, let us return to the family saga. Joseph's father Jacob and his brothers in Canaan had been suffering from the widespread famine

> *When Jacob saw that there were food rations to be had in Egypt, he said to his sons . . . "Now I hear . . . that there are rations to be had in Egypt. Go down and procure rations for us there, that we may live and not die."*
>
> —Genesis 42:1–2

Thus begins the unfolding of the series of events that will eventually lead to the reunion of Joseph and his brothers.

Not only has Joseph grown into a man in touch with the Divine, he seems also to have grown kinder. Although the following part of the text may not seem *kind*, let us explore further.

> *And Joseph's brothers came and bowed low to him, with their faces to the ground. When Joseph saw his brothers, he recognized them; but he acted like a stranger towards them and spoke harshly to them.*
>
> —Genesis 42:6–7

We might assume that Joseph would want to punish his brothers for their murderous acts towards him when they were all so much younger, but some sages think he was actually acting out of kindness. Rabbi Levi Yitzchak of Berdichev, an eighteenth-century Hassidic rabbi (also known as the *Kedushat Levi*), believed that Joseph's actions demonstrated his righteousness and kindness:

> It is only natural that when a person triumphs over his fellow, and the other realizes that the latter has beaten him, he feels great sadness and pain. But when one triumphs and the other does not know by whom he has been beaten, the loss is not as painful. . . . Now this was Joseph's righteousness: in the moment that he brothers bowed low to him and he actually triumphed over them . . . he acted like a stranger toward them so that they would not be bitter and it would appear as if they were bowing to someone else . . . .[5]

Rabbi Abraham Twerski, attributing the idea to his deceased brother Rabbi Shlomo Twerski, wrote that Joseph had forgiven his brothers, but understood that to simply forgive them without giving them an opportunity to make amends would leave them still in a position of "owing" him, in a position of subservience to him: "The brothers would have forever been the groveling penitents who would have to eternally bear the guilt of their behavior. They would never again be able to face Joseph or their father and retain their self-esteem."[6] Abraham Twerski points out that "[the] Talmud says that true and effective *teshuvah* (repentance) is achieved only if the person is placed in the same circumstances of his sin and under the same temptation."[7] Thus, Joseph puts his brothers through several tests, first framing them to appear as if they have stolen the possessions they have offered as payment for food. He is testing their honesty to see if they will reveal the possessions, thus revealing their *teshuvah* (repentance for their earlier deeds). Later, and most importantly, Joseph demands that they bring his younger brother, Benjamin, down into Egypt. Knowing that this will crush their elderly father Jacob and destroy his spirit, the brothers do not know what to do, but realize that they have no choice in the matter.

The great temptation for the brothers would have been to bring Benjamin to Joseph and leave him there as a hostage (an echo of what they had done to Joseph himself) in order to obtain food and provisions for their starving families back in Canaan. But one brother, Judah, resists this temptation. When he tells his father Jacob about Joseph's demand that Benjamin be brought to him, the old man is utterly in despair. Judah assures his father:

---

5. Levi Yitzchak of Berdichev, quoted in Green et al., *Speaking Torah*, 148.
6. Twerski, *Twerski on Chumash*, 88.
7. Twerski, *Twerski on Chumash*, 89.

> *I myself will be a surety for him; you may hold me responsible:*
> *if I do not bring him back to you and set him before you, I shall*
> *stand guilty before you forever.*

—Genesis 43:9

Later, after more trials and tribulations, Judah stands before Joseph (who has still not revealed himself to his brothers) and offers himself as a hostage instead of Benjamin (whom, of course, Joseph favors, since Benjamin is his full blood-brother, son of Rachel, whom he has not seen since he was a baby). Judah beseeches Joseph:

> *Your servant my father said to us: "As you know, my wife bore me*
> *two sons. But one is gone from me and I said: Alas, he was torn by*
> *a beast! And I have not seen him since. If you take this one from*
> *me too, and he meets with disaster, you will send my white head*
> *down to Sheol[8] in sorrow."*

—Genesis 44:27-29

Judah continues:

> *Now, if I come to your servant my father and the boy is not with*
> *us—since his own life is so bound up with his—when he sees that*
> *the boy is not with us, he will die and your servants will send*
> *the white head of your servant our father down to Sheol in grief.*
> *Now your servant [Judah] has pledged himself for the boy to my*
> *father saying, "If I do not bring him back to you, I shall stand*
> *guilty before my father forever." Therefore, please let your servant*
> *remain as a servant to my lord instead of the boy, and let the boy*
> *go back with his brothers. For how can I go back to my father*
> *unless the boy is with me? Let me not be witness to the woe that*
> *would overtake my father!*

—Genesis 44:30-34

The fact that it is Judah who offers himself as a guarantor for Benjamin's safety is significant. It is symbolic of Judah's redemption and complete *teshuvah*.

Earlier in the story, when Joseph finds his brothers tending to their flocks in Dothan, they said to one another, "Here comes that dreamer! Come now, let us kill him and throw him into one of the pits and we can say, 'a savage beast devoured him.' We shall see what comes of his dreams!" (37:19-20). The oldest brother, Reuben seeks to save Joseph's life and Judah suggests that they sell Joseph to traders who are passing by—"What do we gain by killing our

---

8. Sheol is the dark underworld—a place of death.

brother...? Come, let us sell him to the Ishmaelites, but let us not do away with him ourselves. After all, he is our brother, our own flesh" (37:26–27). So, while Judah saves Joseph's life, he also condemns Joseph to a life of slavery.

In addition, Torah goes to great lengths to show that Judah's deeds around this time are not "clean." During this same time period, Judah leaves his brothers and marries a woman named Shua, and with her he sires three sons: Er, Onan, and Shelah. In the course of time, Er marries a woman named Tamar but soon (for unexplained reasons), *"Er, Judah's first-born, was displeasing to the* LORD *and the* LORD *took his life"* (38:7). Tamar is left widowed.

According to the biblical laws of levirate marriage, if a man dies before he has sired two children, it is his brother's obligation to marry the deceased man's widow in order to sire children on the dead man's behalf. Thus, Er's younger brother, Onan, is now obliged to marry Tamar, but before the marriage can take place, Onan, *"knowing that the seed would not count as his, let it go to waste whenever he joined with his brother's wife, so as not to provide offspring for his brother"*[9] (38:9). As punishment for this sin, God takes Onan's life as well (38:10). This leaves Judah's youngest son, Shelah, still a boy, obliged to marry Tamar once he reaches manhood. Judah, now no doubt "spooked" by the death of two of his sons, must feel that Tamar was a jinx, but nevertheless promises Tamar that when Shelah matures, he will fulfill the marital obligation by sending Shelah to her: *"Then Judah said to his daughter-in-law Tamar, 'Stay as a widow in your father's house until my son Shelah grows up'—for he thought, 'He too might die like his brothers.' So Tamar went to live in her father's house"* (38:11). Years go by, Shelah grows up, but still Judah fails to send him to Tamar to marry her.

In the course of time, Judah's own wife, Shua, dies and after an appropriate time of mourning, Judah seeks sexual satisfaction of his own. He travels toward Timnah, where Tamar is living in her father's house. Hearing of her father-in-law's impending arrival, but without her intended bridegroom Shelah, Tamar *"took off her widow's garb, covered her face with a veil, and wrapping herself up, sat down at the entrance of Enaim,*[10] *which is on the road to Timnah, for she saw that Shelah was grown up, yet she had not been given to him as wife"* (38:14).

---

9. From Onan's act, we get the English word "onanism," which means withdrawal before orgasm, incomplete coitus, or masturbation—i.e., the spilling of semen for non-procreative purposes.

10. Interestingly, "Enaim" means "eyes." It is as if God was watching Judah's actions as Tamar sits there awaiting his arrival.

Judah approaches and *"he took her* [Tamar] *for a harlot"* (38:15), making a deal to have carnal relations with her, offering as a pledge his seal, cord, and his staff. After his time with the "harlot," Judah returns home.

Later, back at home, Judah dispatches a servant to redeem his seal, cord, and staff by sending a goat kid as payment for his time with the "harlot," but she is nowhere to be found. Fearing embarrassment, Judah instructs his servant to return home, lest he *"become a laughingstock"* (38:23).

About three months later, Judah hears that Tamar is *"with child by harlotry."* Outraged, he declares, *"Bring her out and let her be burned"* (38:24), but Tamar is smarter than her father-in-law and brings forth the cord and the staff and says, *"Examine these: whose seal and cord and staff are these?"* Immediately recognizing that these possessions are his, Judah admits his guilt, and says, *"She is more in the right than I, inasmuch as I did not give her to my son Shelach"* (Gen 38:26).

Judah takes full paternal responsibility for Tamar's pregnancy and *"when the time came for her to give birth,"* there were twins in her womb! (38:27). Judah thus sires two sons—Perez and Zerah. Now, years later, as Judah stands before his father and then before Joseph, guilty of a multitude of sins—first having sold Joseph into slavery, then having neglected to give his son Shelah to Tamar as a husband, according to the laws of levirate marriage, and finally of impregnating Tamar, in an act of sex with a woman he thought was a prostitute.

As Judah stands now responsible for Jacob's youngest son, Benjamin, now grown to manhood, he has a chance to redeem himself—to take responsibility for Benjamin and ensure his safety. This is what he does when he says to Joseph,

> *Therefore, please let your servant* [Judah himself] *remain as a servant to my lord instead of the boy, and let the boy go back with his brothers. For how can I go back to my father unless the boy is with me? Let me not be witness to the woe that would overtake my father!*
>
> —Genesis 44:33–34

Judah has finally become a righteous man and a good son and brother, trying his best to protect Benjamin and bring Jacob's youngest son home safely.

Judah has not only redeemed himself but he also speaks movingly to Joseph. Evoking the pathos of his elderly father waiting back in hunger-plagued Canaan with Benjamin, and calling to mind Jacob's anguish at the possibility of losing another son, Judah touches Joseph's heart.[11] In fact, Ju-

---

11. Nehama Leibowitz notes that Judah's speech to Joseph is the "longest oration

dah mentions their father fourteen times in his speech to Joseph,[12] evoking Jacob's hoary head, and almost-broken spirit.

Seeing Judah's loyalty to their father, and protectiveness toward Benjamin, Joseph can no longer maintain the façade that he is a stranger to his brothers. He weeps and finally reveals himself.

> *Joseph could no longer control himself . . . and he cried out, "Have everyone withdraw from me!" So there was no one else about when Joseph made himself known to his brothers. His sobs were so loud that the Egyptians could hear, and so the news reached Pharaoh's palace. Joseph said to his brothers, "I am Joseph. Is my father still well?" But his brothers could not answer him, so dumbfounded were they on account of him. Then Joseph said to his brothers, "Come forward to me." And when they came forward, he said, "I am your brother Joseph, he whom you sold into Egypt. Now do not be distressed because you sold me hither; it was to save life that God sent me ahead of you. . . . God sent me ahead of you to ensure your survival on earth and to save your lives in an extraordinary deliverance. So it was not you who sent me here, but God; and He has made me a father to Pharaoh, lord of all his household, and ruler over the whole land of Egypt."*

—Genesis 46:1–8

Joseph instructs his brothers to return to Canaan and bring his father and the entire family back to Egypt where he will ensure that they will have all that they need (Gen 46:9–13).

> *With that he embraced his brother Benjamin around the neck and wept, and Benjamin wept on his neck. He kissed all his brothers and wept upon them; only then were his brothers able to talk to him.*

—Genesis 46:14–15

And so the loving reunion takes place. After the various tests that Joseph has put them through and after a process of *teshuvah* (repentance) that the brothers have experienced within themselves, after the turmoil and the suffering, the brothers are able to embrace and return to love—perhaps a love that wasn't even a return, but felt for the first time now, a love that was devoid of competition, and resentments, but rather grounded in an understanding of the life-and-death struggle that all of them had endured in their own distinct ways.

---

recorded in Genesis." Leibowitz, *Studies in Bereishit: Genesis*, 483.

12. Leibowitz, *Studies in Bereishit: Genesis*, 484.

Eventually, Jacob and all in his tribe come down to Egypt and are protected and cared for Joseph (46:5–7).

Text to Life

Johanna, a spiritual director in a large Canadian city, tells the following story: "I'm very blessed to receive what I consider to be messages from God, especially in times of my life when I am in trouble. One such message came in a two-word dream: "Riding shotgun." The absolute "otherness" of the language—I wasn't even sure what riding shotgun meant—is one of the remarkable gifts of the unconscious, where the Dream Maker resides. I realized that once more the Divine was inviting me to remember that I'm not driving the car, but that I'm in the passenger seat. This remarkable two-word dream highlighted my apparently incurable belief that I control my life when in fact I do not—God is in control.

Another dream sequence gifted me with the understanding that dreams can be life changing. On August 8, 1988, I was diagnosed with cancer in my left breast. I had a lump removed that, blessedly, was surrounded by healthy tissue. My prognosis was good. My lymph nodes were subsequently removed to see if the cancer had spread. I was in hospital for ten days after the removal of my lymph nodes and recovery was slow. During my ten-day hospital stay, my mother came to visit and happened to see Dr. Lyle Green, the son of a friend, in the hallway outside my room. My mother, an inveterate extrovert, hurried out to greet Dr. Green who came into my room to say hello. That night, I had a dream: Dr. Green, who had no connection to my medical case, came into my room and told me, "I looked at your chart and your lymph nodes are clear. You don't need further treatment."

About two days after the dream, Dr. Green did indeed come into my room. "How are you doing?" he asked kindly. I told him I was anxious, because I was still waiting to learn if the cancer had spread to my lymph nodes.

Dr. Green said, "I looked at your chart and your lymph nodes are clear. You don't need further treatment." Exactly the words of my dream.

"That's so nice of you," I had said in my dream, "why did you do this?" "I felt a connection with you." Dr. Green had replied.

> I was in awe. My dream was prophetic. I began to believe even more deeply that my dreams would advise me on how to live. Though my prognosis was good, about two months later my surgeon recommended that I consult with two oncologists to see if I needed chemotherapy treatment to follow-up on the surgery. "Current research is suggesting chemotherapy even if the malignancy has not spread to the lymph nodes," he said. I fearfully asked my dreams what I should do if the oncologists advised chemotherapy.
>
> Soon after I had two dreams. In the first I was told "You don't need it [chemotherapy]." I also dreamed: "An apple a day," and heard the words, "You will live well into your eighties."
>
> I did go to the two oncologists to receive their input and both told me that my pathology report indicated that I did not need further treatment. All my dreams told me what I had subsequently heard from two oncologists. Before I saw the oncologists I wondered whether I would listen to my dreams or the doctors, should the guidance diverge. Luckily I didn't have to choose.
>
> In the Garden of Eden, the apple came from the tree of knowledge of Good and Evil. I understood the "apple a day" dream to be advising me to work for the rest of my life on the awareness of good and evil as both being aspects of life, myself and the Divine.
>
> After this episode of dreams and doctors in my life, I have come to believe that my dreams guide me. My dreams have proven over and over I can trust them because they come from God and are not from my conscious mind. My conscious mind makes many mistakes."
>
> So from Pharaoh to Joseph to Johanna, we see a chain of trust—dreams can be sacred guides to daily living.
>
> JH

Exploring the Text Within

Find a quiet and comfortable place to sit in contemplative silence with the above teachings and with the following questions about you and your life's experience. You may choose to focus on one question or sit with several. Ask yourself: what do the biblical text and these teachings mean to me in my life?

Pharaoh dreamed that he was standing by the Nile when out of the Nile, there came up seven cows, handsome and sturdy, and they grazed in the reed grass. But presently seven other cows came up from the Nile close behind them, ugly and gaunt and stood beside the cows on the bank of the Nile; and the ugly gaunt cows ate up the seven handsome sturdy cows. (Genesis 41:1)

> Can I recall a time in my life when I experienced emotional or spiritual "plenty," and another time when I experienced emotional or spiritual "famine?" How did I celebrate the "plenty" and cope with the "famine?"

> Can I recall a time when a dream has so stirred me that it has inspired a change in the direction of my life? My actions? My relationship(s) with others?

Now do not be distressed because you sold me hither; it was to save life that God sent me ahead of you. . . . God sent me ahead of you to ensure your survival on earth and to save your lives in an extraordinary deliverance. So it was not you who sent me here, but God.

(Genesis 46:1–8)

> Have I ever found myself in an unexpected situation in which I have sensed that God has put me in for a purpose—for good?
>
> How did I navigate that situation?

Dreams have prophetic qualities: they are 'one-sixtieth of prophecy.' . . . [T]he gift of a dream often comes in disguise. It has to be interpreted: "A dream that is not interpreted is like a letter that is not read."

(Talmud, Berachot 55a)[13]

---

13. Frankiel and Greenfield, *Entering the Temple of Dreams*, 129.

> Have you ever had a dream that you felt has had the power to change your life?
>
> How have you responded to the dream?

And she [Tamar] *added, "Examine these whose seal and cord and staff are these?" Judah recognized them and said, "She is more right than I, inasmuch as I did not give her to my son Shelah."*

(Genesis 38:25–26)

> Like Judah, have you ever had your misdeed(s) revealed to you, and have you regretted your behavior and mended your ways?

Chapter 20

Vayiggash-Vayechi

The Curse of Blessings[1]

"Pharaoh said to Joseph. 'Say to your brothers, Do as follows: load up your beasts and go at once to the land of Canaan. Take your father and your households and come to me; I will give you the best of the land of Egypt and you shall live off the fat of the land.'"

—Genesis 45:17–18 (Vayiggash)

"And Jacob called his sons and said, 'Come together, that I may tell you what is to happen to you in the days that will come.'"

—Genesis 49:1–27 (Vayechi)

"If you want to change someone's life, give them a blessing."

—Anonymous

After Joseph revealed himself to his brothers and Pharaoh invited his entire family to come and live in the prosperity of Egypt, Joseph's kin came down into Egypt and were saved from the famine in Canaan. Jacob learned that his beloved son Joseph was still alive and heard God's voice in a vision that it was the right thing to go down to Egypt—

---

1. I thank to my colleague Rabbi Mitchell Chefitz for the title of this chapter, named for his wonderful book of stories entitled *The Curse of Blessings*. Title used with permission of the author.

> *Fear not to go down to Egypt, for I will make you there into a great nation. I Myself will go down with you and I Myself will also bring you back; and Joseph's hand shall close your eyes.*
>
> —Genesis 46:3–4

The reunion between Joseph and his aged father is poignant:

> *Joseph ordered his chariot and went to Goshen to meet his father Israel [Jacob]; he presented himself to him, and embracing him around the neck, he wept on his neck a good while. Then Israel said to Joseph, "Now I can die, having seen for myself that you are still alive."*
>
> —Genesis 46:29–30

Finally, the family is all together again in harmony. Gone is the hatred and resentment that had torn them apart in earlier years, and an elderly Jacob is content, ready to leave this world with all his sons alive and well, and surrounding him. The family settles down in Egypt, Jacob lives in peace and prosperity for seventeen years before his death. All is well.

Vayechi, the last Torah portion in the Book of Genesis, is a bridge between the history of the first generations of the Israelite people and the story of their enslavement in Egypt after "there arose a king in Egypt who did not know Joseph" (Exodus 1:8). The portion tells us of Jacob's deathbed words to his twelve sons, his desire to be buried in the land of Canaan, his internment there, and finally Joseph and his brothers' return to Egypt.

Here we read of Jacob as a frail old man who is preparing to die. During his final illness, he has a chance to speak to each son from his heart. With death approaching, Jacob's final illness is a gift of time—time to offer a deathbed lesson to each of his sons. In the Talmud, we read that

> Until Jacob's days, nobody became sick before he died; people died suddenly, without warning. Then Jacob prayed that a person should become sick before he died, so that he could convey his last wishes to his children, and sickness came into being.[2]

So Jacob calls together his twelve sons and says to them, "*Come together that I may tell you what is to happen to you in the days to come*" (49:1). Jacob offers an ethical will to his offspring.

Professor Nathaniel Stampfer writes that

> the tradition of bequeathing a spiritual legacy [now known as an "ethical will"] . . . has its roots in the Bible and the Talmud. . . .

---

2. BT Bava Metzia 87a.

> [Parents] sought to write and transmit ... personal reflections on their lives as Jews and on the motivating values and events in their life's experience. They hoped to impart the precepts of God's Law refracted through the prism of a parent's life.[3]

This is what Jacob hopes to do in his last words to his sons. Rabbi Irwin Kula writes that

> *Berakhot* (blessings) interpret our experiences and uncover the deeper dimensions of our actions. ... [They] are reminders that there are no neutral human activities. Everything we do has cosmic significance, moving us either closer to or father from the Jewish dream of a perfect world. [They] are not words we have to say but openings to shape, name and define what we are doing in a different light.[4]

I believe that Jacob wants to bring his sons closer to a perfect world. His intention is to set his sons on a better path for the future. He conveys his most heartfelt emotions—feelings of love, regret, reprimand, and insights into his sons' future based on their actions during his lifetime. He offers a unique and individual message to each son, without comparison to any other son,[5] and addresses each son personally, knowing each man's character and speaking to the specific situation and personal life experience of each.

Would that this were so for all parents and children today—that a parent would know a child (even as an adult) so well that the elder, at a time nearing death, could offer an honest, frank, and customized assessment of each child's life and character and to give that child life wisdom! Too often parents and adult children are distant (both geographically and emotionally), and not involved in each other's lives. But Jacob knew his sons and *did* have wisdom to impart to them, even if sometimes that wisdom appeared harsh.

Sometimes "blessings" that seem harsh are, nonetheless, loving, as I believe Jacob's blessings to Reuben and Simeon and Levi were.

My beloved friend and esteemed colleague, Rabbi Marcia Prager, author of *The Path of Blessing*, writes that "Jewish tradition teaches that the simple act of a *brakha* (blessing) has a cosmic effect, for a *brakha* causes *shefa*, the 'abundant flow of G-d's love and goodness to pour into the world, like a hand on a faucet, each *brakha* turns on the tap.'"[6]

---

3. Stampfer, *So That Your Values Live On*, xiii.

4. Rabbi Irwin Kula, "A Blessing," in Olitzky and Forman, eds., *Restful Reflections*, 180.

5 See Ben David, *Around the Shabbat Table*, 88.

6. Prager, *The Path of Blessing*, 13.

I affirm these wise words and would add that a blessing that is harsh and may seem like a curse is also a source of Divine flow—for it offers wisdom, good advice to live by, to remedy a wrong done in the past, a possibility for *teshuva* (repentance) and changing our ways.

Rabbi Prager reflected that Jacob's harsh words to Reuben and Simeon and Levi were not, of course, blessings in the traditional rabbinic sense, but more like "psychospiritual analyses with some *tochecha* (rebuke) mixed in." Jacob's blessings are, in the words of her husband, Cantor Jack Kessler, "karmic charges." Rabbi Prager continued, "In many of our homes, what is the blessing that a parent gives to a child? It is the three-part priestly blessing:"

יְבָרֶכְךָ ה' וְיִשְׁמְרֶךָ יָאֵר ה' פָּנָיו אֵלֶיךָ וִיחֻנֶּךָּ
יִשָּׂא ה' פָּנָיו אֵלֶיךָ וְיָשֵׂם לְךָ שָׁלוֹם7

> May the One Who is the Sourcing Power of Creation and the Fountain of Blessings bless you and guard you
> May the Face of the One shine Divine radiance upon you and flow grace toward you
> May the radiant Face of the One lift up toward you
> And grant you Shalom: Wholeness, Completion, Fulfillment, and Peace.[8]

This blessing is a trajectory towards *shalom*. When I think about Jacob's harsh blessings to his sons, I think that, as a parent, he hopes that Reuben, Simeon, and Levi can achieve wholeness and integration and fulfillment. He knows that there are personality traits and bits of legacy that could stand in their way to achieving wholeness. There is no reason any longer for him to pretend that this is not true, because he is dying. Rabbi Prager continues,

> When we are dying we no longer have to pretend. Jacob sees with candid clarity, and speaks with candid clarity. It may not seem kind, but his intention is to help each son achieve peace—integration, wholeness, and completion. I feel for all of them—Jacob, Reuben, and Simeon and Levi! They all had rough life stories. One of the things I love about Torah is that it doesn't "dry clean" any of our matriarchs and patriarchs. They are all works-in-progress and that is good for me because I am a work in progress too. *Tochechah—Rebuke—a* "blessing [that] *is sometimes concealed within stern rebuke.*"[9]

---

7. Numbers 6:22–27.

8. Rabbi Prager's translation.

9. Rabbi Yitzchak Ginsburgh—contemporary Hassidic rabbi. https://www.inner.org/parshah/genesis-bereisheet/vayechi/from-rebuke-to-blessing.

Torah teaches in Leviticus 19:17 that when an individual has done wrong, it is necessary to rebuke him or her, in order that the person reform. Usually the rebuke comes *not* because the wrongdoer is disliked or hated. On the contrary, it is because the rebuker cares deeply for the wrongdoer. MaLBiM (Meir Leibush ben Yehiel Michel Wisser, a nineteenth-century Polish rabbi) explained that "rebuke is a sign of love,"[10] a sign that the rebuker loves and cherishes the wrongdoer and is trying to help him or her return to a right path. Rabbi Yitzchak Ginsburgh adds that "a certain measure of chastisement lends the personality more solid 'shape.'"[11]

In this spirit, Jacob begins by speaking lovingly to his eldest son, Reuben:

> *Reuben, you are my first-born,*
> *My might and first fruit of my vigor,*
> *Exceeding in rank,*
> *And exceeding in honor.*

Then, Jacob begins his rebuke:

> *Unstable as water, you shall excel no longer;*
> *For when you mounted your father's bed,*
> *You brought disgrace—my couch he mounted!*

—Genesis 49:3–4

What do these words mean? Reuben had sexual relations with Bilhah, Jacob's concubine (35:22). This so angered Jacob that instead of conferring the birthright of the eldest son to Reuben, Jacob gave the birthright to Joseph.

Reuben was not an entirely bad man, however. Though complicit in the early plot to get rid of Joseph, he convinced his brothers not to kill Joseph. Reuben intended to return and save Joseph. When he came back later, however, he found to his distress that his brothers had sold Joseph into slavery to Midianite traders (37:21–30).

Years later, in the midst of their troubles in Egypt (after Joseph had risen to power there), Reuben concluded that the tribulations they were experiencing were divine punishment for their earlier sin against Joseph. Reuben had a conscience, though it was not strong enough to keep him from doing wrong. His father Jacob's estimation of him was accurate—Reuben was, Jacob

---

10. Multiple sources.

11. Rabbi Yitzchak Ginsburgh. https://www.inner.org/parshah/genesis-bereisheet/vayechi/from-rebuke-to-blessing.

concludes, *"unstable as water"* (49:4)—Reuben is a weak man. Jacob knows him well, and he bestows upon him appropriate final words.

Further punishment to Reuben's descendants came in 722 BCE when the Assyrians conquered Canaan and expelled ten Israelite tribes from their homelands. Reuben's tribe was among those tribes and was one of what came to be known as the "Ten Lost Tribes of Israel." There is little known of Reuben's people after the beginning of the "Assyrian diaspora."

Jacob's last words to Simeon and Levi came in the form of a direct curse. Because it is so difficult for him to find words of love for his sons who he saw has cold-blooded murderers:

> *Simeon and Levi are a pair;*
> *their weapons are tools of lawlessness.*
> *Let not my person be included in their council,*
> *let not my being be counted in their assembly,*
> *for when angry they slay men,*
> *and when pleased they maim oxen.*
> *Cursed be their anger so fierce,*
> *and their wrath so relentless.*
> *I will divide them in Jacob,*
> *scatter them in Israel.*
>
> —Genesis 49:5–7

In Genesis 34, we read of the infamous rape of Jacob's daughter, Dinah, by Shechem, son of Hamor, prince of nearby non-Israelite town (see chapter 14). After having duplicitously come to an agreement with the men of Shechem to circumcise themselves, marry Israelite wives, and join the Israelites, Simeon and Levi took advantage of the Shechemite men who were still healing from their circumcisions. The brothers attacked the town, slaughtering all the recovering men (34:25–26). Jacob's other sons plundered the town, seized the flocks and herds, and took all the women, children, and booty captive (34:27–29). Everyone in Shechem suffered greatly—all the men died, all the women and young ones were taken prisoner, and all the property was stolen.

In his last "blessing" to Simeon and Levi, Jacob sends a clear and unambiguous message to his sons that what they have done in killing all the men of Schechem is wrong. He does not restrain his anguish, his shame, and his loathing for their violent and vicious acts. Now as he lay dying, Jacob cannot escape the brutal reality that his sons Simeon and Levi are mass murderers, motivated by bloodthirsty revenge for their sister Dinah's dishonor. Yet even here, so long after the vicious event, Jacob condemns the *act* of mass murder; he doesn't say that his sons themselves are evil. The *act* is evil—perhaps there is yet hope for the redemption of his sons—this is why he hopes that *tochecha*, rebuke, might actually be efficacious here.

As indicated in chapter 14, the story of Dinah is a complicated tale and should not simply be reduced to a tale of rape and revenge. This diminishes the complexities of power and sexual violence, the possibilities of true romantic love between Dinah and Shechem, Dinah's own self-determination, and much more. Whatever the case, blood revenge on Simeon and Levi's part is unacceptable under any circumstances.

What we know of Simeon in particular earlier in the family story is not good. Midrash tells us that Simeon was so envious of his half-brother Joseph that when his brothers plotted against Joseph, it was Simeon who urged his siblings to kill Joseph, and that he was angry when he learned that they had sold Joseph into slavery rather than slaying him.

Later, Simeon seems to have gotten his comeuppance in Egypt when Joseph held him hostage until Joseph's younger brother Benjamin is brought to him: *"But he* [Joseph] *came back to them; and he took Simeon from among them and had him bound before their eyes"* (42:24).

The ancient midrash Genesis Rabbah (91:6) elaborates on Simeon's situation:

> He took Simeon and bound him before their eyes, because it was he who had pushed him [Joseph] into the pit, and separated him from Levi, lest they should devise a plot against him. . . . "Throw this man into prison," Joseph ordered them. But as they approached him, he [Simeon] cried out loud at them; on hearing his voice they [the other brothers] fell on their faces and their teeth were broken, as it says "When the lion roareth and the fierce lion howleth, the teeth of the young lions are broken" (Job 4:10). . . . He [Joseph] then said to them: "He will remain imprisoned until you will bring your brother [Benjamin] . . . ."

An Addendum That Should Not Be an Addendum

The Blessing That Never Came from Jacob's Lips

Jacob's words to his sons were complete it seems, yet there was one glaring omission—this wise father had no words of blessing, no advice, no wisdom for his *daughter*, Dinah! Just as Dinah is silent in her own story,[12] so there is resounding silence from Jacob here. Rabbi Sue Levi Elwell offers

---

12. See *Vayishlach*—Genesis, chapter 34.

a contemporary corrective and healing to this silence in her poem, "Jacob Blesses Dinah:"[13]

> I have wrestled with the words with which to
> bless you,
> Dinah, daughter of Leah.
> A child, you went out to see the daughters of
> the land.
> You returned a woman.
> Did you raise your voice? Your cries were not
> heard.
> Blood flowed through the streets of Shechem
> and I was afraid.
> Like your mother,
> you walk among the people with head
> unbowed.
> May that strength and clarity of vision
> continue in the generations to come.
> To you, my daughter, belong the blessings
> of the breast and the womb,
> blessings of justice and care.
> Your offspring will learn many tongues
> and practice healing arts.
> They will build cities of righteousness
> and none shall make them afraid.

Text to Life

> Cecilia, a woman in her thirties, and an active member of my congregation, came to see me in my office. She had been working hard on some personal issues and told me the following story:

---

13. Rabbi Sue Levi Elwell, *Jacob Blesses Dinah*, in Eskenazy and Weiss, eds., *The Torah: A Women's Commentary*, 301. Reprinted with permission of author.

"A few years ago, I had one of my many terrible arguments with my much-older sister, who had been a second mother to me. I found myself yelling loudly, out of control of my emotions and unable to not stop myself from hurling invectives at my sister. I loved her deeply, but we had frequent conflicts and we just couldn't find a peaceful way to get along.

In the middle of my tirade, my sister yelled back at me, 'Cecilia, don't you realize how ugly you are when you get this angry? No one can reason with you! Don't you see how ugly you are?!'

After I went home, those words, which stung deeply, stayed with me. They never left me and now, as I work on my anger issues, they continue to echo within me. It is ironic that it was my big sister who said these words to me, since she, too, is an angry person—but her words were true. And the truth of her statement to me sunk very deep inside me and remained as a warning, a kind of a curse, a kind of a reminder that I *had* to do something about this problem.

Over the years I have worked on this challenge and now, Rabbi, I need your help to keep on the road of peace."

I was very moved by Cecilia's words and I promised to help her as much as I could in staying on an even keel. As Cecilia continued to be active in the community, on committees and in projects, I gently helped her stay even-tempered and over time her angry disposition dissipated. Today she is not known as an angry person; her sister's *tochecha*—the rebuke that certainly came from love—helped turn anger into peace.

LGB

Exploring the Text Within

Find a quiet and comfortable place to sit in contemplative silence with the above teachings and with the following questions about you and your life's experience. You may choose to focus on one question or sit with several. Ask yourself: what do the biblical text and these teachings mean to me in my life?

> [T]he tradition of bequeathing a spiritual legacy [now known as an "ethical will"] ... has its roots in the Bible and the Talmud. ... [Parents] sought to write and transmit ... personal reflections on

their lives as Jews and on the motivating values and events in their life's experience. They hoped to impart the precepts of God's Law refracted through the prism of a parent's life.

—Nathaniel Stampfer

> If you were writing your own ethical will to your children or to other loved ones, what would you say?

Tochechah—Rebuke—*a "blessing [that] is sometimes concealed within stern rebuke."*

—Rabbi Yitzchak Ginsburgh

> Are there loved ones in your life to whom you feel called to offer loving *tochecha* in the hope of guiding them to a better path in life?

> Has there been a time in your life when someone has offered you unwelcome *tochecha* that, in the end, proved to be valuable and helpful to you?
>
> What was your response?

Guidelines for Group Facilitation of Kriat Hakodesh

As there are "seventy faces to the Torah," so too there are many ways to facilitate a group experience of *kriat ha-kodesh* experience. Following is one suggested format. A group facilitator is encouraged to adapt and adjust this format as s/he feels is appropriate.

Preparing Yourself to Lead

It is important that the group leader her/himself be in a comfortable and grounded state of heart, mind, and soul to facilitate a group well.

- Get good rest in the hours before you facilitate.
- Make sure to center yourself through your own daily spiritual practice.
- If it is your custom to do body work, such as yoga or receiving a massage, prior to facilitating a *kriat ha-kodesh* session is an ideal time to do this.
- Do not rush to arrive at the group meeting place. Make sure you have plenty of time to arrive early, set up your sacred space, get a "feel" for the space, and begin chanting a selected *niggun* (wordless tune).
- Know that you are engaged in *avodat kodesh*, holy work, and that the Presence of all that is sacred in the universe is embracing you now.

Frequency and Size of Meetings

Ideally, a committed group of eight to ten participants meets twice a month for three months for a series of *kriat ha-kodesh* sessions.[1] Meeting regularly over a period of time enables the participants to grow accustomed to one another and to the rhythm and flow of *kriat ha-kodesh*. Having gained a growing familiarity with the method, participants are better able to enter more quickly and deeply into a contemplative state, without being overly distracted by the "how-tos" of the experience.

Creating Sacred Space

Aesthetics are important: *Kriat ha-kodesh* is sacred work, and the space at which a group meets should convey the sanctity of the inner work that will take place in it. Try to find a room that is far away from the common noise of passersby and traffic. Ideally, the room should have comfortable chairs, good ventilation, and windows that look out on trees or bushes. The room should be of adequate size for the number of participants so that each member of the group has space to spread out a bit. This is especially true for participants who will be sitting on the floor and who choose to draw or write. Sometimes, they may be in a reclining position and may need extra room, thus a well-carpeted space is ideal. Often rooms in churches or synagogues have such spaces. If possible, however, the room should be devoid of religious symbols that might discomfort some participants.

Using Music

Beautiful sound (beyond the human voice in chant) might sometimes enhance a *kriat ha-kodesh* session. The format offered here makes no use of electronic music or musical instruments, though they might be used judiciously. As I have trained facilitators in the *kriat ha-kodesh* method, I have observed some of my students use guitar, harp, and *shruti* boxes to lovely effect.

Imagine: a group of eight to ten people sitting silently in a pleasant room with windows, in a building surrounded with trees. The group leader has created a small *mishkan* (sanctuary) in the center of a circle of a wide circle of chairs, leaving space for folks who wish to sit on the floor. The *mishkan* might have objects representing the four natural elements—earth, air, fire, and water:

---

1. Some groups choose to continue meeting after the initial three months.

some smooth stones (earth), a bird's feather (air), a lit candle (fire), and a bowl of clear water. A *hamsa* (a palm-shaped Middle Eastern amulet that symbolizes safety, protection, or good fortune in one's home or life) might be placed in the center of the mishkan, and any other objects that represent love, the human-divine connection, and self-affirmation might be added.

Chanting

The leader, who has arrived early, is already seated and is chanting a quiet, *niggun*, a wordless tune that is easily learned. Soon, each person joins in to the chanting. The chant continues for about five or six minutes. The leader then pauses, makes friendly eye contact with each participant, and blesses the group:

ברוכים אתם בבואכם וברוכים אתם בצאתכם

Bruchim atem b'vo'achem u-bruchim atem b'tzeytchem!
Blessed may you be as you enter and blessed may you be
as you go forth!

The "Spine" of the Kriat Ha-Kodesh Session

The leader then introduces her/himself and briefly explains the *kriat ha-kodesh* method. This explanation should take no more than three or four minutes. The leader then explains that the "spine" of the *kriat ha-kodesh* format consists of the following elements:

- A brief summary of the context of the biblical verse(s) chosen for the session.
- A clear and mindful reading of the selected biblical verse(s).
- Three midrashic teachings that illuminate or interpret the selected biblical verse(s). This should take no more than fifteen minutes.
- Three questions that the participants are invited to sit with and meditate on in contemplative silence. These are the questions in each chapter that are offered under the rubric of "Exploring the Text Within."

The leader explains that each of these four elements will be separated with a wordless tune (*niggun*) and that the group will be listening to and hearing the same biblical text three more times. The leader may choose to explain that one of the core principles of *kriat ha-kodesh* is that *repeated listening to a text offers the listener an opportunity to delve deeper into the text.*

I am reminded of a Talmudic teaching regarding the second paragraph of the blessings of the *Sh'ma*—*v'haya im shamo'ah*—which can be translated literally as "when you listen, you will hear [or understand]." The point of the teaching is that if one has listened in the past, one will "really listen" (and understand) in the future. Another interpretation is that "if you listen to what is old, you will listen to what is new, but if you turn your heart away, you will not hear (or understand)."[2] In the context of *kriat ha-kodesh,* one might say that if one allows (or is offered) as many opportunities as possible to listen, new insights and understandings will most likely emerge.

Often people experience the listening and the hearing differently each time. You might give an example offer an example that evokes how one might "hear" a text differently upon repeated listening. For example, in Psalm 46:10, we read, "Be still, and know that I am God." In their original context, the words were a warning to a people from the tribe of Korah to desist in their rebellion against Moses. Taken out of context, however, one might hear and understand these repeated words differently each time, depending on one's emotional or spiritual need.

In one group I led, a participant later told me that he experienced this verse as follows:

- Upon listening silently the first time during the teachings, he "heard" and understood the words to mean: *Stay calm and quiet and know that I, God, am with you (to comfort you).*

- Upon listening a second time, he felt the words meant: *In silence and stillness, you will discover My essence, you will know Me (and through this knowledge, you will be fulfilled).*

- Upon a third hearing, the meaning of the verse might shift in his mind to mean: *Do not rebel against God's rule (and be an obedient son of your faith).*

- Finally, upon listening and hearing the verse a final time, he experienced a profound moment of understanding: *Be still and unafraid, because I am [the] God (who dwells within you).*

After explaining the value of repetition, the leader also explains that after the final listening to the text and silent contemplation of the final question, there would be time allotted for sharing one's experience, first in dyads and then in the larger group.

During the group sharing, respectful practice is:

---

2. Both Talmudic teachings may be found in the Babylonian Talmud, tractate *Berachot* 40a as commentary on Deuteronomy 11:13.

- No "cross-talking," that is, no interruption when someone is speaking.
- When someone finishes speaking s/he indicates this by saying the Hebrew word *"dibarti"* (I have spoken) and the group acknowledges her/his words by saying together *"shamati"* (I have heard [you])
- When one speaks, s/he should speak about her/his own reaction to the verses, the questions, and the silence, rather than respond (negatively or positively) to another participant's experience. The goal is to learn how the *kriat ha-kodesh* experience has affected each member of the group rather than "react" to another person's experiences.

After the dyadic and group sharing, the leader begins the same *niggun* for the final time and when s/he fades it out, ends the two-hour session with the same blessing as at the beginning:

ברוכים אתם בבואכם וברוכים אתם בצאתכם

Bruchim atem b'vo'achem u-bruchim atem b'tzeytchem!
Blessed may you be as you enter and blessed may you be
as you go forth!

The leader then thanks the group and quietly walks from the room. This indicates that any chatting about the session will take place outside the "sacred space" in which the session took place.

Checklist

- When possible, pre-registration is advised.
- Ideal group size is eight to ten participants.
- Small bottles of water might be provided for participants.
- A letter should be sent to each participant with an introduction briefly describing the "feel" of the session, emphasizing its quiet, gentle, and contemplative nature and explaining that unlike conventional "Torah study" or interactive classes, the majority of our time will be spent in silence or listening to the leader's teachings. Note that there *will* be individual and group interaction and "sharing." The letter should also impart the following information:
    - exact date, beginning and ending times, and location of the group meeting.
    - request that participants arrive on time and plan to stay until the end of the session.
    - recommendation to wear comfortable, casual clothing.

- recommendation to bring only water bottles or mugs with a beverage, as no food is permitted in the session, except when medically necessary.
- recommendation to bring yoga pillows, footstools, or anything else that would make sitting on the floor or in a chair comfortable.
- recommendation to bring pencils, pens, notebook, sketch pad, sketch pencils, etc.
- no electronic devices (smart phones, cameras, recorders, etc.) will be permitted during the session.

- The group leader is seated at least ten minutes prior to the assigned start time.
- Sign on the door as participants enter:

> Welcome to *Kriat Ha-Kodesh*: Contemplative Torah.
>
> Our meeting today will last two hours. We will end promptly at _____.
>
> Please come in quietly and sit down, either on a chair or on the floor, as is comfortable for you.
>
> Please bring only water or a travel mug with another beverage into the room.
>
> Please do not bring food, unless it is medically necessary for you.
>
> Please honor silence unless instructed by your leader that this is a time for sharing.
>
> Please hold your questions until the leader indicates that it is time for them.
>
> If you need to go to the restroom during our session, please leave and return very quietly.

- Send an evaluation or feedback form to each participant after each session. In addition to specific questions, make sure to leave space for open-ended comments.

Bibliography

Barenblat, Rachel. *Seventy Faces: Torah Poems*. Montreal: Phoenicia, 2010.
Ben David, Aryeh. *Around the Shabbat Table: A Guide to Fulfilling and Meaningful Shabbat Conversations*. Northvale, NJ: Aaronson, 2000.
Ben-Shahar, Tal. *Choosing the Life You Want: The Mindful Way to Happiness*. New York: McGraw-Hill, 2007.
Ben-Shahar, Tal. *Choose the Life You Want: The Mindful Way to Happiness*. Reprint, New York: The Experiment, 2014.
———. *Happier: Learn the Secrets to Daily Joy and Lasting Fulfillment*. New York: McGraw-Hill, 2007.
Binz, Stephen J. *Conversing with God in Scripture: A Contemporary Approach to Lectio Divina*, Ijamsville, MD: The Word among Us, 2008.
Birnbaum, Ellen. "On the Life of Abraham." In *Outside the Bible: Ancient Jewish Writings Related to Scripture*, edited by Louis H. Feldman, James Kugel and Harvey Schiffman, 939–41. Philadelphia: Jewish Publication Society, 2013.
Bok, Sissela. *Lying: Moral Choice in Public and Private Life*. London: Vintage, 1999.
Boorstein, Sylvia, Alan Brill, Andrea Cohen-Keiner, and David Cooper. *Meditation from the Heart of Judaism: Today's Teachers Share Their Practices, Techniques and Faith*. Woodstock, VT: Jewish Lights, 1997.
Boorstein, Sylvia. *That's Funny, You Don't Look Buddhist: On Being a Faithful Jew and a Passionate Buddhist*. New York: HarperOne, 1998.
Brodie, Rachel. "When Gender Varies: A Curious Case of *Kere* and *Ketiv—Parashat Chayei Sarah* (Genesis 23:1—25:18)." In *Torah Queeries: Weekly Commentaries on the Hebrew Bible*, edited by Gregg Drinkwater, Joshua Lesser. and David Shneer, 34–37. New York: New York University Press, 2009.
Carasik, Michael, ed. and annotator. *The Commentators' Bible: Genesis, The Rubin JPS Miqra'ot Gedolot*. Philadelphia: Jewish Publication Society, 2018.
Carstens, Daren. *The Secret to Blended Families Marriage and Parenting Success: Making Peace, Escaping the Drama, and Successfully*. Loc?: Carwayne Publishers, 2013.
The Catholic Prayer Bible: Lectio Divina Edition (NRSV). Mahwah, NJ: Paulist, 2005.
Chefitz, Mitchell. *The Curse of Blessings*. Philadelphia: Running Press, 2006.
Cohen, Norman J. *Self, Struggle and Change: Family Conflict Stories in Genesis and Their Healing Insights for Our Lives*. Rev. ed. Woodstock, VT: Jewish Lights, 1996.
———. *Voices from Genesis: Guiding Us through the Stages of Life*. Woodstock, VT: Jewish Lights, 1998.

Cooper, David A. *God Is a Verb: Kabbalah and the Practice of Mystical Judaism*. New York: Riverhead, 1998.

———. *The Handbook of Jewish Meditation Practices: A Guide for Enriching Sabbath and Other Days of Your Life*. Woodstock, VT: Jewish Lights, 2000.

———. *A Heart of Stillness: A Complete Guide to Learning the Art of Meditation*. Woodstock, VT: Skylight Paths, 1999.

———. *Silence, Simplicity and Solitude: A Complete Guide to Spiritual Retreat*. Woodstock, VT: Skylight Paths, 1999.

———. *Three Gates to Meditation Practice: A Personal Journey into Sufism, Buddhism and Judaism*. Woodstock, VT: Skylight Paths, 2000.

Densmore, Dana. *Reb Zalman Gathers Figs: A Study of Reb Zalman Schachter-Shalomi's Reading of Biblical Text to Re-vision Judaism for the Present Day*. Santa Fe, NM: Green Lion, 2013.

Dysinger, Luke, O.S.B., "Accepting the Embrace of God: The Ancient Art of Lectio Divina." http://www.valyermo.com/ld-art.html.

Eskenazi, Tamara Cohn, and Andrea L. Weiss, eds. *The Torah: A Women's Commentary*. New York: Women of Reform Judaism, 2008.

Felder, Leonard. *Here I Am: Using Jewish Spiritual Wisdom to Become More Present, Centered, and Available for Life*. Boston: Trumpeter, 2011.

Frankiel, Tamar, and Judy Greenfield. *Entering the Temple of Dreams: Jewish Prayers, Movements, and Meditations for the End of the Day*. Woodstock, VT: Jewish Lights, 2000.

Friedman, Nathalie. *The Jewish Factor in Remarriage and Stepparenting*. New York: Jewish Communal Service Association of North America, 1994.

———. *Remarriage and Stepparenting in the Jewish Communit.*, American Jewish Committee (AJC), 1993: http://www.bjpa.org/Publications/details.cfm?PublicationID=2565.

Gefen, Nan Fink. *Discovering Jewish Meditation: Instruction and Guidance for Learning and Ancient Spiritual Practice*. 2nd ed. Woodstock, VT: Jewish Lights, 2011.

Glick, Yoel. *Living the Life of Jewish Meditation: A Comprehensive Guide to Practical Experience*. Woodstock, VT: Jewish Lights, 2014.

Gold, Shefa. *The Magic of Hebrew Chant: Healing the Spirit, Transforming the Mind, Deepening Love*. Woodstock, VT: Jewish Lights, 2013.

———. *Torah Journeys: The Inner Path to the Promised Land*. Teaneck, NJ: Ben Yehuda, 2006.

Goldenberg, David M. *The Curse of Ham: Race and Slavery in Early Judaism, Christianity and Islam*. Princeton, NJ: Princeton University Press, 2003.

Goldstein, Elyse, ed. *The Women's Torah Commentary*. Woodstock, VT: Jewish Lights, 2000.

Goldstein, Joseph. *Insight Meditation: The Practice of Freedom*. Boston: Shambhala, 1993.

Goleman, Daniel. *Varieties of the Meditative Experience*. New York: Dutton, 1977 (Reissued under the title, *The Meditative Mind*. Los Angeles: Tarcher, 1987).

Green, Arthur. *Ehyeh: A Kabbalah for Tomorrow*. Woodstock, VT: Jewish Lights, 2004.

———. *Radical Judaism: Rethinking God and Tradition*. New Haven: Yale University Press, 2010.

———. *Seek My Face, Speak My Name: A Contemporary Jewish Theology*. Lanham, MD: Aaronson, 1994.

———. *These Are the Words: A Vocabulary of Jewish Spiritual Life*. Woodstock, VT: Jewish Lights, 1999.

———. *Tormented Master: The Life and Spiritual Quest of Rabbi Nahman of Bratslav*. Woodstock, VT: Jewish Lights, 1992.

Green, Arthur, with Ebn Leader, Ariel Evan Mayse, and Or N. Rose. *Speaking Torah: Spritiual Teachings around the Maggid's Table*. Woodstock, VT: Jewish Lights, 2013.

Hall, Thelma. *Too Deep for Words: Rediscovering Lectio Divina with 500 Scripture Texts for Prayer*. Mahwah, NJ: Paulist, 1988.

Hammer, Jill, with Shir Yaakov Feit. *Omer Calendar of Biblical Women*. New York: n.p., 2012.

Haralick, Robert. *The Inner Meaning of the Hebrew Letters*. Northvale, NJ: Aaronson, 1995.

Held, Shai. *The Heart of Torah, Vol. 1, Essay on the Weekly Torah Portion: Genesis and Exodus*. Philadelphia: Jewish Publication Society/University of Nebraska Press, 2017.

Isaacs, Ronald H. *Ascending Jacob's Ladder: Jewish Views of Angels, Demons and Evil Spirits*. Northvale, NJ: Aaronson, 1998.

The Jewish Study Bible (JPS TaNaKH). Edited by Adele Berlin and Marc Zvi Brettler, with Michael Fishbane, consulting editor. New York: Oxford University Press, 2004.

Johnson, Sylvester A. *The Myth of Ham in Nineteenth-Century American Christianity*. New York: Palgrave Macmillan, 2004.

JPS Hebrew-English TaNaKH. Philadelphia: Jewish Publication Society, 1999.

Jung, Leo. *Fallen Angels in Jewish, Christian and Mohammedan Literature*. Whitefish, MT, Kessinger, 2011.

Kamenetz, Rodger. *The Jew in the Lotus: A Poet's Rediscovery of Jewish Identity in Buddhist India*. San Francisco: Harper San Francisco, 1994.

Kaplan, Aryeh. *Inner Space: Introduction to Kabbalah, Meditation and Prophecy*. Edited by Abraham Sutton. Jerusalem: Moznaim, 1990.

———. *Meditation and the Bible*. York Beach, Maine: Weiser, 1981.

———. *Meditation and Kabbalah*. York Beach, Maine: Weiser, 1986.

Kierkegaard, Søren. *Fear and Trembling*. New York: Penguin Classics, 1986.

Kravitz, Leonard, and Kerry M. Olitzky. *Pirke Avot: A Modern Commentary on Jewish Ethics*. New York: UAHC Press, 2004.

Kugel, James L. *The Bible as It Was*. Cambridge, MA: Belknap, 1997.

Kushner, Lawrence. *The Book of Words: Talking Spiritual Life, Living Spiritual Talk*. Woodstock, VT: Jewish Lights, 1993.

———. *Eyes Remade for Wonder: A Lawrence Kushner Reader*. Woodstock VT: Jewish Lights, 1998.

———. *God Was in This Place and I, i Did Not Know: Finding Self, Spirituality and Ultimate Meaning*. Woodstock, VT: Jewish Lights, 1991.

———. *The River of Light: Spirituality, Judaism, Consciousness*. Woodstock, VT: Jewish Lights, 1990.

Kushner, Harold. *When Bad Things Happen to Good People*. London: Pan, 2002.

Kushner, Lawrence S., and Kerry M. Olitzky. *Sparks Beneath the Surface: A Spiritual Commentary on the Torah*. Northvale, NJ: Aaronson, 1993.

Lamott, Anne. *Bird by Bird: Some Instructions on Writing and Life*. New York: Anchor, 1995.

———. *Grace (Eventually): Thoughts on Faith*. New York: Riverhead, 2008.
———. *Help, Thanks, Wow: The Three Essential Prayers*. New York: Riverhead, 2012.
———. *Plan B: Further Thoughts on Faith*. New York: Riverhead Trade, 2008.
———. *Traveling Mercies: Some Thoughts on Faith*. New York: Anchor, 2000.
Leib, Yehuda. *The Language of Truth: The Torah Commentary of the Sefat Emet—Rabbi Yehuda Leib Alter of Ger*. Translated and interpreted by Arthur Green; Hebrew texts prepared by Shai Gluskin. Philadelphia: Jewish Publication Society, 2012.
Leibowitz, Nechama. *Studies in Bereshit—Genesis*. 7th ed. Jerusalem: World Zionist Organization, 1985.
Levi Yitzchak of Berdichev. *Kedushat Levi, The Torah Commentary of Levi Yitzchak of Berdichevm. vol. 1—B'reyshit—Vayechi*. Translated and annotated by Eliyahu Munk. Madison, WI: Lama, 2009.
Lew, Alan. *Be Still and Get Going: A Jewish Meditation Practice for Real Life*. New York: Little Brown, 2005.
Margolies, Morris B. *A Gathering of Angels in Jewish Life and Literature*. New York: Ballantine, 1994.
Marsolini, Maxine. *Blended Families: Creating Harmony as You Build a New Home Life*. New ed. Chicago: Moody, 2000.
Menachem Nachum Twersky. *Me'or Eynayim*. Translated and introduced by Arthur Green with a preface by Samuel Dresner as *Menahem Nahum of Chernobyl: Upright Practices, The Light of the Eyes*. Ramsey, NJ: Paulist, 1982.
Merton, Thomas. *The Inner Experience: Notes on Contemplation*. San Francisco: Harper San Francisco, 2004.
———. *New Seeds of Contemplation*. New York: New Directions Reprint Edition, 2007.
———. *No Man Is an Island*. New York: Fall River, 1955.
Metzger, Deena. *What Deena Thought*. New York: Viking, 1989.
Michaelson, Jay. *Everything Is God: The Radical Path of Nondual Judaism*. Boston: Trumpeter, 2009.
———. *God in Your Body: Kabbalah, Mindfulness, and Embodied Spiritual Practice*. Woodstock, VT: Jewish Lights, 2006.
Midrash Rabbah. Translated by Rabbi Dr. H. Freedman. 3rd ed. New York: Soncino, 1983.
Midrash Tanchuma, Bereishis I and II, (Metsudah). The Wallerstein Edition, translated and annotated by Avrohom Davis, edited by Yaakov Y.H. Pupko. Monsey, NY: Metsudah, 2005.
Mordechai Yosef Leiner of Izbica. *Mei HaShiloach*. Published in English as *Living Waters: The Mei HaShiloach: A Commentary on the Torah by Rabbi Mordechai Yosef of Isbitza*. Translated and edited by Betsalel Philip Edwards. New York: Rowman and Littlefield, 2001.
Navon, Mois A. "The Kiss of Esau." *Jewish Bible Quarterly* 35.2 (2007) 127–31.
Nouwen, Henri J. M. *Making All Things New and Other Classics*. Grand Rapids: Zondervan, 2000.
Olitzky, Kerry, and Lori Forman, eds. *Restful Reflections*. Woodstock, VT: Jewish Lights, 2001.
Oratz, Ephraim, ed. *The Hirsch Commentary*. Translated by Gertrude Hirschler. New York: Judaica, 1990.
Ostriker, Alicia. *The Nakedness of the Fathers: Biblical Visions and Revisions*. New Brunsiwck, New Jersey, Rutgers University Press, 1997.
Patton, Laurie L. *Angel's Task: Poems in Biblical Time*. Barrytown, NY: Station Hill, 2010.
Pennington, M. Basil. *Centering Prayer: Renewing and Ancient Christian Prayer Form*. New York: Doubleday, 1982.

———. *Lectio Divina: Renewing the Ancient Practice of Praying the Scriptures.* New York: Crossroad, 1998.

The Pentateuch. Translated and explained by Samson Raphael Hirsch. 2nd ed. New York: Judaica, 1971.

Person, Hara E., ed. *Voices of Torah: A Treasury of Rabbinic Gleanings on Weekly Portions, Holidays, and Special Shabbatot.* New York: Central Conference of American Rabbis, 2011.

Pinson, DovBer. *Meditation and Judaism: Exploring the Jewish Meditative Paths.* Northvale, NJ: Aronson, 2004.

Pitzele, Peter. *Our Father's Wells: A Personal Encounter with the Myths of Genesis.* San Francisco: HarperSan Francisco, 1995.

Prager, Marcia. *The Path of Blessing: Experiencing the Energy and Abundance of the Divine.* Woodstock, VT: Jewish Lights, 2003.

Rabow, Jerry. *The Lost Matriarch: Finding Leah in the Bible and Midrash.* Philadelphia: Jewish Publication Society, University of Nebraska Press, 2014.

Rapp, James D. *Sandals: The Journey of Abraham and Sarah & Hagar—A Suite of Poems by James D. Rapp.* Eau Claire, WI: EC Printing, 2010.

Rashi. *Pentateuch with Rashi's Commentary.* Edited by M. Rosenbaum and A. M. Silbermann. 5 vols. New York: Hebrew Publishing Co., 1870.

Ribner, Melinda. *Everyday Kabbalah: A Practical Guide to Jewish Meditation, Healing, and Personal Growth.* New York: Citadel, 2000.

Riemer, Jack, and Nathaniel Stampfer, eds. *So That Your Values Live On: Ethical Wills and How to Prepare Them* Woodstock, VT: Jewish Lights, 1991.

Rinkewich, Mindy. "Sarah: Cheshbon Nefesh." In *Sarah's Daughters Sing*, edited by Henny Wenkart, 10. Hoboken, NJL KTACV, 1990.

Rohr, Richard. *Contemplation in Action.* 2nd ed. New York: Crossroad, 2006.

———. *Dancing Standing Still: Healing the World from a Place of Prayer; A New Edition of a Lever and a Place to Stand.* Mahwah, NJ: Paulist, 2013.

———. *Everything Belongs: The Gift of Contemplative Prayer.* New York: Crossroad, 2003.

———. *Silent Compassion: Finding God in Contemplation.* Cincinnati, OH: Franciscan Media, 2014.

———. *Yes, and . . . Daily Meditations.* Cincinnati, OH: Franciscan Media, 2013.

Roth, Jeff. *Jewish Meditation Practices for Everyday Life: Awakening Your Heart, Connecting with God.* Woodstock, VT: Jewish Lights, 2009.

———. *Me, Myself and God: A Theology of Mindfulness.* Woodstock, VT: Jewish Lights, 2016.

Rubin, Aharon. *Eye to the Infinite: A Jewish Meditation Guidebook—How to Increase Divine Awareness.* 3rd ed. No loc: CreateSpace Independent, 2014.

Salkin, Jeffrey K. *The Modern Men's Torah Commentary.* Woodstock, VT: Jewish Lights, 2009.

Schachter-Shalomi, Zalman M. *All Breathing Life Adores Your Name: At the Interface Between Poetry and Prayer.* Edited by Michael L. Kagan. Santa Fe, NM: Gaon, 2011.

———. *From Age-ing to Sage-ing: A Profound New Vision of Growing Older.* New York: Grand Central, 1997.

———. *Gate to the Heart: A Manual of Contemplative Jewish Practice.* Boulder, CO: Albion-Andalus, 2013.

———. *The Gates of Prayer: Twelve Talks on Davvenology.* Boulder, CO: Albion-Andalus, 2011.

Schachter-Shalomi, Zalman M., with Donald Gropman. *First Steps to a New Jewish Spirit*. Woodstock, VT: Jewish Lights, 2003.

Schachter-Shalomi, Zalman M., with Joel Siegel. *Davening: A Guide to Meaningful Jewish Prayer*. Woodstock, VT: Jewish Lights, 2012.

Schneerson, Shalom Dov-Ber, and David Sterne. *Love Like Fire and Water (Kuntres Ha-Avoda): A Guide to Jewish Meditation*. New York: Moznaim, 2011.

Schultz, Karl A. *How to Pray with the Bible: The Ancient Prayer Form of Lectio Divina Made Simple*. Huntington, IN: Our Sunday Visitor, 2007.

Sefer Ha-Aggadah, The Book of Legends. Edited by Hayim Nahman Bialik and Yehoshua Hana Ravnitzky, translated by William Braude. New York: Schocken, 1992.

Shalva, Benjamin. *Spiritual Cross Training: Searching through Silence, Stretch, and Song*. Grand Haven, MI: Brilliance, 2016.

Shapiro, Rami. *Amazing Chesed: Living a Grace-Filled Judaism*. Woodstock, VT: Jewish Lights, 2012.

———. *The Angelic Way: Angels through the Ages and Their Meaning for Us*. Chicago: BlueBridge, 2012.

———. *Embracing Esau*. No loc: Lighthouse, 1994.

———. *Guide to Forgiveness: Roadside Assistance for the Spiritual Traveler*. Lanham, MD: Spirituality and Health, 2011.

———. *Minyan: Ten Principles of Living a Life of Integrity*. New York: Harmony, 1997.

———. *Perennial Wisdom for the Spiritually Independent: Sacred Teachings—Annotated and Explained (co-authored with Richard Rohr)*. Woodstock, VT: Skylight Illuminations, 2013.

———. *The Sacred Art of Lovingkindness: Preparing to Practice (The Art of Spiritual Living)*. Woodstock, VT: Skylight Paths, 2006.

Sherman, Charles S. *The Broken and the Whole: Discovering Joy after Heartbreak—Lessons from a Life of Faith*. New York: Scribner, 2014.

Shlomo ben Yitzchak (RaSHI). *The Pentateuch with RASHI's Commentary*. Translated and annotated by M. Rosenbaum and A. M. Silbermann. Jerusalem: n.p., 1929.

Slater, Jonathan. *Mindful Jewish Living: Compassionate Practice*. New York: Aviv, 2004.

———. *A Partner in Holiness: Deepening Mindfulness, Practicing Compassion and Enriching Our Lives through the Wisdom of R. Levi Yitzchak of Berdichev's Kedushat Levi*, volumes 1 & 2. Woodstock, VT: Jewish Lights, 2014.

Sullivan, Kevin P. *Wrestling with Angels: A Study in the Relationship between Angels and Humans in Ancient Jewish Literature and the New Testament*. Leiden: Brill, 2004.

Taitz, Emily, and Sondra Henry. *Written Out of History: Our Jewish Foremothers*. New York: Bloch, 1997.

Torah Education and Culture in the Diaspora. 4th rev. ed. Jerusalem: The Jewish Agency, n.d.

Twerski, Abraham J. *Twerski on Chumash*. New York: Shaar, 2003.

Waskow, Arthur. *Godwrestling*. New York: Schocken, 1987.

———. *Godwrestling, Round 2*. Woodstock, VT: Jewish Lights, 1998.

Wiesel, Elie. *The Town Beyond the Wall*. New York: Schocken, 1995.

Zajonc, Arthur. *When Knowing Becomes Love: Meditation as Contemplative Inquiry*. Great Barrington, MA: Lindisfarne, 2009.

Zohar: The Book of Enlightenment. Translated by Daniel Chanan Matt. Classics of Western Spirituality. Mahwah, NJ: Paulist, 1983.

Index

Adam/adamah, 22, 24
Adat Shalom Reconstructionist Congregation, 19n19
Addison, Howard (Avruhm) (Rabbi), xii, xv, 15
"Age-ing to Sage-ing", 80
Akiba (Rabbi), 94
Alcoholism, 56, 57, 58
ALEPH: Alliance for Jewish Renewal, xiin1, 19n19
Androgynos, 22
Attar, Chayim ben (Rabbi), 162
Azariah (Rabbi), 94

Ben David, Aryeh (Rabbi), 210
Ben-Shahar, Tal, 34
Berlin, Adele, 52n16, 102n2
Berner, Ilana, xvii
Bialik, Hayim Nahman, 164n11–13, 165n15
Birnbaum, Ellen, 63n2
Bok, Sisela, 191–92
Boorstein, Sylvia, xi
Breitman, Barbara, xii, xv, 15
Brettler, Marc, 52n16, 102n2
Brodie, Rachel, 141
Buber, Martin, 13

Carlebach, Shlomo (Rabbi), 32n1
Carstens, Daren, 189n5
Chefitz, Mitchell (Rabbi), 221n1
Cohen, Norman J. (Rabbi), 52n15
Contemplatio, 14, 16

Cook, Alan (Rabbi), 104n6, 107

Dysinger, Luke (Fr.), xiin3, 13–14, 17

Einstein, Albert, 197
Elber, Mark (Rabbi), xvi–xvii
Eleazar (Rabbi), 94
Elwell, Sue Levi (Rabbi), 227–28, 228n13
Eskenazi, Tamara Cohn, 182n3, 183n8

Felder, Leonard, 33n4
Frankiel, Tamar, 208n1, 219n13
Friedman, Debbie, 81
Friedman, Nathalie, 189n5
Fuss, Gerald (Reverend), xvi

Gan Kagan, Ruth (Rabbi), xv
Geller, Laura (Rabbi), 182, 183n8
Ginsburg, Yitzchak (Rabbi), 224n9, 225, 230
Godwrestling, 19, 19n20
Goldenberg, David, 53n18
Green, Arthur (Rabbi), 12n7, 34f6, 37, 66, 72
Greenfield, Judy, 208n1, 219n13

Hagar, 8–9, 20, 73–75, 77–79, 82–89, 93–98, 100–101, 111, 113–16, 130–31, 139
Ham, curse of, 52–53, 55–57
Hammer, Jill (Rabbi), 166, 167n25
Harelick, Robert M., 208n2–4

Hassidism, 11n5
Held, Shai (Rabbi), 165n18, 166, 166n21–22, 166n24
Henry, Sondra, 182
Heschel, Abraham Joshua (Rabbi), v, 35
Hirsch, Samson Raphel (Rabbi), 64, 65, 154, 154n9, 162, 174, 175n8, 189, 195
Hirschhorn, Linda, 82
Hoffman, Jennifer (Jinks), xvii, 24
Homosexuality, 102n2

"Isaac and Ishmael" (song), 122–27
Isaacs, Ronald H., 85n1
Ishmael, 8–9, 75, 82, 85–87, 93–101, 111–16, 131, 139–40
Ishmael (Rabbi), 94

Jabbok (river), 172–73, 177
Jacob ben Asher, 75n3
John, Gospel According to 1:1, 17n18
Johnson, S., 53n18
Jonah ben Abraham Gerondi (Rabbi), 191
Jung, Carl Gustav, 174n6
Jung, Leo, 85n1

Kaplan, Aryeh (Rabbi), xi
Khan, Sanober, 161, 165, 169
Kierkegaard, Soren, 130, 130n3–4
Kramer, Ilyse (Rabbi), xvi, 113n4
Kravitz, Leonard (Rabbi), 38n12
Kriat Hakodesh, 19, 231
Kula, Irwin (Rabbi), 223
Kummer, Judy (rabbi), xvi
Kushner, Harold (Rabbi), 104n7
Kushner, Lawrence (Rabbi), 10, 150n1, 157, 198

Landsman, Irene (Dr.), xvii
Langner, Gilah (Rabbi), xvi
Laytner, Anson (Rabbi), 17n17
Lectio, 13, 16
Lectio divina, xii–xiii, 12–14, 16, 18, 19
Leibowitz, Nechama, 183, 196, 215n11, 216n12

Lev Shomea, Institute for the Training of Spiritual Directors in the Jewish Tradition, xii
Levi (Rabbi), 94
Levi Yitzchak of Berdichev (Rabbi), 62–63, 71, 204, 211, 212
Levitt, Joy (Rabbi), 113n5, 119

Machloket l'shem shamayim, 17
Maimonides (RaMBaM) xvi, 75n3, 184, 196
Mann, Belle, xvi
Mann, Jason (Rabbi), xvi
Meditatio, 13, 16
Meir Leibush ben Yehiel Michel Wisser (MaLBiM), 225
Menecham Mendel of Kotzk (Rabbi), 197–98, 198n9
Midrash, xxiiin1
Miriam, 2–4
Mordechai Yosef Leiner of Isbitza (the Ishbitzer Rebbe), 65
Morei Derekh Jewish Spiritual Direction Program, xiin1
Moses, Burning Bush, 9–10, 64

Nachman of Bratslav (Reb), 33
Nachmanides (RaMBaN), 104n8
Nathans, Hannah (Rabbi), xvi
Navon, Mois A., 176
Nierman, Leonardo, 67–68
Nouwen, Henri, 173, 178

Olitzky, Kerry (Rabbi), 38n12, 157, 198
Oratio, 13–14
Ostriker, Alicia, 55–56

Patton, Laurie, xvi
Peltz Weinberg, Sheila (rabbi), xi
Philo Judeus of Alexandria, 63, 154
Piercy, Marge, 29
Pitzele, Peter, 144
Plumb, Marcia (Rabbi), xvi
Prager, Marcia (Rabbi), xvi, 223–24

Rabbi Berakiah, 67, 79, 182
Rabbi Hanan, 54
Rabbi Hanina, 47

Rabbi Judah ben Rabbi Simon, 54
Rabbi Rehumai, 132
Rabbi Samuel bar Nachman, 153
Rabbi Samuel ben Rabbi Isaac, 54
Rabbi Yohanan, 47, 162
Rabow, Jerry, 162, 163n10, 165n14, 167
RaMBaM (see *Maimonides*)
Rapp, James. D., 87
RaSHI (Rabbi Shlomo ben Yitzhak), 76, 112, 115n7–8, 190, 195n1, 196, 203
Ravnitzky, Yehoshua Hana, 164n11–13, 165n15
Redfield Jamison, Kay (Dr.), 156n12
Rinkewich, Mindy, 79–80
Rohr, Richard (Fr.), xii, 12, 13, 17, 27
Rosenberg, Joel, 20n24
Rosenthal, Avraham Yisroel (Rabbi), 115n9
Rosenzweig, Franz, xn1
Roth, Jeff (rabbi), xi
Ruddell, Franna, xvii

sacred arguing, 17
Salkin, Jeffrey, 177
Satan, 117–18, 129
Sax-Bolder, Eva (Rabbi), xvi, 19n19
Schachter-Shalomi, Zalman (Rabbi), xvii, 37, 80n11
Shakespeare, William—*Richard III* 27
Shalva, Benjamin (Rabbi), xvi, 152, 155
Shapiro, Rami (rabbi), xii, 33, 65, 85n1, 174
Shapiro, Rona (Rabbi), 130n4
Shechinah, 21n1, 104n8
Shema, 19
Shenhar, Aliza, 121n19
Sherman, Charles S. (Rabbi), 97

Shlomo of Radomsk (Rabbi), 157, 159
Shneur Zalman of Liadi (Rabbi), 184
Simeon bar Abba (Rabbi), 111
Simeon bar Yohai (Rabbi), 94
Slater, Jonathan (Rabbi), xii
Sohn, Ruth (Rabbi), xvi, 3–6
St. Benedict of Nursia, 13n9
St. Exupery, Antoine de, 144
Stampfer, Nathaniel, 222, 230

Taglit Birthright Program, 147n10
Taitz, Emily, 182
Targum Onkelos, 162
Thomas-Newborn, Alissa, 116n10
Twerski, Abraham (Rabbi), 212
Twerski, Shlomo (Rabbi), 212
Twersky, Menachem (Rabbi of Chernobyl), 11

Waskow, Arthur (Rabbi), 19n20
Weiss, Andrea L., 182n3, 183n8
Weiss, Zari (Rabbi), 15, 16
West, Avi, xvi
Wiesel, Elie, 44, 45, 63, 113
Woolf, Carl, 44n7

Yedidya Center for Jewish Spiritual Direction, xiin1
Yedidya, Tzviya, xvii
Yehuda Aryeh Leib Alter (Reb) (the *Sefat Emet*), 66
Yisrael ben Yisroel (Israel) ben Eliezer (aka the BesHT), 11

Zalman Sorotzkin (Rabbi), 155, 156
Zeller, David (Rabbi), 15
Zevit, Simcha (Rabbi), xvi, 152

Non-Genesis Biblical, Midrash, and Talmud References

2 Samuel

1:18	117n14

Book of Legends (Sefer Ha-Aggadah),

111n2, 112n3, 164n11–13, 165n15

Deuteronomy

6:4	19n21
6:4–9	20n23
6:5–9	19n22
16:20	38n13

Exodus

1:8	222
20:22	157
24:12	5
3:1–6	9, 10

Genesis Rabbah

12:1	71
19:9	23n2
30:10	47n12
34:2	67n12
34:21	72
36:7	52n17
39:14	76n5
45:2	77n7
45:5	79n9
50:9	103n4
53:11	95 f. 8
58:5	117n11
60:16	136n9
63:10	140n3, 142n5
70:16	163n8–9
78:9	176
80:5	182n4–6
84:13	195n2
84:16	201n1, 202n5
87:7	203n8
91:6	227

Isaiah

2:4	6
5:11	54
56:4-5	75n3, 84

Job (Book of), 104n7

Joshua

10:13	117n14

Lamentations Rabbah, 12

Leviticus Rabbah

20:2	114n6
29:2	153n5

Me'or Eynayim, 11, 12n7

Midrash Aggadah, 8, 23

Midrash Halacha, 8

Midrash Rabbah, 23

Midrash Tanhuma, 34, 35n8, 182n7

Mishna, Pirkei Avot

2:15–16	38n12

Mishneh Torah, De'ot

7:7	184n9

Numbers

19:1–2	12n7
3:1	76
6:22–27	224n7

Or HaChayim

29:16	162n5

Pirkei d'Rabbi Eliezer, 104–105n8, 117n12–13, 132n6

Proverbs

1:8	76
4:9	109
8:34	92
18:21	191
26:18–19	94n7

Psalms

19:1	4
23	7
30:5	6
37:24	135n8
46:10	234
69:34	165n16
93	35

Sefat Emet, 66

Sefer Ha-Aggadah (trans. Braude), 111n2, 112n3

Sefer Ha-Yashar

23:76–86	118n16

Shulchan Aruch HaRav

156:3	184n10

Talmud (Babylonian)
Tractate *Bava Metzia*

87a	222n2

Talmud (Babylonian) Tractate Berachot

55a	208, 219

Talmud (Babylonian) Tractate Chullin

91b	154n8

Talmud (Babylonian) Tractate Sanhedrin

99a	77n6
108a	47n13

Talmud (Babylonian) Tractate Shabbat

55a	44n8

Zohar

57	53n19
79	132n7

www.ingramcontent.com/pod-product-compliance
Lightning Source LLC
Chambersburg PA
CBHW030614230426
43661CB00053B/1975

"For Jews who long to enrich their daily life with the depth and wonder of Torah, for fellow travelers who have long felt that there is a life-changing power in the stories of the Hebrew Bible, these pages are your guide. Rabbi Berner introduces us to *kriat-ha kodesh*—'reading the holy' with a mixture of autobiographical, rabbinical, and midrashic wisdom. The result is a book that gives insights on every page, and a deep practice that can inspire and carry us."

—**Laurie L. Patton**, President, Middlebury College

"We live in a moment of interspirituality where contemplative practices rooted in one faith are shared among seekers of all faiths and none. Rabbi Leila Gal Berner's *Listening to the Heart of Genesis* brings the magic of Ignatius's lectio divina to the deep mystery of Torah, revealing new dimensions of an ancient text. This book is an invitation to discover your own way into the Bible. Accept it; you will not be disappointed."

—**Rami Shapiro**, author of *Embracing the Divine Feminine: Song of Songs Annotated and Explained*

"Rabbi Leila Gal Berner guides us—believers and non-believers alike—on a deep contemplative journey through the book of Genesis, opening gateways of heart, spirit, and soul to surprising discoveries of profound personal meaning. This is a book for all who seek to explore their own inner 'text' through words of Torah. As you walk this path with Rabbi Leila, your heart might just gently open! What a blessing!"

—**Zalman Schachter-Shalomi**, author of *Gate to the Heart: A Manual of Contemplative Jewish Practice*

"Wherever we are on our own journeys, Rabbi Leila Gal Berner welcomes us to join her into a deep, spiritual consideration of how biblical texts can open new and challenging paths in our lives. Berner's scholarship illuminates every page of this accessible volume, which presents a unique and innovative approach to reading and living Jewish text."

—**Sue Levi Elwell**, co-editor of *Chapters of the Heart: Jewish Women Sharing the Torah of Our Lives*

"Rabbi Leila Gal Berner invites seekers of all faiths to engage their hearts and minds with the endlessly intriguing narratives of Genesis. Guided by her innovative approach, we discover how the struggles of ancient Hebrew Bible characters can directly inform our own contemporary life challenges. These stories, accompanied by probing questions for contemplation, will touch the hearts of anyone wishing to enrich their own spiritual journey. Readers will welcome the opportunity to encounter Genesis with fresh eyes."

—**Marcia Prager**, author of *The Path of Blessing*

"Rabbi Leila Gal Berner's book makes a lovely contribution to opening the Torah contemplatively to people of all backgrounds and levels of belief. Her writing reveals the depth of her spirit and the breadth of her erudition."

—**Howard Avruhm Addison**, author of *Show Me Your Way: The Complete Guide to Exploring Interfaith Spiritual Direction*

"The process that Rabbi Leila Gal Berner offers in her book—the text, midrashic teachings, and guiding questions—helped me reflect and focus attention on what is most important in my life. I recommitted to slowing down, listening more carefully, and concentrating to appreciate the good that surrounds me."

—**Julie K. Gordon**, Rabbi Educator, Hill Havurah

"Rabbi Berner's *Listening to the Heart of Genesis* breathes life into Torah and into sacred texts from all traditions. With a method of reading the holy into the text of our own lives, this book teaches its readers and practitioners through a process of illumination, self-reflection, deeper wholeness, and integration. It is an essential tool for spiritual leaders, clinicians, and educators. For those of us who are committed to moving into a rich landscape of personal reflection and repair via the Bible, Rabbi Berner provides a clear and engaging path."

—**Rochelle Robins**, Dean of the Chaplaincy, School Director of Clinical Pastoral Education, The Academy for Jewish Religion, California